AF600224

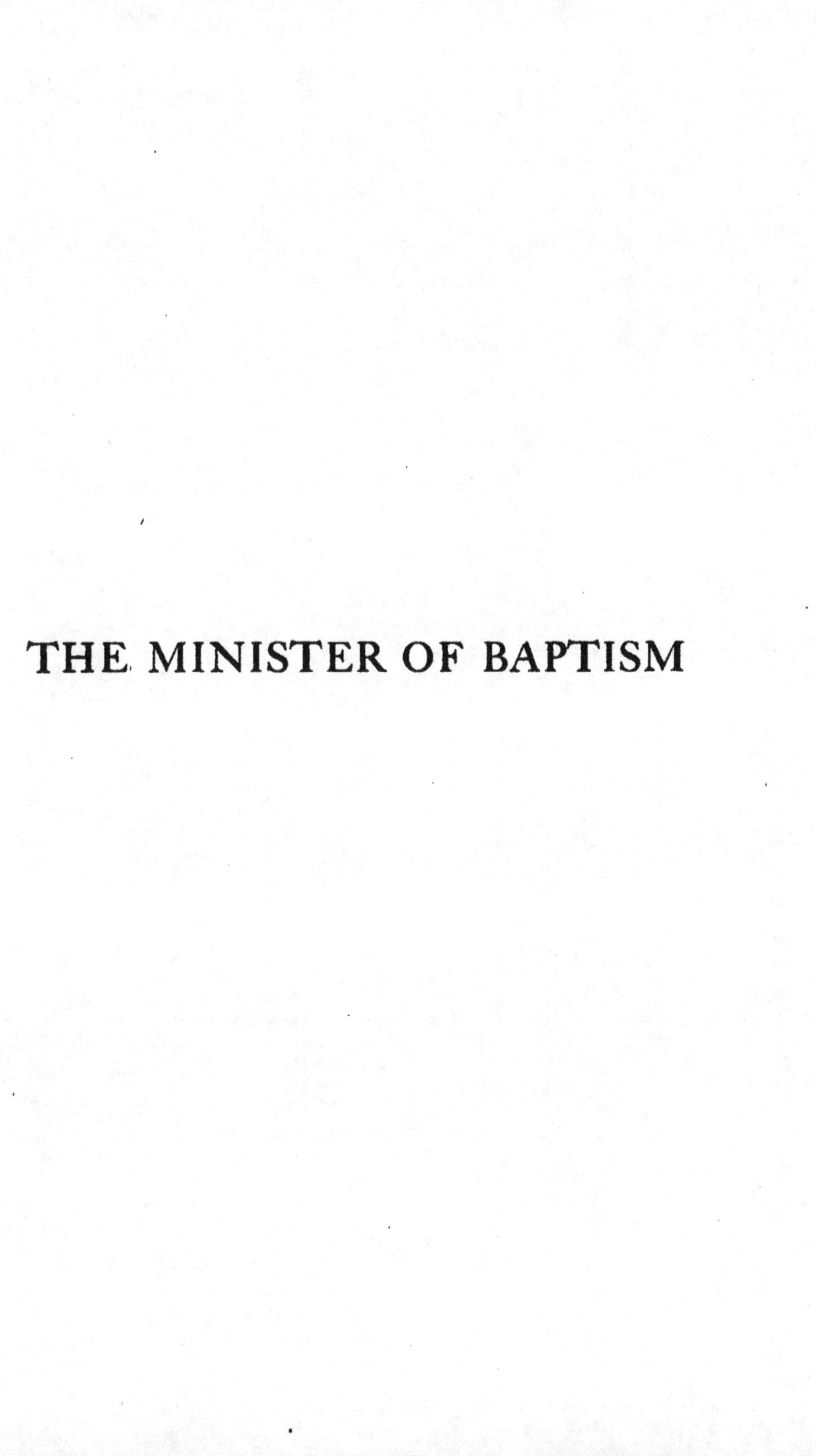

THE MINISTER OF BAPTISM

THE CATHOLIC UNIVERSITY OF AMERICA
CANON LAW STUDIES
NO. 170

THE MINISTER OF BAPTISM

AN HISTORICAL CONSPECTUS AND COMMENTARY

BY

REV. JOSEPH FRANCIS WALDRON, A.B., J.C.L.
PRIEST OF THE ARCHDIOCESE OF PHILADELPHIA

A DISSERTATION

Submitted to the Faculty of Canon Law of the Catholic University of America in Partial Fulfillment of the Requirements for the Degree of

DOCTOR OF CANON LAW

WASHINGTON, D. C.
1942

Nihil obstat:

Clemens V. Bastnagel, J.U.D., S.T.L.
Censor Deputatus

Washingtonii, die VII Maii, 1942

Imprimatur:

✠ D. Card. Dougherty
Archiepiscopus Philadelphiensis

Philadelphiae, die IX Maii, 1942

The Wickersham Printing Company
Lancaster, Pennsylvania

To My Father

and

To The Memory

of

My Mother

TABLE OF CONTENTS

PAGE

CANONICAL COMMENTARY

CHAPTER V

CHAPTER VI

CHAPTER VII

INTRODUCTION

It is axiomatic to state that the beginning of every enterprise is extremely important. Nowhere is this truism more recognized among men than in the realm of human life itself. Science is constantly studying new ways and devising modern methods by which it may assure from the first moment of conception not merely a status of well-being for human life in general, but also a state of vigorous health for the individual human life in particular, initiated under the most favorable circumstances possible in the case.

That which Science has been seeking to do for the natural life, the Church has constantly sought to preserve in regard to the supernatural life of man. Her tender solicitude for the entire sacramental system throughout the centuries bears ample proof of an honest and sincere endeavour to beget in her subjects the finest and most fruitful spiritual vitality.

Certainly if this extreme solicitude is not only warranted, but even demanded, for any particular sacrament in preference to all others, then that sacrament is baptism. For logically baptism, as the door to and the very foundation of all the other sacraments,[1] is tremendously important inasmuch as in reality it is the birth of man into the supernatural kingdom of God, and the means whereby he is granted true membership in the Church of Christ.[2]

Necessarily, then, any study of the essentials of this sacrament is important. In particular, a study of the minister of baptism is warranted, since to him is entrusted the safekeeping of the matter and form, and upon his integrity of

[1] Canon 737, § 1.

[2] Canon 87.

intention depends their proper use. In the mind of the Church he is of importance and interest not merely in that he can confer baptism validly, but inasmuch as he should seek to administer so great a sacrament licitly. Moreover, what amounts to deep interest on the part of the Church in regard to the ordinary Catholic minister of the sacrament, as is patently evident from her numerous conciliar decisions and papal pronouncements, becomes of vital and solicitous concern in regard to the very validity of baptism when conferred by non-Catholics, especially in these modern times.

It is with these thoughts in mind that this historical and canonical treatment of the minister of baptism is proposed. Knowing full well that there can be little additional information furnished to a subject already so widely discussed, and that as a result these pages lack the attractiveness of complete novelty, yet the writer presents the present study with the hope that it may both furnish a necessary background for a better understanding of the Church's legislation in this regard and also serve as a spur towards a complete fulfillment of that legislation on the part of all ministers of baptism.

The author takes occasion to express his gratitude to His Eminence, Dennis Cardinal Dougherty, Archbishop of Philadelphia, for the opportunity of advanced study; to the Faculty of the School of Canon Law; and to all others who in any way contributed by interest and aid towards the completion of this dissertation.

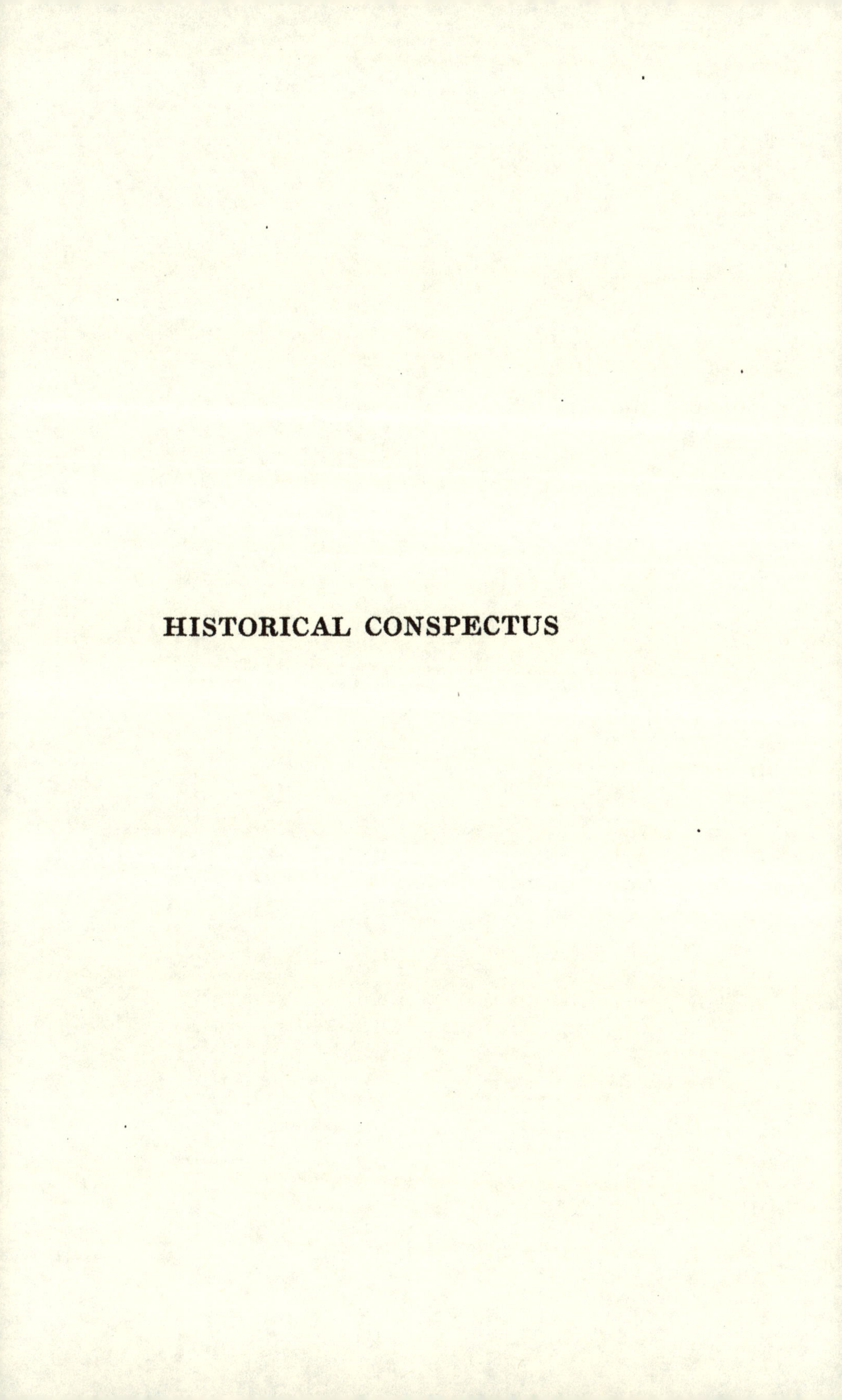

HISTORICAL CONSPECTUS

CHAPTER I

The First Five Centuries of the Church

ART. 1. THE ORDINARY MINISTER OF SOLEMN BAPTISM

"Going therefore, teach ye all nations: baptizing them in the name of the Father, and of the Son, and of the Holy Ghost,"[1] were the solemn words with which Christ sent the eleven Apostles forth as messengers of the Gospel and ministers of the sacrament of baptism. Thus at the very beginning of the Church it was chiefly through their episcopal ministration that baptism was conferred,[2] as Origen (185-254) later bears testimony.[3]

But since baptism, like the other sacraments, was to exist for all time, it was necessary that this power which the Apostles enjoyed as its ordinary ministers should be given also to others. In the early days of the Church it was transmitted to their immediate successors, namely, the bishops.

One of the earliest to bear testimony to this was St. Ignatius of Antioch (c. 50-107),[4] who clearly indicated that the bishop was the ordinary minister and the other clergy

[1] Matthew XXVIII: 19.

[2] Acts X: 47-48.

[3] *Commentarium in Ioannem*, tomus VI, n. 17: "Qui ergo in Actis baptizati erant in Ioannis baptismo, et neque an Spiritus esset audierant, denuo ab Apostolo baptizantur, quia regeneratio non apud Ioannem, sed apud Iesum per Apostolos suos fiebat..."—J. P. Migne, *Patrologiae Cursus Completus, Series Graeca* (161 vols., Parisiis, 1856-1866), XIV, 258. Hereafter referred to as *MPG*.

[4] *Ep. ad Smyrnaeos*, VIII, 1: "Non licet sine episcopo neque baptizare neque agapen celebrare;"—*MPG*, V, 714. *Ep. ad Heronem diaconum*, III, 2: "Nihil sine episcopis agas; sacerdotes enim sunt; tu vero minister sacerdotum. Illi enim baptizant...; tu vero ministras."—F. X. Funk, *Opera Patrum Apostolicorum* (2 vols., Tubingae, 1887), II, 177.

only assisted him in the rite. The writings of Pope Saint Clement (c. 90-100) [5] and Tertullian (160-222),[6] in their insistence upon the absolute right of the bishop alone to baptize, corroborate the statements of Saint Ignatius.

As to the exact reason why the administration was thus ordinarily reserved in the early Church, authors do not agree. Tertullian, in a work written by him as a Montanist,[7] thought that it was in virtue of the episcopal character. Corblet,[8] however, judged it to be but a natural outgrowth of the effect baptism produced. He argued that since baptism gave entrance into the Church, it was only logical that bishops, as heads of the individual dioceses, should admit the new members. On the other hand, Chardon [9] believed that the administration was reserved to the bishops merely because they were the legitimate successors of the Apostles, whom Christ had constituted the first ministers. Though each of these opinions has an element of truth, yet all seem to overlook an important factor: namely, that an intimate association existed between the sacraments

[5] *Ep. III*: "Quapropter cunctis fidelibus et summopere omnibus presbyteris et diaconis et reliquis clericis attendendum est, ut nihil absque episcopi proprii licentia agant. Non utique missas sine eius iussu quisquam presbyterorum in sua parochia agat, non baptizet, nec quidquam sine eius permissu faciat."—J. P. Migne, *Patrologia Cursus Completus, Series Latina* (221 vols., Parisiis, 1844-1864), CXXX, 49. Hereafter referred to as *MPL*. *Ep. I—MPL*, CXXX, 33. These epistles are attributed to Pope Saint Clement in the Pseudo-Isidorian collection. Their authenticity is doubtful.

[6] *Liber de baptismo*, c. XVIII: "Dandi [baptismum] quidem habet ius summus sacerdos, qui est episcopus."—*MPL*, I, 1218; *Corpus Scriptorum Ecclesiasticorum Latinorum* (68 vols., Vindobonae, 1866-), XX, 214. Hereafter this collection will be referred to as *CV* (*Corpus Vindobonense*).

[7] *De exhortatione castitatis*, c. VII—*MPL*, II, 922.

[8] *Histoire du sacrament de baptême* (2 vols., Genève, 1881), I, 300.

[9] *Histoire des sacraments* (6 vols., Parisiis, 1745), I, 315.

of baptism and confirmation.[10] Hence, since the bishop was ever required for confirmation, it was but natural and logical that he should as a rule be the one who administered the sacrament of baptism solemnly.[11]

That the bishop was the ordinary minister of solemn baptism was the belief of the universal Church. This is shown from the individual works of Saint Cyprian of the African Church (200-258),[12] Saint Hilary of Poitiers in France (315-366),[13] Saint Cyril of Jerusalem (313-386) [14] and Saint Gregory Nazianzen (329-389).[15]

Towards the end of the fourth and in the early part of the fifth centuries, however, there are references which at first glance seem to indicate that the priest has equal power with the bishop in the administration of the sacrament. So the Council of Laodicaea (c. 343-381),[16] the Canons of the

10 *Ep. Papae Melchiades (310-314) ad omnes Hispaniae episcopos*: "Ita coniuncta sunt haec duo sacramenta, ut ab invicem nisi morte praeveniente nullatenus possint segregari, et unum sine altero rite perfici non potest."—*MPL*, VII, 1119; Jaffé, *Regesta Pontificum Romanorum* (2nd ed. [by Kaltenbrunner (0-590), Ewald (590-882), and Lóewenfeld (882-1198), and so referred to as *JK*, *JE*, and *JL*], Lipsiae, 1885), *JK*, n. 171.

11 Ermoni, *Le baptême dans l'église primitive* (Paris, 1904), p. 30; Thomassinus, *Vetus et nova Ecclesiae disciplina* (3 vols., Parisiis, 1688), Pars I, lib. II, cap. 23, n. 3.

12 *Ep. ad Fortunatum de exhortatione martyrum*—*MPL*, IV, 654; *CV*, III, 319.

13 *Tractatus in LXVII psalmum*, n. 33—*MPL*, IX, 466; *CV*, XXII, 308.

14 *Catechesis XVII*, De Spiritu Sancto, II, c. 45—*MPG*, XXXIII, 1010.

15 *Oratio XL*, In sanctum baptisma, c. 26—*MPG*, XXXVI, 395.

16 Canon 8: "Eos qui . . . oportet, et baptizari ab ecclesiae catholicae episcopis et presbyteris."—Hardouin, *Acta conciliorum et epistolae decretales ac constitutiones summorum pontificum* (12 vols., Parisiis, 1714-1725), I, 782 (hereafter referred to as Hardouin); Labbe-Cossart, *Sacrosancta concilia ad regiam editionem exacta* (15 vols. in 16, Parisiis, 1671-1674), II, 585 (hereafter referred to as Labbe); Mansi, *Sacrorum conciliorum nova et amplissima collectio* (53 vols., Parisiis, 1901-1927), II, 585 (hereafter referred to as Mansi). Cf. also canon 46—Hardouin, I, 789; Labbe, II, 589; Mansi, II, 589.

Apostles (c. 400),[17] the Apostolic Constitutions (c. 400) [18] and the Canons of Hippolytus (c. 450) [19] linked the names of bishop and priest so intimately when speaking of the minister of baptism that both appear to have been given the same power.

On the other hand, Saint Jerome (342-420) [20] explicitly stated that which Pope Innocent I (402-417) confirmed a few years later,[21] namely, that the bishop alone possessed the exclusive right to baptize solemnly. Moreover, Saint Augustine (354-430) strengthens their position in his narration of the sudden conversion of the dying Martialis, wherein a priest baptized solely because the bishop could not be reached.[22]

Because of this united view as represented by the Western authors, Martene (1654-1739),[23] in commenting on the texts which had their origin in the Eastern Church, advanced the same opinion which Trombelli (1697-1784) later gave [24] in reference to canon seven of one of the Roman synods (402),[25] and claimed that with all such passages

17 Canons 46, 47, 49, 50—*MPL*, CXXX, 19-20.

18 Lib. III, 11—Funk, *Didascalia et Constitutiones Apostolorum* (2 vols., Paderbornae, 1905), I, 201; Lib. III, 16—Funk, *op. cit.*, I, 209; Lib. VII, 23—Funk, *op. cit.*, I, 409. These also appear in Mansi, I, 383, 390 and 499.

19 Canon IV, 32—Hans Achelis, "Die ältesten Quellen des Orientalischen Kirchenrechte. Die Canones Hippolyti,"—Gebhardt-Harnack, *Texte und Untersuchungen zur Geschichte der altchristlichen Litteratur* (Leipzig, 1891), VI, 61-62.

20 *Dialogus contra Luciferianos*, c. 9: "Ecclesiae salus in summi sacerdotis dignitate pendet... Inde venit, ut sine chrismate et episcopi iussione, neque presbyter neque diaconus ius habet baptizandi."—*MPL*, XXIII, 165.

21 *Ep. ad Decentium*, cap. III—*MPL*, LVI, 515; *JK*, n. 311.

22 *Civitas Dei*, L. XXII, c. 8, n. 13—*MPL*, SLI, 767; *CV*, XL, 605.

23 *De antiquis ecclesiae ritibus* (4 vols., Rotomagi, 1700), I, 4.

24 *Tractatus de sacramentis* (13 vols., Bononiae, 1769-1783), III, 366.

25 *Canones synodi Romanorum ad Gallos episcopos*: "Paschae tempore presbyter et diaconus per parochias dare remissionem peccatorum et minis-

which seem to indicate an equality between the bishop and priest in the matter of administration one must understand with reference to the priest the phrase *iubente episcopo.*

Though it is quite possible that this answer may be part of the solution, yet it would seem that the reason for the discrepancy is ultimately to be placed elsewhere. All the texts which seemingly grant the priest equal power with the bishop to baptize solemnly originated in the East. Hence a probable explanation lies in the fact that there was a highly developed parochial organization in the East much earlier than in the West, as shall be seen more fully in chapter III. It was as a consequence of this that the priest of the East had gained more power.

At any rate it can still be said that the bishop was the ordinary minister of solemn baptism in the East as well as in the West, in such a manner as to make his presence in the diocese imperative for this precise purpose. For as late as the Council of Chalcedon (451) the clergy of Edessa besought Bishops Photius and Eustathius for the return of their own bishop in order that he might be with them to baptize solemnly.[26] Finally, even after the close of this period in our history (c. 550), in the West there was a plea made by the clergy of Milan for the return of their own Bishop Dacius who had been detained for many years by Justinian because of a controversy.[27]

terium implere consueverunt, etiam praesente episcopo."—Hardouin, I, 1035; Labbe, III, 1137; Mansi, III, 1137.

[26] Actio XI: "...festinante salutifera sancti diei paschalis imminente, in qua et propter catechismos, et propter eos qui digni sunt sancto baptismate, opus est eius praesentia."—Hardouin, II, 534; Mansi, VII, 251.

[27] *Ep. Legatis Francorum qui Constantinopolim profiscebantur ab Italiae clericis directa*: "...quia cum pene omnes episcopi quos ordinare solet, sicut bene scitis, mortui sint, immensa populi multitudo sine baptismo, moritur."—Mansi, IX, 155. The bishop had been detained by Justinian at Constantinople for fifteen years in connection with the Three Chapter

ART. 2. THE EXTRAORDINARY MINISTER OF SOLEMN BAPTISM

The power to baptize, which Christ directly gave to the eleven Apostles, they could and did communicate to others, as is evidenced by the action of the deacon Philip.[28] In fact, although Sacred Scripture gives no testimony of any greater extension of this power among the minor clergy, yet it is quite probable that at least the other six deacons possessed it. But even in such cases it was understood that the administration really pertained to the apostolic office.[29]

Bingham (1668-1723)[30] is of the opinion that the Apostles possessed a discretionary power whereby they could authorize others when they thought the necessities and emergencies of the infant Church demanded it. This power they could and did recall as soon as the need was over. So the bishops, as successors to the Apostles, were the ordinary ministers, and in virtue of this discretionary power they sometimes permitted priests and deacons to administer.

For, that priests and deacons were extraordinary ministers is evident from the testimony of Saint Clement of Rome for priests,[31] of Saint Ignatius of Antioch for deacons,[32] and of Tertullian[33] and the Council of Elvira (305) in regard to both.[34]

[28] Acts VIII: 38.

[29] Saint Hilary of Poitiers, *Tractatus in LXVII psalmum*, n. 33: "...a diacono ministerium apostolici officii...exigeret."—*MPL*, IX, 466; *CV*, XXII, 308.

[30] *The works of the Reverend Joseph Bingham* (edited by the Rev. R. Bingham in 10 vols., Oxford University Press, 1855), IX (*The History of Lay Baptism*), 11. Hereafter referred to as the *History of Lay Baptism*.

[31] *Ep. III—MPL*, CXXX, 49. This, of course, is pseudo-Isidorian.

[32] *Ep. ad Heronem*, III, 2—Funk, *Opera Patrum Apostolicorum*, II, 177.

[33] *Liber de baptismo*, c. XVIII: "Dandi [baptismum] quidem habet ius summus sacerdos, qui est episcopus. Dehinc presbyteri et diaconi, non tamen sine episcopi auctoritate."—*MPL*, I, 1218; *CV*, XX, 214.

[34] Canon 77. "Si quis diaconus regens plebem, sine episcopo vel presbytero aliquos baptizaverit, episcopus eos per benedictionem perficere

Towards the end of the fourth century, Saint Ambrose († 397) wrote in a tone which indicates that it was quite common for priest to administer baptism.[35] In fact, his contemporary, Saint Cyril of Jerusalem (313-386), spoke of bishops, priests and deacons[36] in such a manner as to cause Bingham[37] to conclude that deacons and priests had ordinary power of themselves to baptize solemnly in country villages. Though it is true that the advent of parochial development in the West and its increasing organization in the East were bestowing greater power upon the minor clergy, yet it seems still too early in this regard to arrogate to priests and deacons such ordinary power.

Martene's[38] explanation is that priests and deacons were understood to have the bishop's permission in any case of necessity. Necessity, he explained, could be taken in a broad sense, as when a large number had to be baptized, or when the bishop was too far distant, and in the strict sense, as when one was dying and the bishop could not be present. Hence, for him these texts were to be interpreted as referring to cases of necessity taken in the broad sense, so that these priests and deacons really baptized solemnly with the permission, at least presumed, of the bishop.

It is important to note, however, that the priest was gradually given even greater latitude in this regard. Tertullian had explained the reservation of solemn baptism to

debebit."—Hardouin, I, 258; Labbe, II, 18; Mansi, II, 18. The deacon here referred to seems to have been placed in charge of a rural chapel, and though usually solemn baptisms were not conferred in these places, yet it seems to have been permitted here—probably because of some necessity.

35 *In psalmum CXVIII expositio—MPL*, XV, 1227; *CV*, LXII, 48.

36 *Catechesis XVII*, De Spiritu Sancto, II, c. 35: "Non circa tempus baptismatis, quando accesseris ad episcopos, vel presbyteros, vel diaconos (omnibus namque locis datur gratia et in pagis et in urbibus); ... tu itaque ad baptizantem accede."—*MPG*, XXXIII, 1010.

37 *History of Lay Baptism*, p. 18.

38 *De antiquis ecclesiae ritibus*, I, 18.

the bishop on the score that episcopal orders were necessary.[39] But less than two centuries later, Saint John Chrysostom (344-407)[40] and Saint Augustine († 430),[41] both of whom lived while the bishop was the ordinary minister of baptism, stated that the priest himself had the right to baptize in virtue of his orders. Saint Augustine especially, who seems to have been the first to have distinguished between validity and licitness with regard to the administration, demanded episcopal permission solely for licitness, so that a priest who had left the Church could still confer valid baptism, even though he would be acting wrongly.

At any rate, with the growth of the Church and the greater demands upon the time of the bishop, priests were more frequently commissioned to baptize, as is evidenced both directly[42] and indirectly.[43]

39 *De exhortatione castitatis,* c. VII—*MPL,* II, 922.

40 *De sacerdotio,* L.III, c. 5: "Nam si non potest quis intrare in regnum caelorum, nisi per aquam et spiritum regeneratus fuerit; ...haec autem omnia non aliter, quam per sanctas illas manus, sacerdotum nempe, perficiuntur."—*MPG,* XLVIII, 643.

41 *Contra Epistolam Parmeniani,* L.II, c. 13, n. 28—*MPL,* XLIII, 71; *CV,* LI, 79. On the whole subject of baptism Saint Augustine is the outstanding authority of this period. He more than any other clarified the teaching of the Church in regard to the minister. The reason why a special section is not devoted solely to his doctrine is that it seemed better to place him chronologically in each section, so that his influence upon the other writers might be more apparent and the general division of the thesis might be better observed.

42 Saint Augustine, *Sermo CCCXXIV*: "Continuo tulit illum ad prebyteros, baptizatus est."—*MPL,* XXXVIII, 1447. Council of Epaône (517), canon 16: "Presbytero, propter salutem animarum,... charismata subvenire permittimus."—Hardouin, II, 1099; Mansi, VIII, 561.

43 Synod of Saint Patrick (c. 450), canon 27: "Clericus episcopi in plebe quislibet novus ingressor, baptizare et offerre illum non licet, nec aliquid agere."—Hardouin, I, 1792; Labbe, VI, 518; Mansi, VI, 518. This rule was laid down under penalty of excommunication, and the use of the word *offerre* shows that it pertained to the priests specifically, for the Apostolic

At the same time the deacon appears less frequently as the extraordinary minister. A text from Saint Epiphanius (315-413) is urged [44] in conjunction with the texts previously cited, wherein the bishop and priest are linked as the administrators of baptism without any mention of the deacon, to prove that deacons no longer had any right whatsoever.

However, it cannot be proved with certainty that Saint Epiphanius stated any more than that the deacon was not the ordinary minister. The failure to mention him in the other texts was perhaps due to the increased number of priests in the Church at the time, and hence the consequent lesser need of calling upon deacons to fulfill that ministration. But this in itself is no denial that he still possessed power. On the contrary, Saint Jerome (342-420),[45] Pope Siricius (384-398),[46] Theodoret of Cyrrhus (393-458) [47] and Pope Gelasius I (492-496) [48] vindicated for the deacon as well as for the priest the right to baptize solemnly with

Constitutions (Lib. III, 20 — Funk, *Didascalia et Constitutiones Apostolorum*, I, 201) stated that priests and bishops were the only clerics possessing the power to sacrifice.

[44] *Adversus haereses*, L. III, t. II, Haeresis LXXIX: "Nam neque diaconis quidem ipsis ullum in ecclesiastico ordine sacramentum perficere conceditur, sed hoc dumtaxat, ut eorum quae perficiuntur ministri sint." — *MPG*, XLII, 746.

[45] *Dialogus contra Luciferianos*, c. IX: "Inde venit, ut sine chrismate et episcopi iussione, neque presbyter neque diaconus ius habet baptizandi." —*MPL*, XXIII, 165.

[46] *Ep. ad episcopos Gallos*: "Paschae tempore, presbyter et diaconus... in fontem quoque descendunt; illi in officio sunt: sed ullius episcopi nomine facti summa conceditur." — Hardouin, I, 1035; Labbe, III, 1137; Mansi, III, 1137.

[47] *Quaest. in II Parell.*, cap. XXXIII—*MPG*, LXXX, 851.

[48] *Ep. IX* (*ad episcopos Lucaniae*), c. VII: "Diaconos quoque propriam servare mensuram...nihil eorum penitus suo ministerio applicare, quae primis ordinibus proprie decrevit antiquitas. Absque episcopo vel presbytero baptizare non audeant, nisi, praedictis fortasse officiis longius constitutis, necessitas extrema compellat."—*MPL*, LIX, 51; *JK*, n. 636.

proper permission, although Pope Gelasius seemingly restricted the use of this power to those cases of necessity wherein it was permitted to all others to baptize privately.

At any rate, the close of this period of our history finds the names of priest and deacon linked together in the I Council of Orleans (509)[49] and the II of Orange (533)[50] in a manner patently indicating that both were still considered capable of being the ministers of solemn baptism.

ART. 3. THE MINISTER OF PRIVATE BAPTISM IN CASES OF NECESSITY

The necessity of baptism for salvation has prompted the Church from earliest times to be most generous in rules regarding its administration in cases of necessity. Priests and deacons, it is true, needed episcopal permission to baptize solemnly in ordinary cases, yet both, as has been seen in the texts already cited, could act without his explicit permission in cases of necessity.

Moreover, though the minor clerics had no power to administer in ordinary cases,[51] yet it was taken for granted that in extreme necessity they could bestow private baptism for which the bishop would later supply the ceremonies.[52]

In regard to the laity, however, the earliest reference seems to have been in that of the baptism which was conferred on Saint Paul by Ananias, who to all appearances

[49] Canon 12—Hardouin, II, 1010; Mansi, VIII, 353.

[50] Canon 16: "Presbyter, vel diaconus, sine litteris, vel si ordinem baptizandi nesciat, nullatenus ordinetur."—Hardouin, II, 1175; Mansi, VIII, 837.

[51] *Apostolic Constitutions*, Lib. III, c. 11: "Immo neque clericis reliquis potestatem baptizandi facimus; ut lectoribus, cantoribus, janitoribus, aut ministris."—Funk, *Didascalia et Constitutiones Apostolorum*, I, 201.

[52] *De Rebaptismate*, c. X: "Si a minore clerico per necessitatem traditum fuerit, eventum exspectemus, ut aut suppleatur a nobis aut a Domino supplendum reservetur."—*MPL*, III, 1195. This work is dubiously attributed to Saint Cyprian.

possessed no clerical orders.[53] Whether or not this was performed solemnly cannot be proved from Sacred Scripture, but it certainly is a unique case.

At any rate the earliest authoritative source permitting all the laity to baptize in cases of necessity is found in the writing of Pope Saint Victor (189-198).[54] The same right is acknowledged by Tertullian [55] and Saint Jerome.[56]

Strangely enough Labauche [57] gathers from Pope Victor's text that at the end of the second century the administration of private baptism was permitted to the faithful on any occasion whatsoever. Yet such does not seem the case. All texts referred solely to necessity. In fact, Tertullian so forcefully insisted upon the obligation of the laity to baptize in extreme cases, threatening with guilt for the spiritual destruction of another when they neglected this duty, that it would seem that the laity, far from baptizing privately at all times, were reluctant even in case of necessity to administer the sacrament.

Of particular interest, because of the requisites in the lay minister which it exacted, is the legislation of the Spanish Council of Elvira (305).[58] First, there had to be a case of

[53] Acts IX: 18.

[54] *Ep. I (ad Theophilum Alexandriae epis.)*, c. I: "... si necesse fuerit, aut mortis periculum ingruerit, gentiles ad fidem venientes quocumque loco vel momento, ubicumque evenerit, sive in flumine, sive in mari, sive in fontibus, tantum, Christianae confessione credulitatis clarificata, baptizentur."—Mansi, I, 701; *JK*, n. 74.

[55] *Liber de baptismo*, c. XVIII: "... Alioquin etiam laicis ius est.... Sufficiat scilicet in necessitatibus utaris."—*MPL*, I, 1218; *CV*, XX, 214.

[56] *Dialogus contra Luciferianos*, c. IX: "Quod frequenter, si tamen necessitas cogit, scimus etiam licere laicis."—*MPL*, XXIII, 165.

[57] *The three sacraments of initiation* (New York: Benziger and Co., 1922), p. 71.

[58] Canon 38: "Placuit peregre navigantes, aut si ecclesia in proximo non fuerit, posse fidelem, qui lavacrum suum integrum habet, nec sit bigamus, baptizare in necessitate infirmitatis positum catechumenum."—Mansi, II, 12.

absolute necessity, when baptism could not otherwise be had. Secondly, the person needed to have his own baptism entire (*integrum*), namely, it must not have been a baptism deferred until he was in danger of death. Thirdly, the minister had to be one who was not a bigamist in the sense of having married successively. The last two conditions seem strange, but Bingham [59] and Corblet [60] think that they were exacted because the council considered the laity by this administration to participate in the sacerdotal power, and so demanded that they be free from defects which would exclude one from the reception of sacred orders.

Here it may be well to note that Saint Basil (330-379),[61] and Saint Gregory of Nazianzus (329-389) [62] evidently considered baptism administered by the laity invalid. Labauche [63] considers their opinion to be but the natural outgrowth of a custom which existed in some of the Eastern Churches in direct opposition to the usage of the primitive Church. The custom resulted from the controversy regarding the validity of heretical baptism—a controversy to be discussed in the next article—and consisted in a rule laid down by part of the East forbidding the simple faithful to administer private baptism, so that by this stringent method the profanation of the sacrament might be prevented. This

59 *History of Lay Baptism*, p. 29.

60 *Histoire du sacrament de baptême*, I, 311.

61 *Ep. CLXXXVIII*: " Quare eos, qui ipsorum partibus stabant, tamquam a laicis baptizatos, iusserunt vero Ecclesiae baptismate ad Ecclesiam venientes expurgari."—*MPG*, XXXII, 663.

62 *Oratio XVIII* (Funebris in patrem), c. XXI—*MPG*, XXXV, 1023. Herein is narrated in detail how as a youth he, more than any of his companions, was terrified when a violent storm threatened them at sea. His fear arose chiefly from the fact that he had not been baptized. Evidently he did not think his companions could validly baptize even in extreme necessity, although they were Christians.

63 *The three sacraments of initiation*, p. 74.

may be the true solution, and since these two citations are practically isolated, they must be considered indicative more of a lamentable error than of a historical discrepancy affecting the general tenor of the thesis.

In the Western Church, far from any denial of this privilege to the laity, is the statement first made by Saint Augustine[64] that baptism given by a lay person even outside a case of necessity, although it is a usurpation of power and should be fittingly punished, is still valid. But though the privilege may have been abused, as Saint Augustine implied, yet it was not forbidden them.[65]

The only restriction found in the West, and even this doubtful one can be urged equally in the East, regarded women. Tertullian, in his works,[66] and later Saint Epiphanius (315-413)[67] said that they were not permitted to administer the sacrament and inveighed against those who attempted to do so. The IV Council of Carthage (398) supported their teaching.[68]

In commenting upon these texts authors either insist that the reference is to solemn baptism only, or they aver that it must be borne in mind that at that time the Church was fighting heretical sects intent upon admitting women into

[64] *Contra epistolam Parmeniani*, L.II, c. 13, n. 29—*MPL*, XLIII, 71; *CV*, LI, 80.

[65] *Ep. IX Papae Gelasii* (*ad episcopos Lucaniae*), C. VII: "Quod et laicis Christianis facere plerumque conceditur."—*MPL*, LXIX, 51; *JK*, n. 636.

[66] *Liber de velandis virginibus*, c. IX: "Non permittitur mulieri in ecclesia loqui; sed nec docere, nec tinguere, nec offerre, nec ullius virilis muneris."—*MPL*, II, 902. The word *tinguere* refers to the act of baptizing. *Liber de prescriptionibus*, c. XLI: "Quam procaces: Quae audeant ... tingere."—*MPL*, II, 56.

[67] *Adversus haereses*, L.III, t. II, Haeresis LXXIX—*MPG*, XLII, 742.

[68] Canon 100: "Mulier baptizare non praesumat."—Hardouin, I, 984; Mansi, III, 959; Labbe, III, 959.

the priesthood. Though there is an element of truth in each of these interpretations, and the latter one is particularly forceful, yet neither opinion completely destroys the seeming restriction. For the writers quoted have themselves made no distinction in the rule, nor did the *Didascalia.*[69]

At any rate, whether women were or were not forbidden to administer baptism in case of necessity, yet the Church did permit them to help the clergy for the sake of modesty in the solemn baptism of women. However, frequent stress is placed on the fact that these deaconesses are not to be considered as the ministers of the sacrament.[70]

ART. 4. BAPTISM ADMINISTERED BY HERETICS AND SCHISMATICS

The next important question regarding the minister of baptism concerns the competence of heretics and schismatics to administer the sacrament validly. All early writers admitted that, inasmuch as these at times usurped a power which did not belong to them, they could not act licitly. In this historical discussion of the question, however, there will be no place for arguments from theology as such. Sufficient for the canonical background of the period will be a simple statement of the controversies as indicated in the early writers and councils, and of the solution that ultimately resulted.

Tertullian was the first of the early Church writers to discuss the question, and though he mentioned the same idea in various places, yet it was in his Catholic work directly regarding baptism that he stated beyond doubt his

[69] Lib. III, c. 9: "Mulierem aut baptizare aut a muliere baptizari non approbamus, quia hoc illegitimum est."—Funk, *Didascalia et Constitutiones Apostolorum*, I, 198.

[70] *Didascalia*, Lib. III, c. 12—Funk, *op. cit.*, I, 210. Saint Epiphanius, *Expositio fidei*, n. 21—*MPG*, XLII, 826. *Constitutiones Apostolorum*, Lib. III, c. 16—Funk, *op. cit.*, I, 211; Lib. VIII, c. 28—Funk, *op. cit.*, I, 531.

belief that baptism administered by heretics and schismatics was invalid.[71]

Some authors think that in this passage Tertullian expressed the opinion of the whole African Church, but the most that can be actually proved is that it was the opinion of the Province of Carthage. For the I (215) and the II (217) Councils held there under the episcopate of Agrippinus, a little later than when Tertullian wrote this (200-206), likewise insisted upon the invalidity of that baptism which had been administered outside the Church.[72] Later the schismatical synods of Iconium in Lycaonia and Sunnada (Tscifût-Kassaba) in Phrygia, both held around the year 235, agreed with the opinion expressed by Agrippinus and ordered the rebaptism of all those who returned from heresy.[73]

But the real controversy regarding the validity of such baptisms did not commence until Cyprian became bishop of Carthage (248-258). He, probably influenced greatly by Tertullian's writings and the earlier decisions of the Carthaginian bishops under Agrippinus, declared that baptism administered outside the Church was invalid. He had this opinion confirmed by an African Council held in the autumn of 255. All this is evident from a synodal letter which Cyprian himself wrote to the eighteen bishops of Numidia who had proposed such a question to him.[74] From the very

[71] *Liber de baptismo*, c. XV: "...ideoque nec baptismus unus, quia non idem; quem cum rite non habeant, sine dubio non habent, nec capit numerari quod non habetur; ita nec possint accipere, quia non habent."—*MPL*, I, 1216; *CV*, XX, 214.

[72] *Ep. Cypriani LXXI*: "Quod quidem et Agrippinus bonae memoriae vir, cum ceteris coepiscopis suis qui illo tempore in provincia Africa et Numidia Ecclesiam Domini gubernabant, statuit et librata consilii communis examinatione firmavit."—*MPL*, IV, 411; *CV*, III², 774. *Ep. LXXII*—*MPL*, III, 1110; *CV*, III², 776.

[73] Eusebius, *Historia Ecclesiastica*, Lib. VII, c. 7—*MPG*, XX, 651.

[74] *Ep. LXX*: "...censentes scilicet et pro certo tenentes neminem baptizari foris extra ecclesiam posse."—*MPL*, III, 1037; *CV*, III², 767.

fact that these bishops had questioned the Carthaginian practice, and needed the reassurance of Cyprian that such was not a complete novelty, it may be deduced that they were more impressed by the contrary practice in force at Rome.

Certainly Cyprian was not without opposition even in Africa. Quintus, Bishop of Mauritania, was not deeply impressed with Cyprian's reasons or with the decision reached by the synod and asked for a better explanation. In answer Cyprian sent Quintus a letter (255), in which he explicitly cited the previous teaching of Agrippinus once more and stated that even though he was supported in his view with this tradition, yet it was to be recalled that this was not a question of traditional usage but of reasoning.[75]

This utter rejection of ancient custom as a guide, it may be noted in passing, would seem to indicate that the work on *Rebaptism,* dubiously attributed to Cyprian by some,[76] was not written by him at all. For this treatise frequently referred to the antiquity of the Roman custom in admitting as valid the baptism of certain heretics who had used the proper form, and did not reprobate such a practice. Hence it seems that this book was written by one of the African bishops who upheld the Roman teaching; that it was composed shortly before the time Cyprian wrote to Quintus, and that it was to this argument of antiquity that Cyprian referred in his letter.

But the discussion did not end here. Since the Bishop of Carthage had not been able to overcome the opposition of some of the other African bishops, the question was again introduced at the Council of Carthage held before Easter in 256. At that synod seventy-one bishops of northern Africa and Numidia signified their agreement with the doc-

[75] *Ep. LXXI—MPL,* IV, 409; *CV,* III², 771.

[76] Cf. Art. 3, page 12, *supra.*

trine proposed by Cyprian and sanctioned by the Council held in 255.[77]

In order to strengthen the argument, Saint Cyprian wrote to Pope Saint Stephen I († c. 257) about the decisions of the African Councils. The fact that his legates were received as heretics leads one to believe that Rome had in some way already decided the question, and so regarded the African Church as opposing its teaching intentionally. The exact correspondence in this period is not available in detail, but from certain attacks made upon Pope Stephen in a letter written by Cyprian to Jubainus in the summer of 256 it can be deduced that there was some form of letter sent to Rome.[78]

It is strange that in Cyprian's own letter to Pope Stephen he referred to the Roman opposition in ill chosen terms, and whereas at an earlier time he had argued with the African bishops that his practice was necessary because of Catholic belief, he herein told Pope Stephen that this was merely a disciplinary question to be decided by the individual bishops.[79]

Pope Saint Stephen answered this attack in a letter of his own. The only extant part of this text shows that he spoke with the primacy of the Apostle and commanded that Cyprian desist from this novel practice.[80] From a letter, moreover, which Firmilian, Bishop of Caesarea in Cappadocia, wrote to Cyprian it is possible to gather that Stephen appealed to Apostolic tradition, to the practice of

[77] *Ep. LXXIII—MPL*, III, 1110; *CV*, III², 778.

[78] *Ep. LXXIII—MPL*, III, 1110; *CV*, III², 778.

[79] *Ep. LXXII—MPL*, III, 989; *CV*, III², 775.

[80] Eusebius, *Historia Ecclesiastica*, L.VII, c. 3: "Si qui ergo, a quacumque haeresi veniunt ad vos, nihil innovetur nisi quod traditum est, ut manus illis imponatur in poenitentiam, cum ipsi haeretici proprie alterutrum ad se venientes non baptizent, sed communicent tantum."—*MPG*, XX, 642; *JK*, n. 125.

Saints Peter and Paul, and, most of all, to the authority which he exercised over all the Churches as the basis for conformity to the practice of Rome in admitting the validity of certain heretical baptisms.[81]

The Council of Africa which met at Carthage in September of 256 decided to answer the letter in its own fashion. Cyprian presided, and after the various letters regarding the controversy, with the exception of the one written by Pope Saint Stephen, had been read, the 87 bishops present voted individually and stated their reasons for their opinion. The baptism of all heretical sects was declared invalid by each of the bishops.[82]

At that very moment Pope Saint Stephen was forwarding to all the Churches of Christendom the decision by which he acknowledged the validity of baptism when it was conferred properly by heretics. The result of this action was a division consisting practically of the Churches of Africa and Asia Minor for rebaptism, and of Rome and Alexandria for the validity of the initially conferred baptisms at the hands of heretics. Eusebius said that all over the East synods were held regarding the question. This dissension existed until the death of Pope Stephen, after which his successors, though following his decision, were not so severe in their treatment of the dissident Churches. Dionysius of Alexandria (✝ 265), who had attempted to lessen the rigor of Saint Stephen by writing to him,[83] revealed a further interest in this question with the succeeding Pope, Sixtus II (257-258).[84] His words helped to consolidate the unity, the restoration of which had already been made less difficult by the election of the new pope. Correspondence between

[81] *MPL*, III, 1158.

[82] *MPL*, III, 1074; *CV*, III³ 82; Hardouin, I, 179; Mansi, I, 965.

[83] Eusebius, *Historia Ecclesiastica*, L. VII, c. 7—*MPG*, XX, 647.

[84] Eusebius, *op. cit.*, L. VII, c. 9—*MPG*, XX, 654.

Rome and Firmilian was resumed, and relations between Africa and Rome were renewed. But though by the time Sixtus was succeeded by Dionysius (259-268) much animosity had been extinguished, still the controversy was not settled.[85]

A tendency toward greater concord with Rome on the part of the other Churches, and the continued insistence of Rome on Stephen's decision is evident in the succeeding century. Pope Eusebius (308), in a letter to the bishops of Campagna, insisted that heretics who had been baptized in the name of the Trinity were to be received without rebaptism.[86] The I Council of Arles (314), the first large council in Western Europe to legislate on this matter, while admitting that the African Church had a peculiar law of its own regarding rebaptism, nevertheless instructed the Church not to baptize those who have been baptized already in the name of the Trinity.[87] A few years later (325) the Council of Nicaea took for granted that not all baptisms conferred by heretics were invalid, but only those which had in some way or other been vitiated. So it decreed that those who were baptized by the Paulianists, a sect which did not believe in the Trinity and hence did not use the correct form, did not have valid baptism.[88] Finally, in the year 348 a council held at Carthage ruled that baptism received in the name of the Trinity should not be repeated, and thus even the African Church evidenced greater concord with Rome.[89]

[85] Duchesne, *Histoire ancienne de l'église* (3 vols., Paris, 1906), I, 429.

[86] *Ep. III*—Hardouin, I, 244; Mansi, II, 424; *JK*, n. 165.

[87] Canon 8: "De Afris, quod propria sua lege utuntur ut rebaptizent, placuit, ut si ad ecclesiam aliquis de hac haeresi venerit, interrogent eum (nostrae fidei sacerdotes) symbolum. Et si perviderint eum in Patre, et Filio, et Spiritu Sancto baptizatum; manus ei tantum imponatur, ut accipiat Spiritum Sanctum. Quod si interrogatus non responderit hanc Trinitatem, baptizetur."—Hardouin, I, 265; Labbe, II, 472; Mansi, II, 472.

[88] Canon 19—Hardouin, I, 331; Labbe, II, 683; Mansi, II, 683.

[89] Cap. I—Hardouin, I, 685; Labbe, III, 145; Mansi, III, 145.

As the Council of Nicaea had distinguished by reason of the form between valid and invalid baptism conferred by heretics, so other councils and popes made distinctions.[90] As a result all baptisms conferred by Arians,[91] Montanists [92] and Photinians [93] were considered to have been invalidly administered.

During the fourth century there originated a schismatical sect known as the Donatists. These were the first Christians to separate from the Catholic Church, as such, on a question of discipline. Pertinaciously did they cling to the doctrine of Saint Cyprian during the entire fourth century. Furthermore, when they had completed their separation from the Church of Rome, they declared invalid not only baptism conferred by a heretic, but also that administered by anyone who had lost the Holy Ghost through sin. Their adversaries were considered by them to be in such a condition, and hence baptism could not be validly conferred by anyone outside their ranks.

In the fifth century, Saint Augustine (354-430) wrote against this disturbing sect. As has been noted previously, he was the first to distinguish between valid and licit administration, and with this distinction as a basis his writings had a tremendous influence in settling the question of heretical and schismatical baptism. Firmly believing that even Saint Cyprian himself had seen the error of his doc-

[90] I General Council of Constantinople (381), canon 9—Hardouin, I, 811; Labbe, III, 563; Mansi, III, 563.

[91] Saint Athanasius of Alexandria (295-373), *Oratio II contra Arianos,* n. 43—*MPG,* XXV, 238; *Epistola Decretalis Papae Siricii ad Hymerium Tarraconensem,* cap. I—*MPL,* XIII, 1134; *JK,* n. 255.

[92] Council of Laodicaea (343-381), canon 8—Hardouin, I, 782; Labbe, II, 585; Mansi, II, 585. Canon 7 admitted the validity of baptism conferred by the Novatians and Quartodecimans.

[93] II Council of Arles (452), canon 17—Hardouin, II, 774; Labbe, VII, 880; Mansi, VII, 880. Canon 16 declared that the Bonosiaci baptized validly.

trine and had retracted before his death,[94] Augustine taught that the admission of possible validity for baptism conferred by heretics was not an admission in any way that such heretics had the true Church.[95] Heretics have true baptism simply because baptism is one, and hence those who have been baptized and later have left the Church still retain their baptism and are also able to administer it to others.[96] This is true not only of heretics, but also of schismatics.[97] So all those schismatics and heretics who baptize according to the evangelical form baptize validly,[98] even though the sacrament they confer does not really attain its perfection until the recipients return to the true Church.[99] Only because all this is true is it indicated that one in danger of death not only can, but actually should, receive baptism from a heretic if no orthodox minister be present.[100]

Arguing more particularly against the Donatists, Augustine stated that there should be no worry about the worthiness of the minister. It is Christ Who baptizes and His baptism can flow through the instrumentality of either Judas or John.[101] Hence, even though two ministers of entirely different merit and grace confer baptism, it is the

94 *De baptismo contra Donatistas,* L. II, c. 7, n. 12—*MPL,* XLIII, 133; *CV,* LI, 186.

95 *Op. cit.,* L. V, c. 23, n. 33—*MPL,* XLIII, 193; *CV,* LI, 290.

96 *Op. cit.,* L. VI, c. 9, n. 14—*MPL,* XLIII, 204; *CV,* LI, 308.

97 *Op. cit.,* L. I, c. 1, n. 2—*MPL,* XLIII, 109; *CV,* LI, 145.

98 *Op. cit.,* L. III, c. 15, n. 20—*MPL,* XLIII, 147; *CV,* LI, 211.

99 *Op. cit.,* L. III, c. 13, n. 18—*MPL,* XLIII, 146; *CV,* LI, 208. *Sermo III*—*MPL,* XXXVIII, 33.

100 *De baptismo contra Donatistas,* L. I, c. 2—*MPL,* XLIII, 110; CV, LI, 147.

101 *In Ioannem,* tractatus V, c. 1, n. 11—*MPL,* XXXV, 1419; c. 3, n. 14—*MPL,* XXXV, 1429.

same sacrament which is given by each,[102] for it is not a question of who administers, but of what is administered.[103]

This doctrine of Saint Augustine, which was, in reality, only a clear explanation of that of Pope Stephen, ultimately prevailed. Little by little the Donatists ceased to be a religious party and become a sect of anarchists, thus arousing the combined opposition of the civil and ecclesiastical authorities.

So at the middle of the fifth century the doctrine concerning baptism by heretics and schismatics had been so well clarified, crystallized and universally accepted, that Pope Saint Leo I (440-461) commanded all the Churches not to repeat baptisms already properly administered by heretics.[104] But even without this text it could be concluded that such a doctrine prevailed in the East from the severity with which the Canons of the Apostles punished by deposition any bishop or priest who negligently failed to baptize a person previously invalidly baptized by heretics, or who administered anew the sacrament to one already validly baptized by such.[105]

So at the end of this period in the history of the question of rebaptism the treatment which Saint Fulgentius (468-533) gave to the matter of heretical and schismatical baptism resolved itself into nothing more than an anti-climactic summary of the doctrine already so ably and amply expounded by Saint Augustine.[106]

[102] *Contra Cresconium,* L. III, c. 6—*MPL,* XLIII, 499; *CV,* LII, 415.

[103] *De baptismo,* L. IV, c. 10, n. 16—*MPL,* XLIII, 164; *CV,* LI, 240.

[104] *Ep. Nicetae Aquileiensi epis.*—Hardouin, I, 1771; *JK,* n. 536.

[105] Canon 47—*MPL,* CXXX, 20.

[106] *Contra Fabianum fragmenta,* XIX—*MPL,* LXV, 795; *De fide ad Petrum,* L. I, c. 41—*MPL,* LXV, 692; *op. cit.,* L. XXXVI, c. 77—*MPL,* LXV, 703; *De Trinitate,* L. I, c. 11—*MPL,* LXV, 506.

CHAPTER II

Roman Law

An intensive search of the Roman law sources fails to disclose any particular legislation implicitly or explicitly stating any additional information in regard to the proper minister of baptism. Such a lack is quite explicable on the score that the Roman legislators were not primarily interested in the Church's sacramental system as such, but were naturally more concerned with the administrative and penal processes of ecclesiastical law. Hence, they were content to have the councils, synods and popes legislate on matters particularly sacramental, and then to adopt such legislation in the nature of civil law by the Emperor's approval. So some of the texts previously cited became, in this manner, an integral part of the Roman law system. Moreover, in reference to the minister of baptism, it must be borne in mind that the institution was more or less firmly determined by the time the emperors began to take an interest in the ecclesiastical organization.

However, from an explicit condemnation of certain abuses connected with the sacrament of baptism in general, several conclusions substantiating the previous statements can be directly deduced from Roman law.

In the Theodosian Code [1] and in the Justinian Code [2] it is the bishop who is censured for wrongly administering the sacrament. This exclusive reference to him supports what has already been shown from the councils—that the bishop was the ordinary minister in that period.

[1] C. Th. (16,6) 1.

[2] C. (1.6) 1: "Antistitem, qui sanctitatem baptismatis illicita usurpatione geminaverit, sacerdotio indignum esse censemus." (c. 375 A.D.)

In several other places of the Theodosian Code [3] and throughout the Justinian *Corpus* [4] heretics, particularly the Donatists, Novatians and Eunomians, were censured and punished severely for baptizing those who had already validly received the sacrament. Yet in none of these texts was it alleged that heretics could not baptize validly, but the sole fault condemned was the repetition of the sacrament. This would seem, then, to furnish indirect evidence in Roman law of the common teaching of the Church—that even heretics could baptize validly if they employed the proper matter and form.

These conclusions in regard to the minister of baptism are the only ones warranted by the Roman law legislation as contained in the sources. Hence, though Roman law adds no further information in regard to the institution, yet it does corroborate in these two instances the ecclesiastical law cited elsewhere.

[3] C. Th. (16.5) 58; (16.6) 4; (16.6) 5.

[4] C. (1.6) 2; (1.6) 3; N. (42.3).

CHAPTER III

To the Decree of Gratian

ART. 1. THE ORDINARY MINISTER OF SOLEMN BAPTISM

WITH the growth and expansion of the Church during the first few centuries it soon became evident that much of the old discipline was inadequate to cope with the development. Earlier the bishop of a diocese had found it comparatively easy to administer to the individual needs of his closely knit community himself; but rapid conversions had pushed the boundaries of his parish far beyond the city limits and into the rural districts. The deacons and priests who had assisted him at the cathedral church in time were sent to the villages in an effort to serve the people in small chapels subordinate to the episcopal church. Year after year this necessary tendency towards decentralization became more apparent.

Such development cannot be detected at once in the whole christian world. It was a gradual process that took place in individual dioceses according to the rapidity with which the seed of faith bore fruit in that locality. Simply because it was not simultaneous and depended in great part on the solution given to problems by bishops in individual instances, it is always difficult to describe the universal development of any ecclesiastical institution. A practice is no sooner stated to be general, when a contrary mode of acting in some single part of the Church is discovered.

So to say that the priest remained the extraordinary minister of solemn baptism for the first five centuries and then became the ordinary minister is not entirely accurate. As has been intimated in Chapter I, the development of this institution was much quicker in the East than in the West.

So time divisions can be set only with a hope of placing stopping points in the discussion.

The parochial organization of the East, Zorell thinks, may have started before the fourth century with the advent of the chorepiscopi or rural bishops, who, in their exercise of jurisdiction outside the episcopal city, were always in some degree dependent upon, if not actually subject to, their respective urban bishops.[1] Whether or not the chorepiscopi needed permission to baptize is not definitely certain. But even if they did not, the practice of having the bishop alone as the ordinary minister of the sacrament would not have been destroyed, since these clerics possessed a real episcopal character. Their importance here is that they were pastors with extensive power, and, as a result, were probably the first to instill into the rural groups a feeling akin to independence from the cathedral church.

When the Council of Sardica (343) [2] discouraged the consecration of chorepiscopi for those sections which could be served as well by a simple priest, this class began to decline. Within fifty years most of the rural churches were in the hands of priests, and were visited for the urban bishop by an itinerant clergy (*periodeutae*).[3] So it seems very likely that these priests were still under the immediate direction of the bishop, and that any ministrations they enjoyed in regard to the sacraments were undertaken with episcopal permission. However, the universal truth of this statement is not so evident as to warrant the conclusion of Hatch [4]— that the people who worshipped in these rural chapels were

[1] "*Die Entwickelung des Parochialsystems bis zum Ende der Karolingerzeit*"—*AKKR*, LXXXII (1902), 74-98 and 258-289.

[2] Canon 6—Hardouin, I, 639; Mansi, III, 10.

[3] Council of Laodicaea (343-381), canon 57—Hardouin, I, 792.

[4] *The Organization of the Early Christian Churches* (London: Longmans Green and Company, 1918), p. 198.

still considered members of the bishop's own church and as his parishioners.

As these extra-urban parishes of the East increased in size and number the permissions granted to priests to administer the sacraments became more frequent, and consequently the priests themselves came to be regarded by the people as the usual, if not the ordinary, minister. This has been noted previously in regard to those texts of Eastern writers and councils wherein the names of bishop and priest are linked in so intimate a manner as to lead one to believe that each enjoyed equal power in regard to the administration of baptism. However, as has been remarked, in the absence of proof to the contrary it must still be maintained that, though the priests of the East enjoyed such great power that the people regarded them as the usual ministers of baptism, as yet they were administering under some form of episcopal permission and were not canonically the ordinary ministers.[5]

In the Western Church parochial organization, on the other hand, was delayed by the savage persecutions before the edict of Constantine (313). Though as early as the fourth century, as is shown from the legislation of the Council of Elvira (305),[6] there was evidence of some form of extra-urban chapel, yet all references indicate that the clergy who assisted there were under the direct supervision of the bishop.

As in the East, so in the West these rural parishes gradually increased, and bit by bit the clerics who ministered there gained a certain independence. From the

[5] Thomassinus, *Vetus et nova Ecclesiae disciplina*, Pars I, lib. II, cap. 23, n. 12: "In ecclesia Graeca ex canonibus Apostolicis, baptismi ministri erant presbyteri, ita tamen ut potestati episcopi obnoxios se esse prae se ferrent."

[6] Canon 77—Hardouin, I, 258; Labbe, II, 18; Mansi, II, 18.

middle of the fifth century these rural churches with resident priests in charge to say Mass were grouped together according to locality. Each group thus united was under the supervision of a main Church (*basilica dioecesana*), and it was in the latter Church that baptism was administered solemnly at Easter and Pentecost by the resident pastor of that Church (*presbyter dioecesanus*). It was because of his right to baptize, as granted by the bishop, that he alone received the chrism, and it was in virtue of the supremacy he exercised over the other priests, exemplified in part by this special permission to baptize, that this man came to be known in the sixth century as the archpriest, and his Church as the *ecclesia baptismalis.* However, shortly before the councils of the sixth and seventh centuries the status of the other rural priests changed also, since the rural parishes to which they ministered had begun to be more independent in form.[7]

Because of these conditions at the beginning of this historical period in the Western Church there was still the same insistence upon the legislation that priests should not baptize solemnly, unless the bishop were impeded or had given his permission.[8] For sometime this permission had been given with greater frequency; but that the bishop should still be the ordinary minister, at least at the time of the Pasch, was shown by the way in which Saint Gregory

[7] Bouix, *Tractatus de Parocho* (3rd ed., Parisiis, 1880); Henri Lesêtre, *La Paroisse* (3rd ed., Paris: V. Lecoffre, 1908), pp. 1-32; Imbart de la Tour, *Les paroisses rurales du IVe au VIe siècle* (Paris: A. Piccard et Fils, 1900); Nicholas Connolly, *The Canonical Erection of Parishes,* The Catholic University of America Canon Law Studies, n. 114 (Washington, D. C.: The Catholic University of America Press, 1938), pp. 16-30; *Realencyklopädie für protestantische Theologie und Kirche* (24 vols., Leipzig, 1896-1913), s. v. "Pfarre, Pfarrer," XV, 240-248.

[8] *Capitula collecta a Martino epis. Bracarensi,* cc. 52-53 — Hardouin, III, 397; Labbe, IX, 856; Mansi, IX, 856. Council of Seville (619), canon 7— Hardouin, III, 560; Labbe, X, 559; Mansi, X, 559.

of Tours (544-594) [9] and Saint Gregory the Great (Pope Gregory I) (590-604) [10] excoriated the secular rulers who obstructed the solemn administrations of baptism at the cathedral baptistery by detaining the bishops in prison. This ire may have been provoked in part by the fact that in the time of the Gregorys there was a dearth of priests. Hence a bishop's absence from his diocese and the consequent need of his parochial labors were more keenly felt.[11]

With the passing years there emerged in spite of episcopal exhortations a general unwillingness on the part of the people to defer solemn baptism until the time of the Pasch or Pentecost.[12] This, coupled with the bishop's inability, because of the increased number of administrative matters clamoring for his supervision, to attend to those who had waited for his ministration, finally brought it about that by the middle of the seventh century [13] baptisms were conferred mostly by priests, and so they began to take a major part in the Apostolic mandate to teach and baptize.[14]

From the middle of the seventh century onwards the parish priest administered solemn baptism whether or not the bishop was present.[15] Though it appears from the legis-

[9] *Historia Francorum*, Lib. X, c. 15—*MPL*, LXXI, 545; *Monumenta Germaniae Historica* (*MGH*) (188 vols. incomplete, Hanoverae, 1826–), *Scriptores Rerum Merovingicarum* (*SSRM*) (7vols., 1884-1920), I (ed. W. Arndt et B. Krusch, 1884), 425.

[10] *Epistolarum Lib. I, Ep. XXXIII*—*MPL*, LXXVII, 485; *MGH*, *Epistolae* (*Ep.*) (7 vols., 1887-1928), I (ed. Paulus Ewald, 1887), 44; *JE*, n. 1101. *Libri Dialogorum*, Lib. IV, c. 26—*MPL*, LXXVII, 360.

[11] Martene, *De antiquis ecclesiae ritibus*, I, 19.

[12] II Council of Macon (585), canon 3—Hardouin, III, 461; Mansi, IX, 951; *MGH, Leges in 4°*, Sectio III (*Concilia*), I (ed. F. Maassen, 1893), 166.

[13] Corblet, *Histoire du sacrament de baptême*, I, 301.

[14] Council of Clovesho (747), canon 9—Hardouin, III, 1955.

[15] IV Council of Toledo (633), canon 6—Hardouin, III, 581; Mansi, X, 618. Cf. also Theodulf of Orleans, c. 797), *Liber de ordine baptismi*, c. 17: "Nam presbyteris, sive absentibus sive praesentibus episcopis, baptizare et baptizatos chrismate ungere licet, sed quod ab episcopo fuerit consecratum." —*MPL*, CV, 236.

lation that there was no longer any need to seek episcopal permission, yet the priest's break from subjection to the episcopal jurisdiction in this matter was not yet complete. Obligations still existed on each side. The priest, for his part, was to baptize in the diocese for which he had been ordained. He was not to perform the sacrament in any other bishop's territory without first seeking permission. Moreover, each year at Lent he was obliged to render to his proper Ordinary an account of the baptisms he had administered during the past year.[16] The bishop, on the other hand, was to safeguard the sacrament in his diocese [17] by carefully instructing his priests in the administration of it.[18] Then on his episcopal visitation he was to make prudent inquiries from his priests concerning the essentials and rites of the sacrament,[19] correcting completely any mistakes found.[20]

Thomassinus stated [21] that after the time of Charlemagne churches other than the cathedral were permitted to have baptismal fonts, and that these were under the supervision

[16] Council in Germany (743), canon 3—Hardouin, III, 1920; Mansi, XII, 366; *MGH, Leges in 4°*, Sectio III (*Concilia*), II (ed. A. Werminghoff, 1904), 3. Council of Vernum (755), canons 7-8—*MGH, Leges in 4°*, Sectio II (*Capitularia Regum Francorum*), I (ed. A. Boretius, 1883), 32. *Capitulary of Benedict the Levite*, Lib. V, c. 60—*MGH, Leges in folio*, II² (ed. G. H. Pertz, 1837), 49. Though most of the authorities quoted up to the present reflect particular sources, yet they must be understood as indicative of a general trend.

[17] Charlemagne (768-814), *Capitulare Ecclesiasticum* (789), cap. LXIX—*MGH, Leges in folio*, I (ed. G. H. Pertz, 1835), 64; *MPL*, LXXXXVII, 295.

[18] II Council of Tours (813), canon 18—*MGH, Leges in 4°*, Sectio III (*Concilia*), II, 288.

[19] Haito Basiliensis (822), *Capitularia*, cc. 5-7—*MGH, Leges in 4°*, Sectio II (*Capitularia Regum Francorum*), I, 363.

[20] Ivo of Chartres (1040-1117), *Decretum*, Pars I, cap. 75—*MPL*, CLXI, 83.

[21] *Vetus et nova Ecclesiae disciplina*, Pars I, lib. II, c. 5, n. 8.

of an archpriest. However, it would seem that Thomassinus spoke of the *ecclesia baptismalis* previously mentioned, and that he placed their date of origin a few centuries late. For certainly he could not mean that these churches were found in the city, since a particular council of that period proves otherwise.[22] So it would seem, and Chardon agrees with this,[23] that Thomassinus referred to the baptismal churches, and while he mentioned the archpriest in particular, yet he failed to note that by the end of the ninth century priests attached to the minor rural churches also had fonts.[24]

Before the eleventh century city parishes as distinguished from the bishop's church, with the exception of the churches in Rome and Alexandria, had been unknown, and so the baptisms were performed in the city at the cathedral by the bishop himself or by the priests whom he had delegated. But around the year 1000, because of the increase in urban populations, bishops began to erect a few parishes around the cathedral, and to give their priests the right to baptize.[25] It was to churches such as these that the Council of Limoges (1032) had reference.[26]

So, though the bishop had previously retained some vestige of his erstwhile exclusive right in his capacity of sole

[22] Council of Meaux (845), canon 48: "Ut nemo presbyterorum baptizare praesumat, nisi in vicis et ecclesiis baptismalibus."—Hardouin, IV, 1491.

[23] *Histoire des sacraments*, I, 323.

[24] "Invaluit utique post nonum praesertim saeculum consuetudo concedendi parochis usum baptisterii, sed in ruralibus solummodo ecclesiis, haud vero in civitatibus, in quibus residebat episcopus ..."—Pallottini, *Collectio Omnium Conclusionum et Resolutionum quae in causis propositis apud S. Cong. Cardinalium S. Concilii Tridentini Interpretum prodierunt ab anno 1564 ad annum 1860* (18 vols., Romae, 1868-1893), XVI, 4.

[25] *Realencyklopädie für protestantische Theologie und Kirche*, s. v. "Pfarre, Pfarrer," XV, 245.

[26] Sessio II—Mansi, XIX, 543.

ordinary minister of baptism by having the cathedral church as the only place of baptism for the city, now even that semblance was relinquished. Soon it became common for the bishops to leave the administration of baptism entirely to the priests of the city. Yet as a reminder of the former reservation the custom arose, says Mabillon,[27] for the bishop to baptize two or three infants on Holy Saturday, even though the priests baptized all the rest on that day.

At the same time, it may be noted, the administration of the sacrament became so definitely parochial, that any infringement upon this right was challenged. In the general progress of the Church oratories had arisen on private estates and in monasteries. Though these had assisted the Church by caring for a certain portion of the neighbouring people, yet oftentimes the principal reason why individuals maintained them was for the financial gain that could be realized from the revenues. With the rise of the parochial system the pastors fought this infringement upon their rights and sought to restrict the rights of these quasi-parishes. On the other hand, the lords and religious were loath to relinquish such a lucrative practice. Eventually laws were passed in the various districts, so that it was forbidden for any priest to baptize outside the actual parish church,[28] and the monks and regulars could minister to the people only with the consent of the bishop.[29]

[27] *Musaeum Italicum* (2 vols., Parisiis, 1724), II, 95 and 137.

[28] *Ecclesiastical laws of King Edgar* (967), c. 15: "Docemus etiam, ut quilibet sacerdos baptismum peragat, simul ac requiritur; et deinde in parochia sua . . ."—Hardouin, VI A, 661; Labbe, XVIII, 515; Mansi, XVIII A, 515. Burchard of Worms (✝1025), *Decretorum Libri Viginti*, lib. IV, cc. 4, 44 et 47—*MPL*, CXL, 731 and 736.

[29] Connolly, *The Canonical Erection of Parishes*, p. 40. Cf. also the Council of Poitiers (1100), canon 10: "Ut clericis regularibus iussu episcopi sui baptizare . . . liceat "; canon 11: " Ut nullus monachorum parochiale ministerium presbyterorum, id est, baptizare . . . praesumat."—Mansi, XX, 1124.

Thus such a great change had been wrought in this institution throughout the centuries, that at the end of this period the priest, and particularly the parish priest, was almost exclusively referred to as the ordinary minister of solemn baptism.[30]

ART. 2. THE EXTRAORDINARY MINISTER OF SOLEMN BAPTISM

The noticeable lack of mention of the deacon as the extraordinary minister of baptism, and an increased insistence upon the power of the priest which prevailed during the fifth century, continued through the following centuries.

The decree by which Pope Gelasius (492-496) instructed deacons to baptize, in all likelihood solemnly, but only in those cases of extreme necessity which would permit even the laity to act, was frequently quoted during this period.[31] Probably the number of priests had so increased that there was little need to call upon the ministrations of the deacon.

So there is rare mention that he still retained his right to baptize,[32] and for the greater part his competence in this regard seems to have been relegated to the assignment of assisting the priest in the administration of baptism.[33]

[30] Ivo of Chartres, *Panormia*, Lib. I, cap. 23: "Quod soli sacerdotes debent baptizare."—*MPL*, CLXI, 1052. Honorius Augustodunus (✝ 1136), *Gemma Animae*, Lib. III, c. 116—*MPL*, CLXXII, 674. Hugh of Saint Victor (✝ 1142), *De officiis ecclesiasticis*, Lib. I, c. 13—*MPL*, CLXXVII, 389.

[31] Burchard of Worms, *Decretorum Libri Viginti*, Lib. IV, c. 57.—*MPL*, CXL, 738. Ivo of Chartres, *Decretum*, Pars I, cap. 67 and 252—*MPL*, CLXI, 82 and 119.

[32] *Canones Aelfrici*, canon 16: "Diaconus est . . . ei liceat baptizare."—Hardouin, VI A, 981; Labbe, XIX, 699; Mansi, XIX, 699.

[33] Atto of Vercelli, *Capitulare*, c. XX: "Ut in nulla ecclesia cuiuslibet dioeceseos ubi baptismus celebratur, presbyter absque diacono esse reperiatur. Unde omnis presbyter non habens diaconum, eligat sibi personam et plebi innotescat: tunc ad pontificem suum consignans deducet, cuius vitam probatam habeat, et diaconus consecretur . . . Tantum est ut sine diacono non sit."—*MPL*, CXXXIV, 32.

ART. 3. THE MINISTER OF PRIVATE BAPTISM IN CASES OF NECESSITY

The fundamental rules laid down in the first five centuries did not change in this period. In cases of necessity not only minor clerics but also the laity were permitted to baptize. As a matter of fact, none of the authors speaks of this subject without referring to it as a discipline of the earlier popes and councils.[34]

However, this permission to baptize was to be used only in extreme cases. The non-ordained who rashly baptized were excommunicated, placed under severe penances before they were readmitted to ecclesiastical communion, and forever excluded from the reception of orders.[35]

The necessity of this strict prohibition for people in general cannot be readily understood in view of the numerous texts in which priests are censured for permitting people to die without baptism.[36] From these it would seem that the laity, far from abusing the privilege, did not use it as regularly as they should in cases of necessity.

[34] *Collectio Hispana*, Lib. IV, tit. 22—*MPL*, LXXXIV, 70. Council of Mainz (813), canon 4—Mansi, XIV, 66; *MGH*, *Leges in 4°*, Sectio III (*Concilia*), II, 261. Council of Tribur (895), canon 12—Mansi, XVIII A, 138. Ivo of Chartres, *Panormia*, Lib. I, cap. 24 et 26—*MPL*, CLXI, 1052; *Decretum*, Pars I, cap. 64—*MPL*, CLXI, 82. Algerus (1070-1133), *Libri tres de sacramentis*, Lib. III, c. 6—*MPL*, CLXXX, 838. Honorius Augustodunus, *Gemma Animae*, Lib. III, c. 116—*MPL*, CLXXII, 674. *Beati Lanfranci Arch. Cantuarensis Ep. X* (*ad Domnaldum Hiberniae epis.*)—Mansi, XX, 32.

[35] This is quoted as being in the Penitential of Theodore of Canterbury (Lib. I, c. 9, n. 11) in McNeil-Gamer's *Medieval handbook of penance*, Record of Civilization: Sources and Studies, edited under the auspices of the Dept. of History, Columbia University, n. 29 (New York: Columbia University Press, 1938), p. 193. It is also found in the spurious book taken from this work of Theodore—*Gregorii Papae III* (*731-741*) *Iudicia*, n. 30—Mansi, XII, 295.

[36] Such texts will be cited in Article 5 of this chapter.

In regard to women, the prohibition placed by the IV Council of Carthage (398) was frequently repeated.[37] However, Corblet remarks that Saint Isidore of Seville († 636) interpolated the phrase *nisi necessitate cogente,* and in this introduced a new but logical interpretation for the ancient text.[38]

It may also be noted that the repugnance to the parents' baptizing of their own children and to their consequent assuming of both the corporal and spiritual paternity did not refer to cases of necessity.[39] Early in the twelfth century Hugh of Saint Victor (c. 1096-1141) permitted the mother to baptize if no one else were there to act,[40] while the same permission seemingly had been granted to the father as early as the ninth century.[41] It is of interest also to note a particular twelfth century custom existing in Ireland, where, as Corblet says, the father very often baptized the new-born babe. No reasons for such a practice have been cited.[42]

ART. 4. BAPTISM ADMINISTERED BY HERETICS, SCHISMATICS, PAGANS AND JEWS

The effect which Saint Augustine strove to produce in the fifth century evidently had been achieved with lasting re-

37 So it is included in the writings of Ivo of Chartres (*Panormia,* Lib. I, c. 25—*MPL,* CLXI, 1051; *Decretum,* Pars I, c. 65—*MPL,* CLXI, 82).

38 *Histoire du sacrament de baptême,* I, 320. Corblet does not cite the source from which he gathered this, nor can it be found among Isidore's writings. Neither is it mentioned by any other commentator.

39 Pope Urban II (1088-1099), *Ep. CCLXXII—MPL,* CLI, 529; *JL,* n. 5742.

40 *De officiis ecclesiasticis,* Lib. I, cap. 13: "Absentibus altaris ministris, et clericis omnibus et urgente necessitate, laicus baptizare potest. Si nec laicus praesto fuerit, mulier baptizet. Si nulla alia reperiri potuerit, mater ipsa baptizet. Nec propter haec a viro suo separabitur, quia per necessitatem excusatur."—*MPL,* CLXXVII, 389.

41 Council of Constantinople (814), canon 16—Hardouin, IV, 1054; Mansi, XIV, 122. Pope John VIII (872-882), *Ep. LXXXIV—JE,* n. 3258.

42 *Histoire du sacrament de baptême,* I, 325.

sults. All controversy regarding baptisms administered by heretics and schismatics appears to have been settled finally. During this period the validity of baptism when conferred with the proper matter and form was acknowledged.[43]

That any doubt existed as to what this proper form was there can be no question. All agreed that the invocation of the Blessed Trinity was both necessary and sufficient, so that if the sacrament was conferred in this manner, regardless of the worthiness or dignity of the minister, it was valid.[44]

It was on this basis that distinctions were frequently drawn with regard to the baptisms administered by the various heretical sects, and if they were valid by reason of the form, then the reception into the Church of such people who had received the sacrament in this way differed only

[43] Saint Gregory the Great, *Epistolarum Lib. VI, Ep. XXXVII — MPL*, LXXVII, 828; *MGH, Epistolae*, I, 413. Council of Rouen (649), canon 5 —Mansi, X, 1200. *Capitulary of Benedict the Levite*, Lib. VII, c. 403—*MGH, Leges in folio*, II², 127. Ivo of Chartres, *Decretum*, Pars I, cc. 160-161—*MPL*, CLXI, 96-97; *Panormia*, Lib. I, c. 87—*MPL*, CLXI, 1064. Abbot Rupert Tuitensis († 1135), *De Trinitate et operibus eius, In Levit.*, Lib. II, c. 25 — *MPL*, CLXVII, 275; *De divinis officiis*, Lib. X, c. 5 — *MPL*, CLXX, 265.

[44] Pope Gregory II (715-731), *Ep. XIV*, n. 8—*MPL*, LXXXIX, 525; *JE*, n. 2157. Pope Zachary (741-752), *Ep. X* (*ad Bonifacium Arch.*)—Mansi, XII, 339; *JE*, n. 2274. *Capitulary of Benedict the Levite*, Lib. VI, c. 68—*MGH, Leges*, II² 77. Burchard of Worms, *Decretorum libri viginti*, Lib. IV, cc. 39 and 41—*MPL*, CXL, 734. Ivo of Chartres, *Decretum*, Lib. I, c. 233—*MPL*, CLXI, 115. Worthy of special notice is the text reproduced verbatim in many authors among whom are: Bede (who seems to have been the first to cite it), *In S. Ioannis Evangelium expositio*, c. 3—*MPL*, XCII, 668; Alcuin, *Commentarium in Ioannem*, Lib. II, c. 5—*MPL*, C, 779; and Rabanus Maurus, *Homiliae in evangelia et epistolas*, Homilia LXXII—*MPL*, CX, 283. The text reads the same in all three: "Nequaquam videlicet eam, postquam semel expleta fuerit, posse repeti: sive enim haereticus, sive schismaticus, sive facinorosus quisque in confessione sanctae Trinitatis baptizet, non valet ille, qui ita baptizatus est, a bonis catholicis rebaptizari, ne confessio vel invocatio tanti nominis videatur annullari."

because of the beliefs they had formerly held.[45] As a result those who received baptism from the early heretics could be classified in three ways.[46] First, those who had to be baptized on entrance, as did the Paulianists, because the form was vitiated. Secondly, those who had received valid baptism (Apollinarists, Macedonians, Novatians and Quartodecimans), but who had to be anointed with chrism upon entrance into the true Church. Thirdly, those whose baptisms were valid and who were received simply by an abjuration of their former beliefs (Nestorians, Eutychians, Manichaens, Valentinians and Marcionites).

Apparently, however, not all the opinions expressed by Saint Augustine were immediately accepted. He believed that anyone, even if unbaptized, who used the Trinitarian form baptized validly. But Augustine hesitated to express it outright without reservation, and so he uttered it subject to correction if the Church should choose to teach differently.[47]

Some did disagree with this doctrine and considered baptism conferred by pagans to be invalid.[48] Stranger still,

[45] Concilium Quinisextum, canon 95—Hardouin, III, 1694; Mansi, XI, 968. Fulgentius Ferrandus, *Breviatio Canonum*, cc. 173, 175, 193—*MPL*, LXXXVIII, 827. Saint Gregory of Tours, *Historia Francorum*, Lib. II, c. 1—*MPL*, LXXI, 192; *MGH, SSRM*, I, 59. Pseudo-Isidore, *Decreta Siricii Papae*, cap. I—*MPL*, CXXX, 678 and Hinschius, *Decretales pseudo-Isidorianae et capitula Angilrammi* (Lipsiae, 1863), p. 520. *Ep. Innocentii Papae ad episcopos Macedoniae*—*MPL*, CXXX, 718, and Hinschius, *op. cit.*, p. 550, and *JK*, n. 303.

[46] *Epistolarum Gregorii Magni Lib. XIV*, Lib. VI, ep. 67—*MPL*, LXVII, 1205; *MGH, Epistolae*, I[2] 325. The classification is made in Migne in the commentary on this text.

[47] *De baptismo contra Donatistas*, Lib. VII, c. 53, n. 102—*MPL*, XLIII, 242; *CV*, LI, 338.

[48] *Capitulary of Benedict the Levite*, Lib. VII, c. 401: "Praecipimus ut qui a paganis baptizati sunt, denuo a Christi sacerdotibus in nomine Sanctae Trinitatis baptizentur, et postea ab episcopis chrismentur, quia aliter Christiani nec dici nec esse possunt."—Mansi, XVII B, 1112; *MGH, Leges*, II[2],

even a priest mistakenly ordained without being baptized was practically classed as a pagan, since all those whom he had baptized were to be rebaptized as soon as the error had been detected. Though the matter might be explained, in reference to outright pagans, by saying that in all probability they did not use the correct form, yet it is difficult to allege the same reason for the supposed invalidity of the sacraments conferred by a priest, who certainly must have acted correctly and in good faith.[49]

That the whole question concerning baptisms conferred by the unbaptized was far from settled was evidenced by the difficulty presented to Pope Nicholas I (858-867) in reference to the validity of a baptism conferred by an unbaptized Jew. The papal response to this question was so decisive that all future doubts in this regard seem to have been dispelled.[50]

Thus later authors indicated that pagans,[51] Jews,[52] unbaptized priests,[53]—in fact any person using the Trinitarian formula—conferred valid baptism.

127. The text, although changed in part, was taken from Pope Gregory III (731-741), *Ep. ad Bonifacium*—Mansi, XII, 278; *MGH, Epistolae*, III, 279; *JE*, n. 2239. This is proved by Emil Seckel, "Studien zu Benedictus Levita. VIII," in *Neues Archiv der Gesellschaft für ältere deutsche Geschichtskunde*, XLI (1917), 213.

[49] Council of Compiegne (759), canon 9: "Si presbyter ordinatus deprehenderit se non esse baptizatum, baptizetur, et ordinetur iterum, et omnes quos prius baptizaverit."—Mansi, XII, 657. This is also quoted in the *Capitulary of Benedict the Levite*, Lib. VI, c. 94—*MGH, Leges*, II^2, 78; and the *Penitentiary of Egbert of York*, cc. VII and XVII—Mansi, XII, 435-436. A further study of the authenticity of these texts will be made in Article 4 of the next chapter.

[50] *Responsa ad consulta Bulgarorum*, nn. 14 et 15—Hardouin, V, 360; Mansi, XV, 432; *JE*, n. 2812.

[51] Ivo of Chartres, *Panormia*, cc. 27, 29—*MPL*, CLXI, 1052.

[52] Algerus, *Libri tres de sacramentis*, Lib. III, c. 6—*MPL*, CLXXX, 838.

[53] Burchard of Worms, *Decretorum libri viginti*, Lib. IV, c. 100—*MPL*, CXL, 749.

ART. 5. LEGISLATION INCIDENTAL TO THE MINISTER OF BAPTISM

In addition to the texts previously cited to determine the actual minister of baptism, the early councils, synods and writers contained other legislation incidental to this institution. Hence, though it does not directly concern the status of the ministers as such, yet it does prove of sufficient interest to mention.

A. *Money*

Throughout the centuries one important matter was frequently repeated, and that was in regard to exacting money for the administration of the sacrament. Lactantius († c. 320) [54] and Pope Saint Gelasius (492-496) [55] were the only ones in the first period to mention it, the latter stating that though money could not be exacted, yet if people gave it willingly it could be accepted.

But in this later period of the institution there was frequent mention of the question, and most of the texts are of the same tenor as that of Pope Saint Gelasius. The insistence at this time may have become so evident either because there were more abuses in this regard, or because the increased number of ordinary ministers demanded constant repetitions of the established rule and usage. At any rate the councils [56] and the various authors of the Penitentials and Capitularies [57] stressed this so very much that it was

[54] *Divinae Institutiones*, Lib. III, c. 26—*MPL*, VI, 433.

[55] *Ep. ad universos Lucaniae episcopos*, cap. 7—*JK*, n. 636.

[56] III Council of Braga (572), c. 7—Mansi, IX, 840; Council of Bourges (1031), c. 12—Mansi, XIX, 504; Council of Rheims (1049), c. 5—Mansi, XIX, 742; Council of Rouen (1050), c. 16—Mansi, XIX, 753; Council of Rheims (1119), c. 4—Mansi, XXI, 236; Council of London (1125), c. 2—Mansi, XXI, 330; Council of Tours (1163), c. 6—Mansi, XXI, 1178; and many others.

[57] *Excerptiones Ecgberti*, c. 12—Mansi, XII, 414. Charlemagne, *Capitula presbyterorum*, cap. 5—*MGH, Leges*, I, 138. *Capitulary of Benedict the*

made a matter of investigation for the bishop on his canonical visitation.[58] In fact, those who violated this precept were often punished by the stated penalty of excommunication for two or three months.[59]

B. *Unnecessary deferring of baptism by a priest*

Additional legislation concerned the priest who refused to baptize a sick child when it was brought to him. In regard to this most of the texts contented themselves with warning such a minister that he would be answerable to God if the child died without baptism.[60] But one minor council ruled that he should be suspended for a length of time to be determined by the bishop,[61] and the Penitential of Theodore of Canterbury suggested that he be deposed.[62]

C. *Disposition, time, and status of the priest*

Other legislation which was insisted on with less stress may be summed up by a simple noting that the priest who baptized had to be, in the ordinary administration, fasting,[63] and that he was not to confer the sacrament except during

Levite, Lib. V, c. 172 and Lib. VI, c. 183—*MGH, Leges*, II² 55 et 80. *Capitula Rodulfi*, c. 18—Mansi, XIV, 952. *Capitularia Herardi Turonensis*, c. 31—Mansi, XVII B, 1287. Regino, *De ecclesiasticis disciplinis*, Lib. I, cc. 121 et 127—*MPL*, CXXXII, 215 et 217.

[58] Regino, *op. cit.*, Lib. I, c. 1, n. 19—*MPL*, CXXXII, 188.

[59] Council of Merida (666), c. 9—Mansi, XI, 81. XI Council of Toledo (675), c. 8—Mansi, XI, 142. *Excerptiones Ecgberti*, c. 40—Mansi, XII, 417. Council of London (1138), c. 1—Mansi, XXI, 511.

[60] *Gregorii Papae III Iudicia*, n. 30—Mansi, XII, 295. *Capitulary of Theodulf of Orleans*, c. 17—Mansi, XIII, 998. *Liber Legum Ecclesiasticorum (994)*, n. 17—Mansi, XIX, 183. Burchard of Worms, *Decretorum libri viginti*, Lib. IV, cc. 46 et 49—*MPL*, CXL, 736. Atto of Vercelli, *Capitulare*, c. 19—*MPL*, CXXXIV, 34.

[61] Council of Berghamsted (697), c. 7—Mansi, XII, 112.

[62] Cap. 88—*MPL*, LXXXXIX, 957.

[63] Council of Rouen (1072), c. 5—Mansi, XX, 36.

the times properly designated.[64] Moreover, though it be true that baptisms conferred by criminal priests were valid,[65] yet a degraded priest was to baptize only in a case of extreme necessity.[66]

[64] Council of Auxerre (578), c. 18—Mansi, XIX, 914. These times occurred at the Pasch and at Pentecost. At the time this council was held there was still prevalent the effort to make these the sole times for solemn baptism, but with the passing centuries such a regulation was abandoned, and is found only in isolated instances. The Council of Auxerre placed a three month excommunication on a priest who acted contrary to this rule.

[65] *Responsa Stephani Papae II* (who ruled for three days in 752, and hence this may be spurious), n. 10—Mansi, XII, 561. Pope Urban II (1088-1099), *Ep. XVII (ad Lucium praepositum S. Juventii)*—Mansi, XX, 661; *JL*, n. 5743.

[66] Council of Verberie (752), c. 15—Mansi, XVII B, 164; *MGH, Leges in 4°*, Sectio II (*Capitularia Regum Francorum*), I, 41.

CHAPTER IV

To the Code of Canon Law

The development in regard to the minister of baptism as outlined in the preceding chapter practically completes the historical evolution of the institution. From Gratian until the Code of Canon Law nothing of particular importance was changed. Though the period was unproductive of any major development, yet it is important for consideration. The collections made during those centuries, the papal pronouncements, the multitude of synods and councils convened throughout the Church—all combine to evidence that that which had previously been legislated in regard to the minister of baptism for one or more localities now actually became the universal rule. At the same time in accordance with the further development of canonical science throughout this long period, the decretalists and canonists were not content with merely stating who was the proper minister, but sought also to determine the more specific matters pertaining to him.

Art. 1. The Ordinary Minister of Solemn Baptism

Though the bishop was still regarded as one of the ordinary ministers of baptism, yet, as a rule, he did not perform the ceremony. The occasions upon which he did act were usually those that seemed to merit greater solemnity, as in the case of children of the royal family. However, around the seventeenth century it was considered that the baptism of adults converted to the Church was worthy of such added solemnity, and so it was generally required that such cases be referred to the bishop of the diocese, so that he himself might baptize them, or else authorize their pastor with the permission to do so in his name.[1] It was constantly maintained that it was his duty to safeguard the proper administration of the sacrament among the priests of his diocese,[2] concerning which obligation, however, the Council of London (1237) at the very beginning of this period had declared that it might be fulfilled by a constant surveillance on the part of the archdeacon.[3]

In reference to all this Gratian merely collected the material already cited in the preceding chapters. So for him the priest undoubtedly was an ordinary minister of solemn baptism,[4] a fact accepted in like unanimity by the theologians of his time,[5] by even the earliest of the decretalists,[6] and later by Pope Eugene IV (1431-1447).[7]

[1] Synodal Constitutions of the Province of Naples (1699), Tit. I, cap. II, n. 12—*Acta et decreta sacrorum conciliorum recentiorum, collectio Lacensis* (7 vols., Friburgi Brisgoviae: Herder, 1870-1890), I, 160 (hereafter *Coll. Lac.*). Provincial Council of Avignon (1725), Tit. XXV, cap. VIII—*Coll. Lac.*, I, 525. Schmalzgrueber, *Ius Ecclesiasticum Universum* (5 vols. in 12, Romae, 1843-1845), Lib. III, tit. 42, n. 45.

[2] Pax Jordanus, *Elucubrationes diversae* (3 vols., Coloniae Allobrogum et Lugduni, 1729), I, 145.

[3] Cap. II—Mansi, XXIII, 445.

[4] C. 19, D. IV, *de cons.* This is taken from St. Isidore's *De Officiis*, Lib. II, c. 24.

[5] Peter Lombard, *Sententiarum Libri Quattuor* (2nd ed., 2 vols., Ad Claras Aquas prope Florentiam: Ex Typographia Collegii S. Bonaventurae, 1916), Lib. IV, dist. VI. Hugh of Saint Victor, *De officiis ecclesiasticis*, Lib. I, cap. 13—*MPL*, CLXXVII, 389.

[6] Hostiensis (Henricus de Segusia), *Summa Aurea* (Venetiis, 1570), p. 310. Ioannes Andreae, *In quinque decretalium libros commentaria* (Venetiis, 1581), Lib. III, tit. 42.

[7] Eugenius IV (in Conc. Florentin.), const. "*Exultate Deo*", 22 nov. 1439, § 10: "... Minister huius sacramenti est sacerdos, cui ex officio competit baptizare."—*Fontes*, n. 52. These words were later embodied in many councils and synods, among which were the Council of Mainz (1451), tit. *de baptismo*—Mansi, XXXII, 121, and the Council of Besançon (1571), tit. *de baptismo*—Mansi, XXXVI B, 49.

Gratian's adoption of practically all of the previously cited writings of Saint Augustine is shown in his canons referring to the fact that the individual merits of the priest, whether he be good or bad, in no way affect the sacrament itself.[8]

As was evidenced at the close of the immediately preceding period, the custom of conferring the sacrament in the local parish church had become rather widespread. This practice became even more common in the present period, for with the increase of population the right of having an individual baptistery was quite freely granted to even the smaller churches. Quite naturally with this development the pastor likewise became the ordinary minister of baptism for every member of his flock, and to him was entrusted the sacred task of seeing that none of them died without that sacrament.[9]

So to the pastor and to the bishop alone pertained this ordinary administration of solemn baptism, and they alone could delegate another priest to perform it.[10] Grana-Nieto (17th century) in particular defended the pastor's right by arguing that Christ had confided baptism to the Apostles because they had charge of the flock, rather than because of their episcopal character. So since pastors now had a shepherd's duty in regard to their people, to them likewise pertained the right to baptize.[11]

[8] C. 25, 26, 27, 39, 41, D. IV, *de cons.*

[9] I Council of Fermo (1590), cap. XIII—Mansi, XXXVI B, 901. IV Provincial Council of Milan (1579), Pars I, cap. 7—Mansi, XXXIV A, 361. Council of Aix (1585), canon 6—Mansi, XXXIV B, 944. Synod of Mount Lebanon (1736), Pars II, c. 2—*Coll. Lac.*, II, 117.

[10] S. C. Ep. et Reg., *Bituntina*, 4 sept. 1772—*Analecta Iuris Pontificii*, XII (1873), 120.

[11] *Catena Iurium Utriusque Iurisprudentiae* (Lugduni, 1678), Lib. III, tit. 42, n. 3.

He further stated,[12] and in this he was joined by Schmalzgrueber (1663-1735),[13] that solemn baptism pertained to the priest-pastor in a special manner, since for the lawfulness of the act of baptism it was requisite that the minister be both *de iure* (*qua sacerdos*) and *ex officio* (*qua parochus*) qualified. Hence, though they did not state that the conferring of baptism was solely a jurisdictional act, so that if it were conferred by one without such jurisdiction it would be null, yet they did maintain that it was an act which for the lawfulness of its performance must be posited by one with either ordinary or delegated jurisdiction.

It was in view of these requisites that a pastor, simply because he was a pastor, could not at will baptize everyone licitly. For a fully lawful procedure a person had to be baptized by the pastor of the place in which he had his domicile, or by a pastor who otherwise had obtained jurisdiction over him by custom or prescription.[14] So it was wrong for a pastor to baptize another's subjects when they were brought to him, if they could easily be presented to their proper pastor for the administration of the baptism. It may also be noted that no bishop or pastor could act licitly outside of his territory, unless he had obtained the necessary permission.[15]

In view of all this insistence upon the necessity of jurisdiction for the proper administration of the sacrament of

[12] *Op. cit.*, Lib. III, tit. 42, n. 4.

[13] *Ius ecclesiasticum universum*, Lib. III, tit. 42, n. 41.

[14] Schmalzgrueber, *op. cit.*, Lib. III, tit. 42, n. 42.

[15] La Croix, *Theologia Moralis* (3 vols., Venetiis, 1761), T. II, L. VI, Pars I, art. 1, n.1. Caponi, *Institutiones canonicae* (2nd ed., 2 vols., in 1, Coloniae Allobrogum, 1734), I, 227-228. II Plenary Council of Baltimore (1866), Tit. V, cap. 2, *de baptismo—Concilii plenarii Baltimorensis II in ecclesia metropolitana Baltimorensi a die VII a die XXI Octobris A. D. MDCCCLXVI habiti et a Sede Apostolica recogniti acta et decreta* (editio altera, Ioannes Murphy: Baltimore, 1894), n. 227.

baptism, it is not strange that Lancelotti (1522-1590) maintained that if any simple priest should presume to baptize solemnly in ordinary circumstances without this requisite delegation or permission, though he would not become irregular, yet he would sin gravely.[16] And in support of this opinion it may be noted that though the Constitutions of Padua (1339) had cited a common law of the fourteenth century to the effect that anyone who disobeyed these restrictions should be punished severely,[17] yet later Basso († 1713) insisted that such severity should not be expressed in the infliction of an excommunication or of an irregularity.[18]

Evidently the pastor had only with some opposition received this exclusive right to baptize. As has been seen in the previous chapter, the cathedral had possessed exclusive urban rights in regard to the administration of baptism up until the eleventh century. At that time other baptisteries were set up in some of the parishes, but as yet not every city church did have one. Moreover, even though these baptisteries did exist, the cathedral church still maintained a cumulative competence over the diocese, and the archpriest and canons thereto attached enjoyed extraordinary rights. Consequently, as the number of parishes with baptisteries increased, and as it became more and more common that in each parish the pastor baptized his own subjects, the archpriests, canons and cathedral chapters, who thought they had gained some sort of jurisdiction in the matter either by custom or prescription, sought to restrict the parochial power. But against the archdeacons,[19] still later

[16] *Institutiones Iuris Canonici* (Venetiis, 1704), Lib. III, tit. 3, n. 3.

[17] Canon 12—Mansi, XXV, 1138. Constitutions of Lucca (1345), canon 53—Mansi, XXVI, 276.

[18] *Bibliotheca Iuris Canonico-Civilis Practica* (4 vols., Mutinae, 1757), I, 61.

[19] S. R. C., *Neritonen.*, 9 maii 1606—*Fontes*, n. 5223.

in opposition to several cathedrals and mother churches,[20] and finally against the canons of the cathedrals, the Sacred Congregation of the Council insisted that the pastor was the ordinary minister and that he was to be preferred to all others with regard to his own subjects, and thus effectively destroyed all the contrary customs that existed.[21] The only prominent decisions adverse to the pastor's right was that by which the competence of Saint Peter's at Rome was acknowledged for all the people of the city,[22] and that by which it was logically stated that a vicar-general whose faculties had not been limited by the bishop could baptize licitly anywhere in his diocese without the permission of the pastor or even in spite of his refusal.[23]

In fact, so strongly had the pastor's right been built up throughout the centuries, because of the almost exclusive competence that had been acknowledged time and time again for the parish, that in 1891 the Sacred Congregation of the Council seemed intent upon destroying once and for all any contrary practices when it declared that thenceforth every parochial church, large and small, should have its own baptismal font.[24]

In regard to the administration of baptism, one may note in passing, that the religious never had any real right that could conflict with the pastor's. For, though Pope Paul III (1534-1549) had permitted the Jesuits to administer all the

[20] S. C. C., *Neapolitana,* 6 et 27 sept. 1687—*Fontes,* n. 2903; 21 febr. et 28 aug. 1688—*Analecta Iuris Pontificii,* VIII (1866), 1593; *Savonen.,* 16 dec. 1713—Pallottini, *Collectio omnium conclusionum et resolutionum,* XIV, 4; *Fabrianen.,* 24 maii et 21 iun. 1732—*Fontes,* n. 3392; *Burgen.,* 2 maii 1733—*Fontes,* n. 3401; *Aesina,* 15 iul. 1797—*Fontes,* n. 3905.

[21] S. C. C., *Galtellinoren.,* 7 sept. 1895—*Fontes,* n. 4295.

[22] S. C. C., *Romana,* 15 maii 1700 — *Analecta Iuris Pontificii,* VIII (1866), 1594.

[23] S. R. C., *Senogallien.,* 16 apr. 1639—*Fontes,* n. 5374.

[24] *ASS,* XXIV (1891-1892), 358.

sacraments in missionary lands wherein parishes had not yet been established—a privilege communicated also to the other religious—, yet they were forewarned that whenever parishes were erected in these places the pastor's right would prevail.[25] As a matter of fact this supremacy of the pastor over the Orders was later formally acknowledged in other documents; [26] and eventually Pope Innocent X (1644-1655) insisted upon the same, even to the extent of forbidding religious to administer baptism, matrimony and extreme unction in their own houses without the permission of the pastor of that territory.[27]

Finally, it may be mentioned here, that the Sacred Congregation of Rites declared that baptism should not be conferred through a plurality of ministers, although it did not state with certainty that a sacrament so administered was of itself invalid.[28] Moreover, a suspended or interdicted priest was not permitted to baptize solemnly; even when he had to baptize on account of necessity he was to do so in a merely private capacity as would any lay person.[29]

25 Const. "*Cum inter edita*"—quoted by Schmalzgrueber (*Ius Ecclesiasticum Universum*, Lib. III, tit. 42, n. 46) as appearing in 1545, but this Constitution could not be found in any of the collections available to the writer. The same Constitution is referred to in a general way by Petrus Leurenius (*Forum Ecclesiasticum* [3 vols., Venetiis, 1729], II, 526) and La Croix (*Theologia Moralis*, Tom. II, Lib. VI, Pars I, quaest. 47, n. 3).

26 I Provincial Council of Lima (1582), caput 12—Mansi, XXXVI B, 200. S. C. de Prop. Fide, 13 iun. 1633—*Fontes*, n. 4450.

27 Const. "*Cum sicut*", 14 maii 1648 (ad 17)—*Fontes*, n. 232.

28 S. R. C., *Florentin.*, 19 dec. 1665—*Fontes*, n. 5533. The same is also noted in the following: Hieronymus Nicolius, *Lucubrationes utriusque iuris* (Romae, 1662), Lib. V, tit. 9, n. 2; Fermosini, *Opera Omnia* (editio altera, 14 vols., Coloniae Allobrogum, 1741), III (*De officiis et sacris ecclesiae*), Lib. I, tit. 22, n. 7; S. C. de Sacr., 17 nov. 1916—*AAS*, VIII (1916), 479 et *Fontes*, n. 2116.

29 S. C. de Prop. Fide, 21 ian. 1789, ad 2—*Collectanea S. Congregationis de Propaganda Fide* (Romae, 1893), n. 535.

ART. 2. THE EXTRAORDINARY MINISTER OF SOLEMN BAPTISM

Though Gratian [30] and many of the councils of the twelfth and thirteenth centuries,[31] by the special mention they made of the deacon, acknowledged him to be the extraordinary minister of solemn baptism, yet the condition of grave necessity which they exacted before he could act licitly even with authorization was such as would permit any lay person to baptize privately. So the Council of Rouen (1231) provided an outstanding exception when it enumerated additional circumstances of a naturally less severe restriction for the exercise of his ministry by the deacon.[32]

It is with this milder opinion that the commentators agreed, since they averred that the deacon could baptize solemnly outside of grave absolute necessity as long as he had the proper permission or authorization. However, they did insist upon the need of some permission and upon the simultaneous presence of some necessity for licit action, since they argued that of itself the diaconate did not give one the power to baptize solemnly, but only made its subject capable of extraordinary deputation. For the deacon as such was neither *ex iure* (*qua sacerdos*) nor *ex officio* (*qua parochus*) the proper minister.[33]

30 C. 13, D. XCIII (from the letter of Pope Gelasius to the bishops of Lucania); c. 19, D. IV, *de cons.* (from Isidore's *De officiis*, Lib. II, c. 24).

31 Council of York (1195), c. 4—Mansi, XXII, 653; Council of London (1200), c. 3—Mansi, XXII, 715; Council of Oxford (1222), cap. *de baptismo*—Mansi, XXII, 1173; Provincial Council of Treves (1227), cap. I—Mansi, XXIII, 26; Provincial Council of Mainz (1261), c. 2—Mansi, XXIII, 1081; Council of Cologne (1280), cap. IV—Mansi, XXIV, 348.

32 Canon 36; "Nullus diaconus... baptizet, nisi cum sacerdos absens fuerit; ita quod eius adventus commode exspectari non possit, vel idem presbyter gravi infirmitate vel alio incurabili impedimento fuerit impeditus." —Hardouin, VII, 189.

33 Barbosa (1589-1649), *Collectanea decretorum, tam veterum quam recentiorum, in Ius Pontificium Universum* (6 vols. in 3, Lugduni, 1716) in c. 19, D. IV, *de cons.*

Otherwise, if the deacon were capable of baptizing solemnly in view of his very order, he would differ in no way from the simple priest to whom a parish has not yet been entrusted. Yet he did. For the latter, though he was incapable *ex officio* (*qua parochus*), he was qualified *ex iure* (*qua sacerdos*), and because by his very order he did possess the power to baptize solemnly he could be authorized to act even though no actual necessity was present.[34] The deacon, on the other hand, inasmuch as he did not actually possess the power, but only a limited potentiality for it, was not to be given the permission or authorization unless some necessity arose. This necessity would not need to be the actual danger of death. It could arise from the fact that a mulitude were to be baptized at one time, or that the priest who was to baptize had been taken sick and was unable to act, or that the proper minister was under a censure of excommunication or suspension, but had authorized the deacon so that the sacrament might be conferred licitly to those who sought it.[35]

It was in view of this deficiency, which the canonists considered to exist in the sacrament of the diaconate, that they, in commenting on the Decretals of Pope Gregory IX (1227-1241),[36] speculated as to the possibility of a deacon incurring an irregularity, when, having disregarded the stated requirements, he baptized solemnly. Caponi succinctly proposed the opinion of the overwhelming majority when he stated that, though a deacon who baptized privately would not incur any irregularity even though he would be guilty of grave sin, yet a deacon who administered baptism solemnly

[34] Grana-Nieto, *Catena iurium utriusque iurisprudentiae,* Lib. III, tit. 42, n. 6; Schmalzgrueber, *Ius ecclesiasticum universum,* Lib. III, tit. 42, n. 43.

[35] Schmalzgrueber, *op. cit.*, Lib. III, tit. 42, n. 43.

[36] C. 1, X, *de clerico non ordinato ministrante,* V, 28: "Clericus ministrans in pertinentibus ad ordinem quem non habet, deponendus est, et amplius non ordinandus."

would incur an irregularity.[37] This effect obtained because in so acting the deacon usurped a power which was not his, *neque ex iure neque ex officio.*[38]

As a matter of fact, in spite of La Croix's statement to the contrary,[39] it would seem that a deacon could not baptize solemnly even when he was a pastor unless he had specifically received a general authorization from the bishop. For though he was capable of acting *ex officio* (*qua parochus*), yet he was still unqualified *ex iure* (*qua sacerdos*), and a general authorization was requisite to free him from this latter inhability.[40] This opinion of the commentators appears almost with certainty to have been the correct one in view of the dispensation *ad cautelam* from irregularity which the Sacred Congregation of the Council had earlier granted in the case of a deacon-pastor who had performed such solemn actions without any special authorization.[41]

ART. 3. THE MINISTER OF PRIVATE BAPTISM IN CASES OF NECESSITY

The extraordinary faculties to baptize, which through the mercy of the Church had been granted to all in cases of necessity during the preceding centuries, were in no way curtailed at this time. Gratian himself testified to this,[42]

[37] *Institutiones canonicae*, I, 227.

[38] Lancelotti (1522-1590), *Institutiones iuris canonicae*, Lib. II, tit. 3, n. 3; Barbosa, *Collectanea decretorum*, Lib. V, tit. 28, n. 3.

[39] " Parochus vero diaconus, et necdum sacerdos potest iure ordinario etiam solemniter baptizare."—*Theologia Moralis*, T. II, L. VI, Pars I, quaest. 47, n. 5.

[40] Schmalzgrueber, *Ius ecclesiasticum universum*, Lib. III, tit. 42, n. 44; Giraldi, *Expositio iuris pontificii iuxta recentiorem ecclesiae disciplinam* (2 vols., nova Romana editio, Romae, 1830), Lib. V, tit. 28.

[41] S. C. C., *Carnoten.*, 2 dec. 1679—*Fontes*, n. 2852.

[42] Cc. 21, 36, D. IV, *de cons.* (These are taken from the writings of Saint Augustine.)

and in the centuries that followed synods, councils and papal constitutions—all too numerous to cite completely and individually—repeated the already familiar law.[43] Caponi in the early eighteenth century summed up this doctrine concerning the general authorization of power for the cases of necessity by stating that at such a time any person having the use of reason, who knew and was able to employ the required matter and form, baptized validly and licitly.[44]

This absolute authorization was further exemplified in the express permission given to women to baptize in cases of necessity. Earlier, as has been mentioned, there was some doubt on the part of the historians as to whether the severe prohibition laid down against women by the IV Council of Carthage (398) was to be understood so absolutely that it obtained even in cases of necessity. Certainly it appears that such a strict interpretation must be favored in consideration of the way in which Peter Lombard,[45] Gratian [46] and Pope Eugene IV [47] explicitly singled her out as capable of this power, even after they had already made the general statement which should have been sufficient to

[43] To mention a few throughout the centuries: Council of Lambeth (1281), cap. III—Mansi, XXIV, 476; Council of Nimes (1284), cap. *de baptismo*—Mansi, XXIV, 522; Provincial Council of Salzburg (1420), c. 28 —Mansi, XXVIII, 999; Pope Eugene IV (in Conc. Florentin.), Const. "*Exultate Deo*", 22 nov. 1439, § 10—*Fontes*, n. 52; Council of Spain (1512), cap. III—Mansi, XXXII, 582; Pope Benedict XIV, const. "*Nuper ad nos*", 16 nov. 1743—*Fontes*, n. 335.

[44] *Institutiones canonicae*, I, 227.

[45] *Sententiarum libri quattuor* (Quaracchi edition), Lib. IV, dist. 6.

[46] C. 4, C. XXX, q. 3 (cites the letter of Pope Urban II to a certain Vitalis, priest in the diocese of Brescia); c. 20, D. IV, *de cons.* (quotes the IV Council of Carthage, but with the added phrase *nisi necessitate cogente.*)

[47] (In Conc. Florentin.), const. "*Cantate Domino*", 4 febr. 1441 (§ 13) —*Fontes*, n. 54.

show that all of the laity could so act. It appears that they definitely intended to remove all doubts.

As a matter of fact, from the fourteenth century onward women very frequently administered the sacrament in cases of necessity, since in their capacity of midwives and obstetricians they were very often the only ones at hand to confer the needed baptism. Because of this many synods and councils insisted that all women who professionally offered their services at childbirth undergo instruction as to the proper manner of baptizing,[48] and several councils threatened with ecclesiastical penalties any midwives who refused to submit to this instruction and to the subsequent examination they were required to take from their pastor.[49] Indeed, so frequently did these women baptize that at times they acted even when the danger of death to the child was not admittedly probable, and the Holy Office had to insist that before private baptism could be lawfully administered it was required that a positive danger be present for the life of the new-born child.[50]

In like manner, there is explicit mention that among the laity who could baptize in these cases of extreme necessity were to be included the father and the mother.[51] But it

[48] Some of these are: Synod of Mount Lebanon (1736), Pars II, cap. 2—*Coll. Lac.*, II, 117; Council of Bourges (1584), Tit. XIX, c. 8—Mansi, XXXIV A, 878; Provincial Council of Cambrai (1631), Tit. VIII—Mansi, XXXVI, C, 174.

[49] V Provincial Council of Milan (1579), Pars I, cap. 7—Mansi, XXXIV A, 361; Council of Aix (1585), c. 6—Mansi, XXXIV B, 944; Council of Salerno (1596), cap. XI—Mansi, XXXV B, 983; Council of Narbonne (1609), cap. XIV—Mansi, XXXIV B, 1491; *et alii.*

[50] S. C. S. Off., 11 ian. 1899—*ASS*, XXXI (1898-1899), 690 *et Fontes*, n. 1214.

[51] C. 7, C. XXX, q. 1 (from the letter of Pope John VIII (872-882) to Bishop Anselm of Limoges); Council of London (1200), c. 3—Hardouin, VI B, 1958; Hostiensis, *Summa Aurea*, p. 310; Idem, *In quinque libros Decretalium commentaria* (3 vols., Venetiis, 1581), Lib. III, tit. 42, n. 7.

seems that these could licitly proceed to baptize their child, even in case of necessity, only then when anyone else who could properly baptize was absent.[52]

As has been indicated in the preceding sentence, there was a definite order of precedence to be followed by those who ministered in cases of necessity. The bishop and pastor came before all others, then came the simple priest, and then the remaining clerics according to their proper rank. Among the laity men were to be preferred to women, catholics to non-catholics, and good catholics to bad catholics.[53] However, this order could be inverted for good reasons. Thus a women was preferred to a man, even to a cleric, if she possessed more skill or knowledge for the proper dispensation of the sacrament amid circumstances attendant upon her assistance as a midwife, as in the case of uterine baptisms,[54] or whenever any similar demand for the safeguarding of Christian modesty and fundamental decency suggested her prior claim over others.[55] Caponi, moreover, stated that a layman in good standing was to be preferred to an excommunicated or otherwise censured cleric, and, since he admitted that this teaching was opposed by some commentators, he offered the authority of Barbosa in support of his own doctrine.[56]

[52] Council of Besançon (1571), cap. *de baptismo*—Mansi, XXXVI B, 49; Council of Cologne (1280), cap. IV—Mansi, XXIV, 348; Synod of Nimes (1284), cap. *de baptismo*—Mansi, XXIV, 522.

[53] Synod of Nimes (1284), cap. *de baptismo*—Mansi, XXIV, 522; Council of Oxford (1287), cap. II—Mansi, XXIV, 786; II (1312) and III (1314) Provincial Councils of Ravenna—Mansi, XXV, 456 and 547; Provincial Council of Salzburg (1420), c. 28—Mansi, XXVIII, 999; Provincial Council of England (1509), cap. *de baptismo*—Mansi, XXXI A, 422; I Provincial Council of Milan (1565), Pars II, cap. 2—Mansi, XXXIV A, 15; *et passim.*

[54] Lancelotti, *Institutiones iuris canonici*, Lib. II, tit. 3, n. 3.

[55] La Croix, *Theologia Moralis*, T. II, lib. VI, pars I, art. 1, no. 3.

[56] *Institutiones canonicae*, I, 228.

Because this general authorization of power to baptize was both so widely used and so frequently abused, various synods and councils throughout the centuries imposed upon the pastor in particular the obligation of instructing the people in the manner of administering the sacrament. These instructions were to be given several times a year in church, and, if necessary, additional private instructions were to be given in the same place, especially to doctors and midwives, who by the very nature of their work needed such specialized instruction most.[57]

It may likewise be noted that in the past two centuries greater latitude has been granted to the laity, particularly to catechists, in mission lands. There these have been permitted to baptize not only when the child was actually in danger of death, but even in those instances wherein the child could be prudently considered as exposed to circumstances which might endanger its life.[58] They could also baptize, even though the child was perfectly well, when it was foreseen that no priest would be present in that vicinity for some time, and that it would be difficult to reach him.[59]

Authors differed in their opinion as to whether or not a lay person incurred an irregularity by baptizing solemnly. Barbosa (1589-1649) thought that he did not, since the penalty which was stated in the Decretals referred only to a

[57] Council of Oxford (1222), cap. *de baptismo*—Mansi, XXII, 1173; Provincial Council of Mainz (1261), c. 2—Mansi, XXIII, 1081; Council of Arles (1260), c. 2—Mansi, XXIII, 1204. IV Provincial Council of Milan (1576), Pars II, cap. 2—Mansi, XXXIV A, 220; Council of Avignon (1594), c. 12—Mansi, XXXIV B, 1337; S. C. C., *Ceneten.*, 12 mai 1753—*Fontes*, n. 3629; S. C. C., *Forosempronien.*, 24 maii 1823—*Fontes*, n. 3981; II Plenary Council of Baltimore (1866), Tit. V, cap. 2—*Acta et decreta*, n. 228.

[58] S. C. de Prop. Fide, 21 ian. 1788—*Fontes*, n. 4618; 21 ian. 1789—*Fontes*, n. 4625.

[59] S. C. de Prop. Fide, 16 ian. 1804—*Fontes*, n. 4677; 11 sept. 1841—*Fontes*, n. 4795.

cleric, and, as a penalty, should be interpreted strictly. Moreover, so he alleged, the penalty suggested for one who so acted was deposition, which could not be effectively applied to a lay person, since such a one possessed no order from which he might be deposed.[60] Pirhing (1606-1679), on the other hand, held the opposite view. Though his opinion appears more logical, yet it is at an evident disadvantage from the viewpoint of a strict interpretation of the text. Pirhing asserted that it could not be argued that the canon treated solely *de clerico non ordinato ministrante*, since many inscriptions of this title in other editions of the *Corpus* contained only the words *de non ordinato ministrante*.[61] At any rate, Pirhing reminded his readers that it is not always valid to argue from the rubric to the text. In addition, the penalty mentioned in the canon was applicable solely to clerics because they were the common offenders in this regard. Pirhing's main point of argument, however, was that if a cleric, who belonged at least to the ministering part of the Church, incurred the irregularity by so acting beyond his power, *a fortiori* a lay person, who was in no way part of the clergy, became irregular by the commission of a like offense.[62]

ART. 4. BAPTISM ADMINISTERED BY HERETICS, SCHISMATICS, PAGANS AND JEWS

The fundamental dogma that baptism rightly conferred with the proper matter and form is valid no matter who the

[60] *Collectanea decretorum*, Lib. V, tit. 28, n. 5.

[61] While the Richter-Friedberg edition of the *Corpus Iuris Canonici* admits that both inscriptions are found in the various editions, yet it adopts the inscription *de clerico non ordinato ministrante* as being the better supported text.

[62] *Ius canonicum nova methodo explicatum* (5 vols., Dilingae, 1676), L. V, tit. 28, n. 4.

minister may be was maintained in this period also.[63] Carried to its logical conclusion, as it was from the days of Gratian to the time of the Council of Trent, and thence to the appearance of the present Code of Canon Law, this meant that valid baptism could be administered by heretics,[64] schismatics,[65] pagans and Jews.[66]

Enough has been said to show that all of these ministers had to use the proper matter (water) and the Trinitarian form for the valid conferring of baptism. This standard was always maintained.[67]

Worthy of particular mention, however, is the question of the intention which the minister of baptism must possess. But since this matter may be treated more effectively in connection with the Code's legislation on the minister of private baptism, the historical development of it will be postponed until then.

[63] IV Lateran Council (1215), cap. I: "Sacramentum vero baptismi, quod ad invocationem individuae Trinitatis, videlicet Patris et Filii et Spiritus Sancti, consecratur in aqua, tam parvulis quam adultis, in forma ecclesiae a quocumque rite collatum, proficit ad salutem."—Mansi, XXII, 982; c. 1, X, *de summa Trinitate et fide catholica*, I, 1.

[64] C. 29, D. IV, *de cons.* (taken from the writings of Saint Augustine). Council of Trent (1547), Sessio VII, *de baptismo*, c. 4—*Canones et decreta sacrosancti oecumenici concilii Tridentini* (Romae: Bernardi Tauchnitz, 1863), p. 44. S. C. C., 27 mart. 1683—*Fontes*, n. 2867. Benedict XIV, ep. "*Singulari*", 9 febr. 1749—*Fontes*, n. 394. S. C. de Prop. Fide, instr. (ad Vic. ap. Siam), 23 iun. 1830—*Fontes*, n. 4748. S. C. S. Off., 20 nov. 1878—*ASS*, XI (1878), 614 and *Fontes*, n. 1058; S. C. de Sacr., 17 nov. 1916—*Fontes*, n. 2116.

[65] C. 40, D. IV, *de cons.* (taken from Augustine, *De baptismo*, Lib. I, c. 1, n. 2). S. C. S. Off., 20 aug. 1671—*Fontes*, n. 746; 5 iul. 1853—*Fontes*, n. 924.

[66] C. 23 (from Isidore), 24 (the response of Pope Nicholas) and 31 (Augustine, *De baptismo*, Lib. VIII, c. 53), D. IV, *de cons.* Eugene IV (in Conc. Florentin.) const. "*Exultate Deo*", 22 nov. 1439—*Fontes*, n. 52; and in many councils and synods.

[67] C. 28, 30, 32, D. IV, *de cons.* (Quotations from Saint Augustine.)

In the consideration of the question as to whether or not it is licit for parents to request heretical or schismatical ministers to baptize their children when their own pastor is absent, most of the remarks made by the commentators are startling, unless it be understood that the parents themselves for some reason or other are unable to administer the sacrament. Pignatelli († 1675)[68] stated that in extreme necessity it would be permitted if (a) no offense would be given to Catholics, (b) the legitimate matter and form and the proper intention were present, (c) there were no communication whatsoever of the parents with the minister in the schismatical ceremony, and (d) it were certain that no error in regard to faith should threaten the ones who received baptism from such ministers. Zoesius († 1627) had previously permitted the same, although he stated that if parents acted thus without real necessity they would sin gravely.[69] It must be borne in mind, however, that at a later time, but still within the same century, the Holy Office in explicit terms strictly forbade such a practice save in cases of absolute extreme necessity.[70]

With regard to the question of the validity of baptisms conferred by a priest who had been erroneously ordained without having been baptized, it is only in the light of the texts of this period that a complete understanding of the previously mentioned difficulty is achieved.[71] For it is only through the Decree of Gratian that one receives an inkling that all the other sources had drawn upon spurious canons.

[68] *Consultationes canonicae* (6 vols., Coloniae Allobrogum, 1700), IV, 237.

[69] *Ius canonicum universum* (Venetiis, 1757), L. III, tit. 42, n. 8.

[70] 20 aug. 1671: "Non permittat (Episcopus) schismaticis administrare Sacram. Baptismatis nisi in casu necessitatis, et deficiente quacumque alia persona catholica."—*Fontes*, n. 746. Cf. also S. C. S. Off., 5 iul. 1853: "Sedulo autem curet idem Episcopus Vicarius Apostolicus admonere catholicos sibi subditos licitum sibi non esse extra casum extremae necessitatis petere pro filiis suis Baptismum a schismaticis vel haereticis."—*Fontes*, n. 924.

[71] Cf. Chapter III, art. 4.

Of the two texts which are found throughout the centuries, the oldest probably originated in the Penitential of Theodore of Canterbury (c. 690),[72] and from there was later copied by Benedict the Levite (c. 845).[73] It was not, however, until the time of Burchard of Worms († 1025) that the text was ascribed to the Council of Compiegne (759).[74] The canon thus titled was then quoted by Ivo of Chartres († 1116),[75] although it appears that even at that time the authenticity of the text was questioned to some degree, since Migne notes that in the margin of one of the oldest manuscripts of the Decretum there were written opposite this text the words, *Hic dubitatur.*

When this text appeared in Gratian it was inserted as a *palea,* and the words *et omnes, quos prius baptizavit* were omitted.[76] It was in this same form that it was quoted in the first of the *Compilationes*[77] and in the Decretals of Gregory IX.[78]

The other text commonly found among the authors was less severe in its doctrine, since it admitted the possible validity of such baptisms. This canon probably owes its

[72] Lib. II, cap. 2, c. 13—McNeil-Gamer, *Medieval Handbook of Penance,* p. 200.

[73] *Capitularia,* Lib. VI, c. 94: "Si quis presbyter ordinatus deprehenderit se non baptizatum esse, baptizetur et ordinetur iterum, et omnes quos prius baptizavit."—*MGH, Leges,* II², 78. That Benedict used Theodore as his source for this is attested by Emil Seckel, "Studien zu Benedictus Levita. VII," *Neues Archiv der Gesellschaft für ältere deutsche Geschichtskunde,* XXXIV (1908), 349.

[74] *Decretorum libri viginti,* IV, 74, has the inscription: "(Ex Concil. apud Compendium, cap. 5)"—*MPL,* CXL, 741.

[75] *Decretum,* I, 268—*MPL,* CLXI, 122; *Panormia,* I, 96—*MPL,* CLXI, 1066.

[76] C. 60, C. I, q. 1.

[77] Lib. V, tit. XXXV, cap. 1.

[78] C. 1, X, *de presbytero non baptizato,* III, 42.

origin to the Penitential of Egbert of York († 767),[79] although in a slightly varied form it was later attributed to Isidore by Burchard [80] and Ivo of Chartres.[81]

Gratian adopted the inscription which these latter authors used and employed the same canon with only minor unimportant changes.[82] Richter-Friedberg noted that the canon seems to contain two sections: the first part, consisting of a proposed question or the recitation of a false opinion; and the second part, beginning with the phrase *Sed Romanus Pontifex,* being in the nature of a true response to the difficulty.

At any rate, it appears evident that the whole problem, which at first glance seems to have arisen from the valid legislation of the Council of Compiegne (759), in reality owed its origin to two Penitentials, and so can be definitely classified as one of the many errors or corruptions which frequently appeared in these books.

This solution seems better and more practical than the one proposed by Martene.[83] He claimed that the entire difficulty arose from a misreading of the abbreviations used in the original manuscript, and that instead of *et omnes, etc.* it should have been copied to read *non omnes, etc.* The

[79] C. VII: "Quicumque presbyter si norit quod non sit baptizatus, baptizetur et omnes illi quos antea baptizaverat. Attamen papa Romanus constituit, si missae administrator vitiosus sit, vel paganus: quod servitium Spiritus sancti esset in dono baptismi, non tamen in hominis alicuius."—Mansi, XII, 435.

[80] *Decretorum libri viginti,* IV, 100: "(Ex dictis S. Isidori episcopi) Si quis presbyter per ignorantiam ordinatur antequam baptizetur, debent ab eo baptizati baptizari, et ipse non ordinetur, sed Romanus Pontifex iudicat non hominem qui baptizat, sed Spiritum Dei subministrare gratiam baptismi, licet paganus sit qui baptizat."—*MPL,* CXL, 748.

[81] *Decretum,* I, 294—*MPL,* CLXI, 130; *Panormia,* I, 97—*MPL,* CLXI, 1066.

[82] C. 59, C. I, q. 1.

[83] *De antiquis ecclesiae ritibus,* I, 21.

actual abbreviations themselves lack the similarity that would make such an opinion probable.

ART. 5. INCIDENTAL QUESTIONS REGARDING THE ADMINISTRATION OF BAPTISM

A. *Rebaptism*

From the preceding chapters it is evident that the Church ever taught that baptism, no matter by whom it might previously have been conferred, should not be repeated in one who doubtlessly had already received it validly. Gratian [84] and the Decretals [85] sufficiently indicated and summed up the same orthodox teaching in this period to make further proof from the later councils, popes and canonical commentators superfluous.

For the general tenor of all is that baptism can be conferred absolutely a second time only when it is certain that the previous baptism for some reason or other was invalid. In other cases, wherein definite proof of validity or invalidity was lacking, so that the whole subject was doubtful, rebaptism was to take place conditionally—which after all is not a second baptism at all.[86]

For those who were guilty of the offense of rebaptizing the commentators expressed a variety of punishments. Basso (✝ 1713) [87] noted at the outset of his treatment that for incurring any of the penalties the offending party must have conferred the sacrament absolutely and not merely

[84] C. 43, D. IV, *de cons.* (taken from the writing of Saint Augustine); c. 51, D. IV, *de cons.* (from Homily XXXVI of Venerable Bede).

[85] C. 6, X, *de baptismo et eius effectu,* III, 42; c. 2, X, *de apostatis et reiterantibus baptisma,* V, 9.

[86] Gaetano Felix Verano (1648-1713), while not the first one by any means to teach this, summed up the whole question in the way shown above. Cf. *Iuris canonici universi commentarius particularis* (3 vols., Monachii, 1703), in c. 1, X, *de sacramentis non iterandis,* I, 16, n. 2.

[87] *Bibliotheca iuris canonico-civilis practica,* I, 62, n. 6.

conditionally. In the civil law such an offense would seem to have been punishable by death (*ultimum supplicium*) or exile.[88] The canonical punishment, according to all, was that the offender became irregular.[89] One decretalist[90] added that such an offender must remain in penance all his life, and be excluded from the prayers of both the faithful and the catechumens.

Boich (1310-c. 1350)[91] particularized the punishments more than the others. He stated that the penalty varied according to the dignity of the offender. A bishop should be deposed and degraded; a cleric should be deposed.[92] For a lay offender he recommended *ultimum supplicium*, which, since he was writing of both ecclesiastical and civil punishments, may have meant either a real corporal death[93] or ecclesiastical death by excommunication.[94] If the one rebaptizing were a catechumen or an orthodox minister, he was to be fined and exiled.[95]

Pignatelli († 1675)[96] noted in a practical fashion that the Catholic pastor, if he foresaw that a child whom he was

[88] Böckhn (1690-1752), *Commentarius in ius canonicum universum* (3 vols., Salisburgi, 1776), Lib. V, tit. 9, n. 10. Zoesius († 1627), *Ius canonicum universum*, Lib. V, tit. 9, n. 6. Both base this punishment upon Roman Law. Cf. C. Th. (16.5) 58; and C. (1.6) 2; (1.6) 3.

[89] Basso, *loc. cit.*; Böckhn, *loc. cit.*; Zoesius, *loc. cit.*; Wex (1645-1711), *Ariadne Carolino-Canonica* (Dilingae, 1708), p. 68; Hieronymus Nicolius, *Lucubrationes utriusque iuris*, Lib. V, tit. 9, n. 2.

[90] Pax Jordanus, *Elucubrationes diversae*, I, 146.

[91] *In quinque Decretalium libros commentarius* (Venetiis, 1576), Lib. V, tit. 9, nn. 1 and 2.

[92] As his source for these penalties he cited C. (1.6) 1 for the bishop, and Hostiensis, *Summa Aurea*, p. 311, n. 16, for the cleric.

[93] This was the penalty recommended in C. (1.6) 2 for those who were responsible by age for their actions.

[94] Since he has already cited Hostiensis as his source above, he may have had the same text in mind here.

[95] His source for this is C. (1.6) 3.

[96] *Consultationes canonicae*, IV, 242.

about to baptize would later be rebaptized in the Catholic rite by a heretic, was not to desist from conferring his baptism since it was a licit thing which he did. However, in such a case the pastor did have an obligation to warn the parents against such a deed.

B. *Money*

The legislation prohibiting priests to exact money for the administration of the sacraments as embodied in the councils of the previous centuries was repeated by Gratian,[97] Gregory IX [98] and a host of synods and councils up to the present day. Priests who persisted in such a practice were threatened with divers punishments—even to the extent of excommunication.[99] The only concession made to the ministers of the sacrament was that they could receive those offerings which the generosity of the people prompted them to extend.[100] Underlying all these safeguards is the obvious reason, expressed by a minor French council,[101] that the taking or exacting of money has prevented many people from having their children baptized.

In spite of all these restrictions, however, evidently there were some abuses. So Felinus Sandeus of Ferrara (1444-1503) stated that if one were dying without baptism it would be licit to give money to a priest who otherwise would

97 C. 97, C. I, q. 1 (Saint Augustine's writings).

98 C. 9, X, *de simonia, et ne aliquid pro spiritualibus exigatur vel promittatur*, V, 3.

99 *Gallonis S. R. E. Card. Constitutiones* (*1208*), cap. II—Mansi, XXII, 763.

100 IV Lateran Council (1215), cap. 66—Mansi, XXII, 1054; Council of Oxford (1222), c. 29—Mansi, XXII, 1160; Council of Besançon (1571), cap. *de baptismo*—Mansi, XXXVI B, 52; S. C. Ep. et Reg., *Nucerina*, 17 sept. 1772—*Analecta Iuris Pontificii*, XII (1873), 117; I Provincial Council of Quito (1863), Decisiones, II, cap. 10—*Coll. Lac.*, VI, 402.

101 Council of Lille (1228), c. 17—Hardouin, VII, 1152.

not confer the sacrament.[102] Later others,[103] while not denying that possibly such a base demand could be made by a priest, taught that the money should not be paid, and that in such a case any other person present would take precedence over the priest as minister. If no one else were there, then it would be better to die with baptism of desire alone than to risk the danger of committing simony by giving the money.

In regard to any offering legitimately made on the occasion of baptism, Wex[104] taught that it belonged to the proper pastor of the person baptized, no matter who it was who administered the sacrament or by what right he had come to do so. On the same subject the IV Provincial Council of Baltimore (1840)[105] decreed that bishops were to make regulations about such matters in their first synod, so that there should be no bickering or dissension among the clergy. The II Plenary Council of Baltimore (1866) incorporated this same rule in its legislation.[106]

C. *Unnecessary deferring of baptism by a priest*

For the priest who refused or deferred baptism when a child was legitimately presented for baptism Gratian[107]

102 *In Decretalium libros quinque* (3 vols., Venetiis, 1570), Lib. V, tit. 3.

103 Fermosini (✝ 1672), *Opera omnia* (2nd ed., 14 vols., Coloniae Allobrogum, 1741), XI (*Criminalium*), 171, n. 8; Caponi, *Institutiones canonicae,* I, 229.

104 *Ariadne Carolino-Canonica,* p. 27.

105 Decreta, Cap. III—*Coll. Lac.*, III, 70.

106 *Acta et Decreta,* n. 94.

107 C. 22, D. V, *de cons.* This *palea* is ascribed to Martin III, but it does not exist in his works. This is vouched for by Antonius Augustinus (1517-1586), *De emendatione Gratiani dialogorum libri duo* (Venetiis, 1778), Lib. I, Dialogus XII, p. 471. However, the text is found, as has been noted, among Theodulf of Orleans (*Capitularium,* c. 17), Burchard (*Decretorum libri viginti,* IV, 27) and Ivo of Chartres (*Decretum,* I, 241; *Panormia,* I, 27).

decreed deposition. Later a council held at Padua (1339)[108] stated merely that such a priest should be punished severely. In commenting on the penalty of deposition, Caponi bound the priest to observe it only after a declaratory sentence had been passed upon him.[109]

D. *Self-conferred baptism*

The Decretals[110] were explicitly definite in stating that no one, even in case of necessity, could baptize himself. Though all the decretalists commented on the text, yet none alleged any stronger reasons for the prohibition than those cited by the Decretals: namely, that the form itself signifies a distinction between the one baptizing and the one baptized; and that just as no man can beget himself in the physical life, so is he incapable of begetting himself in the spiritual life.

108 Canon 15—Mansi, XXV, 1138.

109 *Institutiones canonicae*, I, 229.

110 C. 4, X, *de baptismo et eius effectu*, III, 42.

CANONICAL COMMENTARY

CHAPTER V

The Ordinary Minister of Solemn Baptism

Canon 738, § 1. **Minister ordinarius baptismi sollemnis est sacerdos; sed eius collatio reservatur parocho vel alii sacerdoti de eiusdem parochi vel Ordinarii loci licentia, quae in casu necessitatis legitime praesumitur.**

ART. 1. "MINISTER ORDINARIUS BAPTISMI SOLLEMNIS EST SACERDOS; . . ."

In the sacramental system of the Catholic Church baptism alone possesses a double mode of administration: the ordinary manner called solemn, and the one used in cases of necessity called private. Baptism is solemn when administered with all the rites and ceremonies prescribed in the approved liturgical books; otherwise it is called private.[1]

In legislating about this sacrament the Code follows a logical order in its canons, and so the first canons concern the usual minister of the usual mode of administration, namely, the ordinary minister of solemn baptism. By virtue of sacred orders every priest can administer solemn baptism validly. Any restriction placed upon him so as to hinder his action from being licit arises not from an actual lack of the power of orders, but rather from a deficiency in jurisdiction.[2]

[1] Canon 737, § 2. *Rituale Romanum*, tit. II, c. 1, *de sacramento baptismi rite administrando*, n. 3.

[2] Eugenius IV (in Conc. Florentin.), const. "*Exultate Deo*", 22 nov. 1439, § 10: "... Minister huius sacramenti est sacerdos, cui ex officio competit baptizare."—*Fontes*, n. 52. Likewise Saint Thomas says: "Sicut ad sacerdotem pertinet consecrare eucharistiam ... ita ad proprium officium sacerdotis pertinet baptizare."—*Summa Theologica* (ed. alt. Romana, 6 vols., Romae, 1894), III, q. LXVII, a. 2. The first allocution of the bishop to the candidates for ordination states: "Sacerdotem oportet offerre, benedicere, praeesse, praedicare et baptizare."—*Pontificale Romanum, De ordinatione presbyteri.*

ART. 2. ". . . SED EIUS COLLATIO RESERVATUR PAROCHO . . ."

A. *The Pastor*

The Code of Canon Law reserves the licit administration of solemn baptism to the pastor for his parish and, in like manner, to the local Ordinary for his territory. Under the term local Ordinary are to be included residential bishops, abbots or prelates *nullius*, their vicars general, Apostolic Administrators, Vicars and Prefects Apostolic, and all those who by a prescript of law or in view of approved constitutions succeed to the government of the territory upon the removal of the former.[3]

By the term "pastor" is understood either a priest or a moral person to whom has been conferred in title a parish with the care of souls to be exercised under the authority of the local Ordinary.[4] In those cases, however, wherein a parish is entrusted to a moral person, for instance, to a religious community, the moral person cannot be the actual pastor but merely the parish priest in title. In such instances the moral person must provide a vicar into whose hands the actual care of souls is placed.[5] By virtue of canon 451, § 2, the following may be understood to be included in the term "pastor," enjoying all the rights and subject to all the obligations which such a title connotes, unless the law states otherwise in individual cases:

a) The actual vicar of a parish held in title by a moral person (c. 471);
b) The priest who is in charge of a quasi-parish (c. 216 § 3);
c) The substitute vicar (c. 465, §§ 4 and 5; 474; 1923, § 2);
d) The parish administrator (c. 472, 1°; 473);

[3] Canon 198. II Plenary Council of Baltimore (1866), Tit. V, cap. 2: "Ordinarius baptismi minister est Episcopus in sua dioecesi, parochus in sua paroecia."—*Acta et decreta*, n. 227.

[4] Canon 451, § 1.

[5] Canons 452; 471, § 4.

e) The curate lawfully constituted to act as pastor when the parochial office falls vacant (c. 472, 2°);
f) The adjutant vicar deputed with full powers (c. 475); and
g) The assistant vicar who has a general delegation from the diocesan statutes, from the Ordinary's letter of appointment, or from the commission given him by the pastor himself (c. 476, 6°).[6]

The licit administration of baptism is reserved not merely to the pastor of any parish as such, but rather to the proper pastor of the person to be baptized.[7] So the proper priest for the licit administration of solemn baptism is the pastor of that parish in which one has a domicile or quasi-domicile.[8] Since, however, it is possible for a person to possess several domiciles simultaneously,[9] and certain that one can enjoy a domicile and at least one quasi-domicile concurrently, it is possible for one to have several pastors, each of whom would have an equal right to baptize.[10]

[6] Cf. Henry Davis, *Moral and Pastoral Theology* (3rd ed., 4 vols., New York: Sheed and Ward, 1938), III, 46; Cappello, *Tractatus Canonico-Moralis de Sacramentis* (2nd ed., 3 vols., Romae: Marietti, 1928), I, n. 144; Koudelka, *Pastors, Their Rights and Duties According to the New Code of Canon Law*, The Catholic University of America Canon Law Studies, n. 11 (Washington, D. C.: The Catholic University of America, 1921), pp. 14-16.

[7] Davis, *loc. cit.*; Genicot-Salsmans, *Institutiones Theologiae Moralis* (12th ed., 2 vols., Lovanii: Museum Lessianum, 1931), II, n. 139; Aertnys-Damen, *Theologia Moralis* (13th ed., 2 vols., Taurini: Marietti, 1939), II, n. 50; Bouuaert-Simenon, *Manuale Juris Canonici* (3rd ed., 3 vols., Gandae et Leodii: Dessain, 1930), II, n. 19.

[8] Canon 94, § 1.

[9] Costello (*Domicile and Quasi-Domicile*, The Catholic University of America Canon Law Studies, n. 60 [Washington, D. C.: The Catholic University of America, 1930], 154) cites many authorities to prove that one can possess as many as four domiciles at the same time.

[10] Canon 1216, § 2; Koudelka, *op. cit.*, p. 74; Genicot-Salsmans, *op. cit.*, II, n. 139; Bouuaert-Simenon, *op. cit.*, II, n. 19. Bouuaert-Simenon suggest

Though an adult who in the years of his majority possesses two or more domiciles, or a domicile and a quasi-domicile, may choose any one of his proper pastors to administer the sacrament, yet the same question reflects a different aspect in regard to children who are still in their minority. A minor retains the domicile of the person to whom he is subject,[11] and this constitutes a necessary or legal domicile for the child. There is question, however, among canonists as to whether or not a child, in a situation wherein the father enjoys both a domicile and a quasi-domicile, shares in a necessary or legal quasi-domicile also. One group of authors maintains that the Code entirely eliminated the idea of a necessary or legal quasi-domicile, irrespective of whether the father had a domicile also.[12] Another opinion avers that the family gains both the necessary domicile and quasi-domicile of the father.[13] These authors support their view by citing several decisions of the Roman Rota issued shortly before the appearance of the Code, and they allege that for the complete subjection of dependent parties to those under whose authority they are lawfully constituted it is reasonably required that they retain not merely the domicile but also the quasi-domicile

that if the birth occur in the territory of any individual one of the pastors who could be selected, then the choice should fall upon that pastor in whose parish the subject for baptism was born. They think that such observance should be made binding by custom or by particular law.

[11] Canon 93, § 1.

[12] De Meester, *Iuris Canonici et Juris Canonico-Civilis Compendium* (nova editio, 3 vols. in 4, Brugis, 1921-1928), I, n. 318, nota 7; Toso, *Ad Codicem Juris Canonici . . . Commentaria Minora* (5 vols., Romae: Marietti, 1920-1934), II, 21; Ojetti, *Commentarium in Codicem Iuris Canonici* (4 vols., Romae: Universitas Greg., 1927-1931), II, 50, nota 40; Ayrinhac, *General Legislation in the New Code of Canon Law* (New York, 1925), n. 200.

[13] Bouuaert-Simenon, *op. cit.*, I, n. 245; Wernz-Vidal, *Ius Canonicum* (7 vols. in 8, Romae, 1923-1938), II (ed. altera, 1928), n. 12; Chelodi, *Ius de Personis* (2nd ed., Tridenti, 1927), n. 92; Maroto, *Institutiones Iuris Canonici ad Normam Novi Codicis* (3rd ed., 2 vols., Romae, 1921), I, n. 413.

of the parent or guardian. The third opinion, the chief proponent of which is Vermeersch, steers a middle course. It admits that of itself the new legislation yields no recognition to a legal quasi-domicile. So this opinion asserts that the quasi-domicile of the father becomes the legal quasi-domicile of the child only when the father has no domicile. This view of Vermeersch [14] gains strong support from the fact that the Sacred Congregation of the Sacraments has given it place in the question of the competence of diocesan tribunals in the conduct of trials wherein the validity of a marriage is impugned.[15]

After a careful study of the three opinions Costello [16] concludes that speculatively the opinion which entirely denies the existence of a legal quasi-domicile appears to be the more acceptable one. However, he admits the solid probability of the other two opinions because of the decisions upon which they are based and in view of the outstanding authorities who have defended them. Hence, as long as this discussion among canonists exists, it seems that the pastor of the quasi-domicile of the father has an equal right with the pastor of the father's domicile to baptize the child, and that the ultimate selection of the proper minister remains with the father or guardian.

If the child were posthumous, it would be baptized in the parish which the mother retained by reason of her domicile or quasi-domicile.[17] When the parents do not live together,

[14] Vermeersch-Creusen, *Epitome Iuris Canonici* (3 vols., Romae: Dessain, vol. I [1937], vol. II [1934], vol. III [1936]), I, n. 185.

[15] 15 Aug. 1936—*AAS*, XXVIII (1936), 316. This is found in Bouscaren's *Canon Law Digest* (3 vols., Milwaukee: Bruce Publishing Co., 1934-1941), II (1937), 206: "A wife, not legally separated from her husband, if she has a quasi-domicile of her own, can be sued also before the Ordinary of the husband's domicile, but not of the said husband's quasi-domicile, except in case he has no domicile."

[16] *Domicile and Quasi-Domicile*, p. 177.

[17] Canon 93, § 1.

but have not been legally separated, a child living with its mother could be baptized by the pastor or the parish wherein the father has his domicile,[18] and, since in practice the child is subject to its mother, also by the pastor of the parish wherein the mother has her quasi-domicile.[19] When the parental separation has been legally constituted, it seems that the child will follow not only the mother's quasi-domicile but also her domicile.[20]

Since a pastor can validly and licitly administer solemn baptism to any adult possessing a domicile or quasi-domicile within the confines of his territory if that person seek baptism for him, it is possible for a child who has reached the use of reason and thus has become an adult in relation to baptism,[21] and who at the same time is capable of establishing a quasi-domicile,[22] to be validly and licitly baptized in a parish of which his parents can in no sense whatsoever be considered members.

B. *The Pastor and His Actual Subjects Within the Parish*

The pastor encounters comparatively little difficulty in the licit administration of baptism to the infant members of his parish.[23] The mere fact that the parents or guardians of such infants are legitimate members of the parish assures a licit administration in the baptism of these infants with

[18] Canon 93, § 1.

[19] Canon 93, § 2.

[20] Canon 93, § 2.

[21] Canon 745, § 2, 2°. Adulti autem censentur, qui rationis usu fruuntur; idque satis est ut suo quisque animi motu baptismum petat et ad illum admittatur.

[22] Canon 93, § 2. Minor infantia egressus potest quasi-domicilium proprium obtinere . . .

[23] Canon 745, § 2, 1°. Parvulorum seu infantium nomine veniunt, ad normam canonis 88, § 3, qui nondum rationis usum adepti sunt, eisdemque accensentur amentes ab infantia, in quavis aetate.

reference to the note of territorial subjection. However, there does rest upon the priest an obligation to assure himself in some way or other that the child presented will receive a Catholic training. If both parents are lax Catholics, who have fallen away from the practice of their religious duties, then as a general rule the child may be baptized, if there is a founded hope that the parents will change their ways.[24] In doubt the judgment of the local Ordinary should be obtained. Certainly the pastor cannot lawfully baptize an infant if its parents aver that they will not rear the child as a Catholic.[25]

In her legislation the Church respects the natural rights of the parent, and hence the children of heretics, schismatics, apostates and infidels cannot be licitly baptized against the will of their parents, unless the children are in such a condition of ill health that it can be prudently judged that they will die soon or, at least, before they reach the use of reason. If circumstances to warrant such a judgment are not present, a priest cannot licitly administer the sacrament unless the Catholic rearing of the child is assured.[26] It seems that the child of such parents could also be licitly baptized against their will or without their knowledge, when it is foreseen that the child's mind is so afflicted that there is little possibility of its ever attaining the use of reason.[27]

Even if non-Catholic parents, whether heretics or schismatics, should ask the priest to baptize their children, this

[24] S. C. de Prop. Fide, 31 ian. 1796—*Coll.*, n. 625. Cf. also: *Homiletic and Pastoral Review*, XXIV (1924), 849 and 1063-1064.

[25] Lydon, "The Minister of Baptism and Parental Consent,"—*Homiletic and Pastoral Review*, XXV (1925), 289. Aertnys-Damen, *Theologia Moralis* II, n. 63.

[26] Canons 750 and 751.

[27] Sabetti-Barrett, *Compendium Theologiae Moralis* (27th ed., New York: Frederick Pustet Co., Inc., 1919), n. 662.

in itself would not be sufficient to render the administration of the baptism lawful. From responses of the Holy Office it is evident that the priest cannot baptize a child in such circumstances without some well-founded hope for its future Catholic education.[28] So when a priest is asked by heretics or by schismatics to baptize their child simply because their own priests are not available, he cannot thereupon presume that it will be given a Catholic training.

The decision to be reached in many instances as to the moral certainty of such a Christian education is often difficult, as is deducible from the fine distinctions often drawn by the Sacred Congregations in this respect. Regularly it is not lawful to baptize an infant whose parents are both infidels and intend to remain infidels, even though they promise to tell the child of its Catholic baptism when it grows up and permit it to exercise the faith.[29] Yet the Holy Office approved the baptism of the infants of such infidels when there was some reasonable hope that the parents themselves would later seek baptism.[30] Again, the Holy See insisted that infidel children, if they are well instructed in religion, be baptized at the missions, if their parents consented, even though the children were returning home to an infidel atmosphere.[31]

Vermeersch [32] thinks that the very fact that the parents offer their child for baptism, provided that it is not for a superstitious motive, is in itself a sufficient reason to judge that they consent to a Catholic education. But it seems

[28] 19 sept. 1827—quoted by Sabetti-Barrett, *op. cit.*, n. 662, quaes. 3; 6 mart. 1844—*Fontes*, n. 895; 26 aug. 1885—*Fontes*, n. 1095.

[29] S. C. S. Off. (Promont. Bonae Spei), 22 iul. 1840—*Fontes*, n. 882.

[30] S. C. S. Off. (Vic. Ap. Sandwic.), 11 dec. 1850, ad 4—*Fontes*, n. 913.

[31] S. C. de Prop. Fide, 20 mart. 1933—*Periodica*, XXIII (1934), 17; Bouscaren, *Canon Law Digest*, II, 73.

[32] *Theologia Moralis* (3rd ed., 4 vols., Roma: Universitá Gregoriana, 1933), III, n. 221.

rather that a mere consent is not sufficient in itself to satisfy the Sacred Congregations, and that what is required is some hope that such an education will be actually fostered.

It is in the administration of the baptism of adults that the pastor is obliged to exercise his greatest judgment in order to assure its lawfulness. For baptism an adult, as has been noted, is one who has attained the use of reason.[33] A child who has completed his seventh year of age is presumed by the legislator to have attained this use of reason. But one must not accept this age as an absolute norm of judgment. It is after all only a legal presumption.[34] Such a presumption must of course give way to truth when the latter is firmly established by proof. So a pastor will oftentimes experience doubt as to whether a child younger or older than seven has actually attained the use of reason. It is important to determine in each instance the existence or non-existence of the use of reason, since with it the child as an adult is obliged to certain dispositions which concern not only the fruitfulness but also the validity of the sacrament. The decision rests with the minister of the sacrament.

In determining what is implied by the phrase "use of reason" one must well note that with a view to the reception of baptism this phrase is obviously less comprehensive in its connotation than it is in the case of other actions on the part of adult persons.[35] An instruction issued by the Sacred Congregation for the Propagation of the Faith strove to give practical guidance for the pastor faced with this difficulty. This instruction was directly concerned with such people as idiots and imbeciles (*amentes*) and with children of about five years of age, who either certainly or

[33] Canon 745, § 2, 2°.

[34] Canon 1826.

[35] King, *The administration of the sacraments to dying non-catholics*, The Catholic University of America Canon Law Studies, n. 23 (Washington, D. C.: The Catholic University of America, 1924), p. 11.

doubtfully perceive the principal mysteries of faith. The ultimate test in determining the existing rational status of adulthood must be sought both in the extant knowledge of the difference between good and evil and in the established capacity to commit sin (*culpae se reos reddere valeant*).[36]

If it is once established that a child has reached the use of reason, or if it is a matter of one who is unquestionably an adult, then the Code legislates that such a baptism, wherever it can easily be done, should be referred to the local Ordinary, so that he, if he so desires, either through himself or his delegate may confer the sacrament more solemnly.[37] However, the obligation imposed by this legislation is evidently conditional on the bishop's will to reserve the baptism to himself. When the bishop foregoes the use of his right (as the Code permits him to do by implication), he does not dispense from Code law or suggestion, but simply employs his liberty to decline the use of his right. Here in America such reservation is not usual, and so it is the customary practice for bishops to release pastors from any obligation to report such a forthcoming baptism of adults to the chancery.[38]

When the local Ordinary foregoes the use of his right to baptize an adult, then canon 738 must be observed and the baptism of adults belongs to the proper pastor of the catechumen. So the mere fact of having instructed a convert is in itself not a sufficient reason to justify a pastor in baptizing one who does not reside within the parish. The convert belongs to his proper pastor, unless the local Ordi-

[36] S. C. de Prop. Fide, instr., 17 apr. 1777, ad II—*Fontes*, n. 4575.

[37] Canon 744.

[38] Augustine, *A commentary on the New Code of Canon Law* (8 vols [vol. IV, 6th ed.], St. Louis: B. Herder Book Co., 1931), IV, 45; "National parishes: affiliation and separation,"—*The American Ecclesiastical Review* (hereafter referred to as *AER*), LXXXVII (1932), 531-537; Schaaf, "Right to baptize converts"—*AER*, XCIV (1936), 531-532.

nary in virtue of the power he derives from canon 738, § 1, or canon 744, by diocesan statute or in view of a legitimate custom authorizes the priest who instructed the convert to baptize the same.

In America there does seem to be an immemorial custom granting such a right to the priest who instructed the catechumen. It arose, perhaps, from the fact that in the early organization of the Church in this country every priest exercised, as it were, parochial jurisdiction wherever his missionary work called him. Later, when quasi-parishes or, as they were called, missions began to be organized, the custom of recognizing it as every priest's right to baptize all the converts he had instructed, even if he was not their proper pastor, seems to have continued. When in the judgment of the local Ordinary this custom cannot well be abolished, it may be tolerated,[39] and, until the local Ordinary does issue an ordinance to the contrary, it seems that pastors may on this plea of immemorial custom baptize the converts whom they have instructed even though such converts do not live within the confines of the parish. The Ordinary can likewise grant such authorization by statute or by special delegation.[40]

But the greatest exercise of judgment on the part of the minister takes place when he seeks to determine the existence in the adult subject for baptism of the three conditions requisite for the valid and fruitful reception of the sacrament: (1) the intention of receiving baptism; (2) faith in the principal revealed truths; and (3) contrition or at least attrition for all mortal sins.[41] Adults should not be baptized, therefore, without their consent knowingly and will-

[39] Canon 5.

[40] "National Parishes: Affiliation and Separation"—*AER*, LXXXVII (1932), 531-537.

[41] Canon 752, § 1. Adultus, nisi sciens et volens probeque instructus, ne baptizetur; insuper, admonendus ut de peccatis suis doleat.

ingly given, nor without proper instruction and an admonition to renounce sin. The intention on the part of the subject to receive baptism pertains to the very validity of the sacrament; and the other two conditions pertain to its fruitfulness. This law is based upon the necessity of cooperation in the work of salvation.[42]

With respect to the intention or willingness to receive baptism all theologians agree that it is required for validity. When they strive to determine the precise nature of this intention, however, and the manner in which it should be given expression, they are divided. Surely for the certain validity of the sacrament it is better to have the adult expressly request to receive baptism.[43] But there are theologians who maintain that it is probable that sorrow for sins based on some supernatural motive, and therefore founded on faith, includes the necessary intention of receiving baptism. Since this opinion is merely probable it can be acted upon only in cases of necessity when no surer intention can be elicited.[44]

For the valid reception of baptism the adult recipient need not have an actual intention, but it is necessary that a habitual intention, though it be only implicit, be present. In actual practice, since the sufficiency of this implied intention is questioned by some authors, the common teaching is that one should not be content with it outside the case of danger of death,[45] but that an explicit intention should be sought.[46]

[42] Conc. Trident., sess. VI, *de iustificatione*, c. 6.

[43] Cappello, *De Sacramentis*, I, n. 155.

[44] Davis, *Moral and Pastoral Theology*, III, p. 53; Cappello, *loc. cit.*; Ayrinhac, *Legislation on the Sacraments* (New York: Longmans, Green and Co., 1928), p. 30.

[45] Pruemmer, *Manuale Theologiae Moralis* (2nd et 3rd ed., 3 vols., Friburgi Brisgoviae, 1923), III, n. 135.

[46] *The Clergy Review*, XII (1936), 495.

In the general discussion as to what constitutes this habitual intention, whether implicit or explicit, the following remarks by an anonymous author are particularly noteworthy:

> An intention is habitual when it has been formed in the past, has not been recalled up to the present, and thus continues still in existence for the present. An intention is habitual *and explicit* when it results from an *actual* and never recalled intention of the past. It is habitual *but simultaneously implicit* when it follows upon a *virtual* and never recalled intention of the past.
>
> Thus a habitual intention, whether it be explicit or only implicit, needs to be sharply distinguished from the so-called interpretative intention, in virtue of which an act of the will has never really been formed, but in token of which an act of the will would be formed if proper thought and reflexion were given. And so an interpretative intention is at most a contingently potential intention and since it is merely potential, it is also non-actual. It is the wish that one would have, but as yet does not have.
>
> Precisely, then, because an interpretative intention must of necessity look to the future in order to become something actual, it must not be confused with an intention that may rightly be presumed as present. This presumed intention is present when, for instance, some one would here and now explicitly ask for the sacrament if he were questioned concerning it, because his habitual knowledge and the extant characteristic disposition of his christian way of living manifest virtually what is not expressed explicitly. And this is but another way of pointing to an implicit habitual intention, that is, one which in reality has flowed from a virtual intention and continues for the present because it has never been recalled.
>
> For an adult's valid reception of baptism such an intention is undoubtedly required to meet the essential condition of making the act of reception a voluntary one. But such an intention also plainly suffices. There is not required an

> actual or a virtual intention which, more than a mere condition, really influences the act as its cause or active principle, for the recipient of a sacrament is not its cause, but rather a passive subject in relation to it. Therefore the recipient need not have an intention which is the full equivalent of an operative cause in the production of a free human act with complete imputability: it suffices that the subject have an intention which as a condition makes possible the voluntary reception of the administered sacrament.[47]

Throughout this discussion of the nature of the intention necessary on the part of the recipient it must be borne in mind that the judgment at which the minister arrives as to the presence or absence or insufficiency of an intention in the subject—that such a judgment in itself cannot influence the validity of the sacrament. No matter what the minister thinks, if the intention is not present *ex parte subjecti* the sacrament is null. However, the minister must make the judgment, and it can be very important in its effect. Thus oftentimes he can easily foster the proper intention when he accurately judges it to be absent.

Here also it may be noted that an intention which is *purely* superstitious or temporal is not sufficient while there is time to instruct the person. If no such time remains, no official response exists which would prohibit action on such an intention, in the event that there is an utter impossibility of securing more definite information as to the exact nature of the intention. It will not be a valid baptism, if the intention which is *purely* superstitious is the principal one, and there is a positive exclusion of the right intention. But if further information cannot be obtained, some intention, although doubtful, is present in such a case and baptism should be administered conditionally. When there is doubt about the existence or nature of the intention, or about the

47 "Was there sufficient intention for baptism?"—*AER*, CI (1939), 360-361.

fact or the validity of a possible previous baptism, the conditional form must be used.[48]

It would be permissible to administer baptism to one dying and seeking the sacrament, although that person had no desire to become a Catholic due to the common prejudice which misrepresents the Catholic Church. This could not be done if the person held doctrines directly opposed to the Catholic Church.[49]

Noldin [50] explains that if anyone jokingly receives baptism, or if anyone, though he be entirely ignorant of what a sacrament is, permits baptism to be materially conferred upon himself, such a one does not receive the sacrament, since this willingness to submit to the ceremony cannot be interpreted as indicative of the requisite intention.

Greater difficulty in this regard is encountered by the minister when he deals with dying non-Catholics who are unconscious and can give no sign of their intention. Whether or not to baptize is a question of prudent judgment lest the sacrament be unduly exposed to nullity, since, as has been noted previously, the validity of the sacrament depends on the actual existence of an intention in the subject and is not effected by any conclusion which the minister reaches in regard to the presence or absence of such an intention.

The Code [51] states that if a person cannot now ask for baptism, but either before or in his present state has manifested in some probable manner an intention to receive the sacrament, such a one is to be baptized conditionally.

48 King, *The administration of the sacraments to dying non-Catholics*, pp. 50-51.

49 "'Catholic' and the profession of faith at the hour of death"—*AER*, LXV (1921), 304.

50 *Summa Theologiae Moralis* (26th ed. recognovit et emendavit A. Schmitt, S.J., 3 vols., Ratisbonae: apud Fridericum Pustet, 1940), III, n. 41, 3, c.

51 Canon 752, § 3.

Ayrinhac[52] believes that the evidence of intention required by this canon does not have to be very clear or strong. Such a view is probably correct, since in such instances it will generally be impossible to procure any stronger evidence of intention—a fact of which the legislator must have been cognizant. Vermeersch thinks that a reasonable conjecture of the existence of a desire for baptism can be made in the case of one who has heard of the christian religion, and so thinks that in our civilized nations anyone dying without the use of his senses can be baptized at least conditionally.[53] But this opinion seems rather broad, since mere knowledge of the christian religion would not necessarily imply an inclination, no matter how slight, to embrace that religion. It must be admitted, nevertheless, that the intention of receiving baptism could more readily be presumed in one who had lived and moved in a christian atmosphere than it could in one who had never even heard of Christ.

Some theologians maintain that if an unconscious infidel in danger of death has in no manner expressed or manifested his intention to receive baptism, he should not be baptized.[54] It would seem, however, that according to most authors a more elastic interpretation of canon 752 could be accepted in practice. Genicot would not censure one who in the case of such an infidel proceeded to baptize him conditionally in view of the universal saving will of God.[55] This more

[52] *Legislation on the sacraments*, p. 31.

[53] *Theologia Moralis*, III, n. 223.

[54] E. g., Noldin-Schmitt, *Summa Theologiae Moralis*, III, n. 73, sub. 4, b. Their opinion is based on decisions of the Holy Office given on January 25, 1703 (*Fontes*, n. 764) and May 10, 1703 (*Fontes*, n. 765). It contends that it is licit to baptize only those whom the minister can prudently judge to possess at least an implicit intention to receive baptism.

[55] Genicot-Salsmans, *Institutiones Theologiae Moralis*, II, n. 150: "Nihilo minus censemus non esse reprehendendum qui baptismum condicionate

liberal view seems probable to Cappello also,[56] who interprets canon 752 and the responses of the Sacred Congregations as not conclusively reprobating such a practice, but as merely commending a safer norm to follow. But, he adds, baptism is not to be given to such dying infidels if it entails danger of contempt of the Catholic faith among other infidels. Vermeersch favors the liberal opinion also.[57] They all point out that canon 752 fails to make any mention of those infidels who have given no sign of their intention. It tells only what should be done in case they have expressed some probable indication of a desire for baptism. Hence, since the Code is silent on this point, and does not expressly prohibit the administration of conditional baptism, one is free to baptize conditionally an infidel who has in no way manifested a wish or an intention to receive baptism nor any desire to the contrary.[58]

If the minister can baptize a foundling even in the absence of a sponsor because he may interpret its desire for salvation, and if, as the Roman Ritual allows,[59] he can baptize the insane, certainly he may do so in the case of those who face death within reach of the Catholic help that can secure for them salvation, insofar as he has some presumption of a likely desire on the part of the subject and as long as there are no indications to the contrary.[60]

confert etiamsi signa sufficientis intentionis non compererit, sed ipsam merito praesumens fretus universali voluntate salvifica Dei, quae ad spem concipiendam de necessariis dispositionibus internis invitare videatur, dum ad moribundum ducat eum a quo externum ritum sacramentalem percipere valeat." Nevertheless he admits that the opinion expressed by Noldin is more in conformity with the responses of the Holy Office (18 sept. 1850, ad 2—*Fontes*, n. 912; 30 mart. 1898, ad 2—*Fontes*, n. 1197).

56 *De Sacramentis*, I, n. 159.

57 *Epitome Iuris Canonici*, II, n. 35; *Theologia Moralis*, III, n. 223.

58 "Clandestine baptism to dying Protestants"—*AER*, LXXI (1924), 317.

59 Tit. II, c. 3, *de baptismo adultorum*, n. 9.

60 "Conditional baptism to patients in hospitals"—*AER*, LXIV (1921), 624.

In dealing with the entire question of intention in dying non-Catholics it must ever be borne in mind that the lawfulness of the minister's act depends entirely upon the prudence of his judgment. It is not necessary that he be morally certain of the dispositions of the subject; it suffices that he can proceed with a prudent judgment.[61] If the minister possesses a positive doubt as to the existence of an intention on the part of the subject, he must confer the sacrament, at least conditionally, since in doubt no one is to be deprived of so great a gift of God.[62]

Once it has been prudently decided that the subject possesses the proper intention of receiving baptism, the next concern of the minister of the sacrament is, according to canon 752, to make certain that the person is instructed sufficiently in the faith and has sorrow for his past sins.

In regard to the amount of instruction that should precede baptism it may be stated that it varies with individual cases. Insofar as it is possible an adult should be given a complete course of instruction on Catholic doctrine. Since there can never be too much instruction in preparation for baptism, the minister of the sacrament is quite naturally confronted with the question of what constitutes a permissible minimum. This minimum was carefully summarized by the Sacred Congregation for the Propagation of the Faith as including those doctrines which are usually proposed by the theologians as being *de necessitate medii* and *de necessitate praecepti.*[63] The Code does not specify the

[61] Cappello, *De Sacramentis,* I, n. 154.

[62] The treatment of the various opinions of the canonists and theologians herein presented has admittedly been undertaken in a rather cursory fashion. For a further discussion and an evaluation in much greater detail and clarity the reader is referred to the work already cited: King, *The administration of the sacraments to dying non-Catholics* (Chapter III: The baptism of dying non-Catholics), pp. 27-60.

[63] S. C. de Prop. Fide, instr. (ad Vic. Ap. Sin.), 18 act. 1883, ad XVII: "Quapropter Sacra Congregatio ... statuit, ut cum agitur de ordinariis

degree of the requisite instruction, but theologians agree that the least that is to be required even when death is imminent is belief in the existence of God and in the fact that God rewards good and punishes evil. From the responses of the Sacred Congregations some idea of the importance attached to this instruction can be gained, since there is a constant insistence upon it even in the case of those persons who are at the point of death.

Thus the Holy Office ruled that there would not be present a sufficient cause to baptize lawfully if the dying person merely promised to take instructions upon recovery. Such a one, insofar as he is capable, should be instructed in the existence of God, His remunerative justice, and, if possible, even in the Trinity and Incarnation.[64]

In the case of a Mohammedan dangerously sick but in possession of his faculties, the Holy Office declared it unlawful to give him baptism without first speaking to him of our mysteries, even though one could suppose him to be contrite and to be in good faith in his error.[65]

These and numerous other responses show the importance of giving at least the minimum instruction to one who is capable of receiving it. However, when the state of the dying person does not permit an explanation of the faith, then it would certainly be lawful to omit such instruction as long as the person had manifested a general assent to

casibus conversionis adultorum, et excepto mortis eorum periculo, haec pro oculis a missionariis habeantur, antequam eos ad baptismum admittant, nempe ut catechumeni cognoscant principalia mysteria fidei, Symbolum, Orationem dominicam, decalogum, praecepta Ecclesiae, effectum baptismi, actus virtutum theologalium earumque motiva."—*Fontes*, n. 4903; *Coll.*, n. 1606. Obviously, *cognoscant* in this text must be understood in conjunction with the subject's capabilities.

[64] S. C. S. Off. (Quebec), 25 ian. 1703—*Fontes*, n. 764. A stricter response to the same bishop was made later (10 maii 1703, ad 1 et 2—*Fontes*, n. 765).

[65] 30 mart. 1898, ad 1 et 2—*Fontes*, n. 1197.

Christ's doctrine and such assent involved the implicit promise to live a christian life.[66]

If the minister is doubtful as to whether the amount of instruction is commensurate with the intellectual capacity of the subject, this does not permit him to baptize conditionally. For, since the instruction is a requisite for licitness and not for validity, it would be wrong to attach a condition to the administration of a baptism which would otherwise certainly be valid because of the right intention.[67]

In summary it will be helpful to quote three rules laid down by the Reverend Doctor Francis J. Connell, C.SS.R., in regard to the relation of the act of explicit faith to the four necessary truths in the reception of a convert:

> 1. It is never lawful to administer the sacrament to an adult who has certainly never made an act of explicit faith in the first two, at least, of the four essential truths. (These four truths are the existence of God, His remunerative justice, the Trinity and the Incarnation.)
>
> 2. When there is doubt as to the sufficiency of an adult's explicit belief, the priest is bound to furnish the necessary instruction and assistance for the act of faith; if, however, it is impossible to give instruction and the need is urgent, the sacrament may be conferred.
>
> 3. When there is a doubt whether a subject for baptism has reached the use of reason, he should be instructed, if possible, in the essentials of faith (and the other requisite dispositions) before the sacrament is conferred; if, however, adequate instruction is impossible, and there is grave danger of death, he should be baptized, even though he manifest no dispositions nor the intention of receiving the sacrament.[68]

[66] Bouuaert-Simenon, *Manuale Juris Canonici*, II, n. 34.

[67] S. C. C. Off., instr. (ad Vic. Ap. Tche-Kiang), 1 aug. 1860—*Fontes*, n. 963.

[68] "Priestly Ministry of the Essentials of Faith"—*AER*, LXXVI (1927), 570-579.

In regard to the disposition of attrition or sorrow for sins it is sufficient that the subject be in general sorry for all his sins, at least the mortal ones, and this act of sorrow should be at least habitual. The sacrament must not be conferred upon those who are known to have the intention of persisting in sin.[69] "Real attrition would not exist in a catechumen who would not manifest willingness to obey all the laws of God and of the Church, to give up superstitious practices, dismiss an illegitimate wife, abandon an unlawful trade, etc.; hence the necessity sometimes of mentioning and laying stress on some of these points." [70]

There is still another point worthy of note in respect to the baptism of adult converts, for it is a matter to which the minister must attend. It concerns the reception into the Church by conditional baptism of an adult who received a doubtful baptism in a heretical sect. Such a one first makes an abjuration of heresy and the profession of faith in the external forum; then follows conditional baptism; and finally, there is a sacramental confession with conditional absolution. This is contained in an instruction sent by the Holy Office to the Bishop of Philadelphia,[71] and was later prescribed for the whole United States by the Second Plenary Council of Baltimore (1866).[72]

69 Merkelbach, *Summa Theologiae Moralis* (ed. alt., 3 vols., Parisiis: Desclée, De Brouwer et Cie, 1939), III, n. 144.

70 Ayrinhac, *Legislation on the Sacraments*, p. 30.

71 S. C. S. Off., 20 iul. 1859: ". . . Triplex igitur in conciliendis distinguitur procedendi methodus:

I. Si baptismus absolute conferatur, nulla requiritur abiuratio nec absolutio eo quod omnia abluit sacramentum regenerationis.

II. Si baptismus sit sub conditione iterandus, hoc ordine procedendum erit:

a) abiuratio seu fidei professio;

b) baptismus conditionatus;

c) confessio sacramentalis cum absolutione conditionata.

III. Quando denique validum indicatum fuerit baptisma, sola recipitur abiuratio seu fidei professio, quam absolutio a censuris sequitur."—*Fontes*, n. 953.

72 *Acta et Decreta*, n. 240.

It is noteworthy that this instruction, though it evidently seeks to cite in detail the modes of receiving different types of converts, does not require an absolution in the external forum from the censure of excommunication for converts who are to be baptized conditionally. The fact that the instruction explicitly mentions such an absolution in connection with the profession of faith as being necessary in the reconciliation of converts about the validity of whose previous baptism there can be no doubt, and that the profession of faith alone is expressly prescribed for converts who are to be baptized conditionally, is a clear indication that the Holy Office does not consider doubtfully baptized persons to have incurred the censure of excommunication for heresy.

True it is that there is no such actuality as that of a person who has received a doubtful baptism. The doubtful baptism spoken of here is but a mental evaluation and not an extant fact. However, there is an evident reason why persons should not be bound by ecclesiastical censures when it cannot be definitely determined in actual fact whether they are validly baptized or not baptized at all. The Code itself defines a censure as a penalty to be inflicted upon only baptized persons.[73] Since in regard to penalties the more benign interpretation is to be employed,[74] then the probability is that a doubtfully baptized person does not incur penalties legislated for those definitely baptized.[75] Hence, in practice the factual doubt as to the existence of a valid baptism can be reduced to a legal doubt concerning the person's subjection to ecclesiastical jurisdic-

[73] Canon 2241.

[74] Canon 2219, § 1. Cf. also canon 2246, § 2, which stresses a rule of similar import relative to the factor of reservation when the latter attaches to a censure.

[75] Cappello, *Tractatus Canonico-Moralis de Censuris* (3rd ed., Romae: Marietti, 1933), n. 15.

tion, and so the excommunication may safely be regarded as non-existent.[76]

There are those who maintain that the suggestion of the Holy Office, that the word *forsan* be inserted in the formula of absolution from excommunication in the external forum [77] when it is doubtful whether the excommunication on account of heresy was incurred, weakens this position.[78] However, in view of the fact that the Holy Office in the very same instruction did not exact any conditional absolution from censure for those who are to be baptized conditionally, it is probable that the suggestion of *forsan* may very well be referred to the case where a validly baptized Protestant, for example, may perhaps never have been in bad faith and therefore perhaps never incurred the excommunication.

Since the Holy Office in the instruction of 1859 prescribes a sacramental confession of sins and a conditional absolution for the reconciliation of heretics whose earlier baptism was doubtful, one may be inclined to consider at first sight that this attitude is hardly consistent with that assumed in regard to the non-requirement of absolution from the censure in the external forum. Consistency would seem to demand conditional absolution from the censure in the external forum as well as a conditional sacramental absolution, or no absolution in either forum.

One or two considerations, however, will suffice to show that there is no inconsistency, as there is really no parallelism between the two matters. In the first place the submission of sins to the sacramental keys is regulated by the divine law, whereas the discipline regarding excommunication

[76] Canon 2219, § 1.

[77] "In dubio gravi aut levi utrum poenitens in excommunicationem incurrerit per haeresim professam, sacerdos inserat vocabulum *forsan*."—*Fontes*, n. 953.

[78] E. Leroux, "Les Baptêmes d'Adultes"—*Revue Ecclésiastique de Liege*, XVII (1925-1926), 341-352.

is subject entirely to ecclesiastical authority; hence, since the legislative superior is not the same in the two cases, consistency does not require identity of procedure. But a more important difference still is that the newly converted person has committed sins which he has never submitted to the sacramental keys and, unlike the excommunication which cannot affect the person until it is definitely established that he is validly baptized, these sins continue to exist upon his soul independently of the judgment as to the reception or non-reception of baptism. Hence, since these sins would continue to demand absolution in the event that the previous baptism was valid, conditional absolution is given in the internal forum to definitely remove all possibility of sin remaining upon the soul.[79]

In respect to the abjuration of heresy to be made another question presents itself. May the form set forth in the rescript of the Holy Office to the Bishop of Philadelphia, on July 20, 1859, be still used in the United States,[80] or must the method indicated in canon 2314, § 2, be followed?[81]

If the rescript of the Holy Office granted an indult or a privilege, then this would continue in force, since by the approval of the Second Plenary Council of Baltimore (1866) it would seem to have been extended to the whole country.[82] If it was but an interpretation of the prevailing

[79] "Reception of converts into the church"—*AER*, LXXXVII (1932), 528-530; "Absolution from censure and profession of faith at conversion"—*AER*, LXXXVIII (1933), 419; Böhm, "Taufe und Absolution von der Häresie bei Konversionen"—*Theologisch-Praktische Quartalschrift* (*LQS*), LXXXVI (1933), 789; MacKenzie, *The Delict of Heresy*, The Catholic University of America Canon Law Studies, n. 77 (Washington, D. C.: Catholic University of America, 1932), p. 115.

[80] This required the abjuration of heresy and the profession of faith to be made before the priest only.

[81] This demands the presence of the local Ordinary or of his delegate and two witnesses. The Vicar General cannot take the place of the Ordinary without a special mandate.

[82] Canon 4.

law of the Church, it must now yield to the legislation of the Code. The wording of the rescript of the Holy Office shows clearly that no indult or privilege was intended, but merely an interpretation of the then existing law.[83] Since this was, then, merely an interpretation of the general law, it is replaced by the law of the Code.

Some may still object that, since this method of reconciling converts was prescribed by the Second Plenary Council of Baltimore, it may be called a particular law for this country. But it is a particular law that is opposed to the law of the Code,[84] and therefore it is abolished.[85] These reasons would seem to warrant the conclusion that, unless an indult similar in tone to the instruction of 1859 is obtained from the Holy See, converts in this country also will have to make their abjuration of heresy and profession of faith before the Ordinary or his delegate and two witnesses.[86]

C. *Restrictions upon the Pastoral Right to Administer Solemn Baptism*

The right which the pastor has to baptize those people who possess a domicile or quasi-domicile within his parish boundaries is both personal and territorial. And simply because by its very nature it is such, it can be limited by restrictions which are territorial, or personal, or both.

In respect to territorial limitation, the Code itself confines to the limits of his own parish his ordinary power to ad-

[83] The rescript commences: "*Proposito dubio.*" So the Bishop of Philadelphia did not seek any special concession or grant, but merely presented a difficulty. The doubt was settled by a definite instruction worded: "*Emi. D. D. decreverunt dandam esse instructionem, prout sequitur.*"

[84] Canon 2314, § 2.

[85] Canon 6, 1°.

[86] Throughout the United States it is customary for the bishops to make the diocesan priests to whom faculties have been granted their habitual delegates for the reception of this abjuration.

minister the sacrament solemnly when it legislates that he cannot lawfully baptize even his own subjects in the territory of another priest unless he has the proper permission from the local Ordinary or from the local pastor.[87] In the cases wherein he baptizes with the proper permission the lawfulness of the conferring of the baptism arises solely in view of the permission, and cannot be construed in any way as arising from his pastoral office. Blat [88] remarks that this restriction cannot be considered as one of the exceptions or limitations mentioned in canon 201, § 3,[89] because in this matter it is not exactly a question concerning the exercise of voluntary jurisdiction, but rather a question of the power of the sacred ministry which, although it is connected with jurisdiction, is however circumscribed in its operation by territorial considerations. So, even though the pastor has more extensive rights in respect to the administration of the sacrament of Penance in that he can absolve his subjects anywhere,[90] yet the strict territorial limit placed upon him in the administration of solemn baptism is the same as that imposed for the administration of Holy Viaticum,[91] Extreme Unction [92] and Matrimony.[93] Hence Woywod concludes:

[87] Canon 739. In alieno territorio nemini licet, sine debita licentia, baptismum sollemnem conferre ne sui quidem loci incolis.

[88] *Commentarium Textus Codicis Iuris Canonici* (5 vols. in 6, Romae: ex typographia Pontificia in Instituto Pii IX, 1921-1927), Lib. III, Pars I, n. 22.

[89] Canon 201, § 3. Nisi aliud ex rerum natura aut ex iure constet, potestatem iurisdictionis voluntariam seu non-iudicialem quis exercere potest etiam in proprium commodum, aut extra territorium existens, aut in subditum e territorio absentem.

[90] Canon 881, § 2. Though the jurisdiction exercised in the administration of the sacrament of penance is judicial, yet canon 881 is an exception to the general rule of canon 201, § 2.

[91] Canon 850.

[92] Canon 938, § 2.

[93] Canon 1095, § 1, 2°.

"As a general rule, one may lay down the principle that strictly pastoral functions are by law subject to the authority of the pastor of the place where such functions are to be performed." [94]

The pastor's right to baptize solemnly all his parishioners within the parish may also be restricted territorially even within the very parish confines in two ways: first, by the right which another parish possesses either by law or by custom to baptize these people, and secondly, by the existence within the territory of a national or linguistic parish.

In respect to the first of these two modes of restriction, namely, that a parish should have a right to baptize subjects of another pastor, such a right can arise from custom or legitimate grant. The practice is of long duration, dating back as it does to the time when the cathedral churches had the sole right to baptize the people of the town. Later the right to baptize was given to the individual parish churches, but it often happened that in towns where the growth in population postulated a division of parishes, the new churches retained a filial relation toward the ancient or mother church. This relationship or dependency was evidenced in many cases by the fact that the mother church obtained an exclusive or, at least, a cumulative right to baptize all the people of the town. Blat defines such a cumulative right of a parish as the right by which people may be lawfully baptized in that parish church, as well as in their own proper parish.[95] Such rights could be acquired by parishes through lawful grant or custom. So Fanfani [96] cites, as an example of such a right arising from custom, the fact that people can be baptized in Saint Peter's at Rome no matter to which parish they belong.

94 "The Legislation of the Code on Baptism"—*Homiletic and Pastoral Review*, XX (1920), 1037-1042.

95 *Commentarium*, Lib. III, Pars I, n. 64.

96 *De Iure Parochorum* (Romae: Marietti, 1924), n. 233.

The legislator, recognizing that such rights were all too generally current, so that the maintenance of baptismal fonts was rendered practically useless for such parishes as were located in towns or districts wherein the exclusive right of conferring baptism attached to the mother church, sought to restore to the pastor his right to baptize his own subjects and therefore abrogated any such exclusive right wherever it existed at the time of the promulgation of the Code.[97] The Code commanded, moreover, that in the future every parish church should possess its own baptismal font, and that thenceforth only the cumulative right to baptize could be recognized for any parish.

A further indication of the legislator's desire to restore to the pastor a full parochial right in every detail is shown from the response of the Code Commission, wherein it is stated that in the future such a cumulative right could no longer be acquired by custom, and that any church which theretofore had possessed an exclusive right to a baptismal font now enjoyed merely a cumulative right.[98]

In reference to the second territorial restriction of a pastor's right to baptize all those who have a domicile or a quasi-domicile within his parish, namely, when a national parish exists within the same territory, it must be noted that in spite of a seeming clash of rights there need not be any real parochial conflict. The pastor of the English-speaking parish does not have his rights over certain people restricted; rather, such people are withdrawn from his jurisdiction and are entrusted to the safekeeping of a priest of their own nationality.

[97] Canon 774, § 1. Quaelibet paroecialis ecclesia, revocato ac reprobato quovis contrario statuto vel privilegio vel consuetudine, baptismalem habeat fontem, salvo legitimo iure cumulativo aliis ecclesiis iam quaesito. This canon is so strongly worded that for the future no parish can vindicate for itself the continued use of such a previously enjoyed exclusive right in virtue of any of the claims that canons 4 or 5 may apparently offer.

[98] *AAS*, XIV (1922), 662.

The Holy See has recognized the departure from the constant usage of exclusive territory for each parish, and seemingly has sanctioned and recognized cumulative jurisdiction with other pastors in one and the same territory.[99] It is precisely such a departure from the usual rule of a single and exclusive parish in a given territory for which the Code expressly provides.[100]

While it is true that the pastor of a national parish has cumulative jurisdiction with the pastor of the English-speaking parish, yet their jurisdiction is by no means coextensive. The latter possesses complete pastoral jurisdiction over the entire territory of his parish and over all the people living in it, except those who actually choose to belong to the parish erected for their nationality; but the pastor of the national parish is limited in his parochial jurisdiction not only to the territorial boundaries of his parish, but also to the members of the given nationality within the designated territory as long as they have not chosen to attend the English-speaking parish.[101]

Among the more widely known authors the only one to discuss the question in detail is Augustine,[102] and he expresses opinions which, if held in practice, would certainly

[99] S. C. Conc., 1 febr. 1908—*ASS*, XLI (1908), 109-111.

[100] Canon 216, § 4. Non possunt sine speciali apostolico indulto constitui paroeciae pro diversitate sermonis seu nationis fidelium in eadem civitate vel territorio degentium . . .

[101] It will be noted that here it is taken for granted that national parishes have territorial boundaries and that the pastor's authority is thereby confined. Some maintain that the national pastor's authority abstracts from all territorial limits and hence is merely personal without any reference to place. This latter opinion is espoused by L. Raymond (*Periodica*, XVI [1927], 261*), who maintains that Italian parishes, at least in this country, are more frequently personal than territorial. Cf. "National pastors and assistance at marriage"—*AER*, LXXX (1929), 88-94.

[102] *Commentary*, IV, 40-41; *The Pastor According to the New Code of Canon Law* (2nd ed., St. Louis: B. Herder Book Co., 1924), pp. 56-58.

lead to an actual conflict of rights between the pastor of the national parish and the pastor of the English-speaking parish. He cites the example of an Italian family moving into a section wherein exist an English-speaking parish, a German parish and an Italian parish. Before the family definitely affiliates with the English-speaking parish or the Italian parish, Augustine would give the German pastor a right to baptize any one of the family.[103]

According to our interpretation of the rights of a national pastor, however, the German pastor has no authority whatsoever. He may not baptize the child even if the parents wish to join his parish, for this is not permissible for them, since the parish exists solely for those of German extraction. The family, in spite of its lack of definite affiliation with any parish, belongs to either the Italian or the English parish. The Italian pastor has a right to baptize the child as his parishioner, unless the parents have decided to join the English-speaking church. If they so decide, the Italian pastor cannot deter them and loses all authority over them. It would likewise seem that the English-speaking pastor could lawfully baptize the child if it were presented to him, since it could be legitimately interpreted as a sign on the part of the parents that they wished to join that particular parish in preference to their own national church.[104]

In like manner Augustine holds that the pastor of the German parish could " in justice " baptize an adult whom he has converted, even though such a person were not of

103 " Because by reason of the territory or parochial district, he may claim as much right as the English pastor, and as far as pastoral rights go he is as much entitled to perform the ceremony as the English pastor." — *Commentary,* IV, 41; *The Pastor,* p. 57.

104 For an accurate account of the alien's right to affiliate himself with either the national or the English-speaking parish confer the private declaration of the Sacred Congregation of the Council, January 15, 1938, and the letter of the Apostolic Delegate to the United States, February 17, 1938, as cited in Bouscaren's 1941 *Canon Law Digest Supplement,* pp. 48-49.

the German nationality. The reason he offers in support of this opinion is that " the pastor of the English-speaking congregation cannot claim anyone as his subject before baptism." [105] Such a reason lacks foundation. It is at variance with the mind of the legislator, for canon 738, § 2, rules that a *peregrinus* who, by the very necessity of the case, has not yet been baptized is, nevertheless, to be solemnly baptized by his own pastor (*a parocho proprio*). True it is that before baptism one is not directly bound by the law of the Church.[106] Nevertheless, the Church directly obliges her ministers, and in the case of children born of Catholic parents, the latter; and indirectly the person to be baptized. In like manner it will be necessary to consider a catechumen conditionally subject to the pastor of the place where he resides.

In the writer's opinion the German pastor cannot be considered the proper pastor (*parochus proprius*) for the baptism of a convert who is not of his nationality, and hence cannot confer such a baptism solely on the pretense of not conflicting with any outside parochial jurisdiction. But, as has been noted previously, the German pastor would seemingly have a right to baptize the convert whom he has instructed, even though such a person were not a member of his parish, either on the score that here in America there seems to be an immemorial custom granting such a right, or because quite generally throughout the United States diocesan regulations honor the instructing priest with the right to confer baptism upon his convert.

Since the pastor's right to baptize is both territorial and personal, and thus, as we have seen, can be restricted by certain territorial circumstances, so also can his jurisdiction

[105] *Commentary,* IV, 41; *The Pastor,* pp. 57-58. The only objection to such a practice that he can foresee is a diocesan regulation or a lawful custom to the contrary.

[106] Canon 12.

be personally circumscribed. Hence a pastor can lose his right to baptize solemnly his subjects if he has incurred an excommunication,[107] a suspension *a divinis* [108] or a personal interdict.[109]

In regard to such a pastor thus affected by censure some authors [110] merely state a previous decision rendered by the Sacred Congregation for the Propagation of the Faith [111] and seemingly draw the quite general conclusion that such a pastor no longer has the right to baptize solemnly. Such a conclusion is warranted to the extent that a priest so censured, if he continued to exercise his parochial ministry without any excuse whatsoever, would incur an irregularity; [112] but to make the conclusion altogether general, with-

[107] Canons 2257 and 2261.

[108] Canons 2278 and 2279, § 2, 2°. "A pastor suspended *a iurisdictione*, while he may not administer ecclesiastical property nor hear confessions, because these acts entail jurisdiction, he may nevertheless baptize and administer Holy Viaticum and Extreme Unction." — Eligius G. Rainer, C.SS.R., *Suspension of Clerics*, The Catholic University of America Canon Law Studies, n. 111 (Washington, D. C.: The Catholic University of America, 1937), p. 79.

[109] Canons 2268 and 2275.

[110] Augustine, *Commentary*, IV, 44; Ayrinhac, *Legislation on the Sacraments*, p. 17; Cappello *De Sacramentis*, I, n. 144, sub nota 2; Bouuaert-Simenon, *Manuale Juris Canonici*, II, n. 19.

[111] 21 ian. 1789: "Sacerdotem suspensum et interdictum nullo umquam tempore administrare posse Baptismum cum solemnitatibus, sed, quando propter necessitatem debeat baptizare, baptizet private." — *Coll.*, n. 598; *Fontes*, n. 4625.

[112] Canon 985. Sunt irregulares ex delicto: ... 7° Qui actum ordinis, clericis in ordine sacro constitutis reservatum, ponunt, vel eo ordine carentes, vel ab eius exercitio poena canonica sive personali, medicinali aut vindicativa, sive locali prohibiti. That the pastor under censure who solemnly baptizes without cause is included within the ambit of this canon is vouchsafed by Vermeersh-Creusen, *Epitome*, II, n. 24. Moreover, in regard to incurring this irregularity the following words of Rainer (*Suspension of Clerics*, p. 191) are important: "The ceremonies must be so carried out that those who witness them will realize that objectively they are not

out indicating that circumstances do arise which will permit such a priest to baptize solemnly, is inaccurate.

In the first place, if the pastor has incurred such a penalty as a *latae sententiae* penalty, and it has not been enforced by a condemnatory or declaratory sentence and the crime was not notorious, he is still not bound to observe it in the external forum if such an observance would result in the danger of scandal or the loss of his good name.[113] Such a pastor, though bound by the penalty in the internal forum, would frequently find it necessary to baptize solemnly in cases wherein a refusal to do so would excite astonishment in the minds of his parishioners. In such instances he would act not only validly but also licitly.

Again the Code lays down certain conditions under which ordinary excommunicates, and even *excommunicati vitandi* and those excommunicates upon whom a declaratory or condemnatory sentence has been passed, can licitly administer the sacraments.[114]

Prior to the consideration of these conditions it is practically requisite to show the parallel between such excommunicates and between priests who have been suspended or

feigned, but in keeping with the external rite. Hence, should a priest who is suspended *a divinis* withhold his intention while celebrating Mass or administering Baptism, he would nevertheless become irregular, despite the nullity of the Mass or the ineffective administration of Baptism. His external acts betray no sense-perceptible defect or objective lack of reality which could induce spectators to regard his acts as a mere nugatory performance or, at least as being devoid of the sacred meaning and object which their external rite normally implies. On the contrary, he would incur the irregularity precisely because his acts are in all seeming reality the active performance of a sacred sacrificial function and the fulfillment of a sacred sacramental rite. In a word, his acts are the solemn acts of sacred orders from whose exercise he is barred."

[113] Canon 2232, § 1. For a lengthy commentary on this confer: Conran, *The Interdict*, The Catholic University of America Canon Law Studies, n. 56 (Washington, D. C.: The Catholic University of America, 1930), pp. 51-55.

[114] Canon 2261.

interdicted either apart from or in consequence of a condemnatory or declaratory sentence. This is necessary inasmuch as suspended [115] and personally interdicted priests [116] are governed by the same rules as excommunicates in respect to the administration of the sacraments. Rainer,[117] while admitting that the use of such terms could engender misunderstandings, compares a suspended cleric after a condemnatory or declaratory sentence to an *excommunicatus vitandus,* and a simply suspended cleric to an *excommunicatus toleratus simpliciter.* Certainly the same distinction in regard to the administration of the sacraments can be made for clerics personally interdicted.

Those who are excommunicated simply, or suspended or personally interdicted apart from any declaratory or condemnatory sentence, even though their crime be notorious, can validly and licitly administer the sacrament of baptism solemnly as often as the faithful legitimately seek it from them, and they are not obliged to inquire into the reasons of the one desiring to receive it.[118] It seems that under such circumstances the priest could even show himself ready to administer the sacraments, in such a manner that the people could easily approach him. Furthermore, the petition of the faithful need not be explicit. Even an implicit or reasonably presumed request would suffice, such as would obtain if the good of souls demanded such administration and there were no other priests present.[119]

[115] Canon 2284.

[116] Canon 2275, 2°.

[117] *Suspension of Clerics,* p. 56.

[118] Canons 2261, § 2; 2275, 2°; 2284.

[119] Rainer (*op. cit.,* pp. 84-85) and Conran (*The Interdict,* p. 97) note that the Code does not require a grave cause for such a petition, but merely a just cause, such as can be found when one desires to receive the sacraments and no other priest is present, or any other cause which enhances devotion or is prompted by a real convenience. Hyland (*Excom-

However, *excommunicati vitandi* and excommunicated or suspended or personally interdicted priests upon whom a condemnatory or declaratory sentence has been passed can solemnly administer baptism only to those who are in danger of death, and even then they may do so only when there are no other priests present.[120] At the same time it must be noted that the Code simply requires a *periculum mortis* and not an *articulus mortis*. A *periculum mortis* is present not only when death may probably ensue, but also when no more than a probability is had that death will not ensue. Such a danger of death may arise from various causes: sickness, wound, infirmity of old age, major operations, imminence of battle, dangerous journeys, etc. In case there is a positive doubt as to whether the person is really constituted in danger of death, the benefit of the doubt must be given to the person petitioning the sacrament. It is important to note that an implicit petition will suffice for the priest's action in administering solemn baptism. When such a priest administers baptism on the supposition that the person is in danger of death, although as a matter of fact no danger actually existed, the administration nonetheless is both valid and licit.[121]

Throughout these remarks it must be borne in mind that the lawfulness of the administration of the sacrament under

munication, The Catholic University of America Canon Law Studies, n. 49 [Washington, D. C.: The Catholic University of America, 1928], p. 93) gives as a just cause "the earlier conferring of baptism."

[120] Canons 2261, § 3; 2275, 2°; 2284. The rule that is here stated as applying in the case of solemn baptism obtains also for the administration of the remaining sacraments, save that in the case of confession the requests of the faithful who are in danger of death may be accommodated by the censured priest even if other priests were at hand for receiving the confession.

[121] Hyland, *Excommunication*, pp. 93-99; Conran, *The Interdict*, pp. 98-105.

these circumstances is assured solely from the viewpoint of the Church's requirements in her penal legislation. If the censured priest were simultaneously in a state of mortal sin, his administration of baptism under the circumstances sanctioned by the Church's penal legislation would, of course, on that score not be unlawful, but it would be unquestionably illicit by reason of the unrepented sin which burdens his conscience.[122]

In those circumstances under which the Code permits a cleric temporarily to disregard his suspension, or interdict or excommunication, he cannot be thought to be violating the inflicted penalty to the extent of exercising sacred orders the lawful exercise of which he has been deprived. By force of the law itself he regains the use of those orders. Hence, if he administers the sacraments while under these penalties, either to protect his good name and reputation,[123] or because the faithful have legitimately petitioned such an administration,[124] there is no actual violation of the inflicted penalty and consequently no irregularity is incurred.[125]

D. *The Pastor's Right Over Residents Without Domicile or Quasi-Domicile*

I. *Vagi* and Those with Only a Diocesan Domicile

In regard to those who have only a diocesan domicile or quasi-domicile and those who lack even this, the proper priest for the administration of solemn baptism is the pastor of the parish in which they are actually staying at the time

122 Cerato, *Censurae Vigentes Ipso Facto a Codice Iuris Canonicae Excerptae* (editio secunda recognita, Patavii, 1921), n. 37; Sole, *De Delictis et Poenis* (Romae, 1920), n. 220.

123 Canon 2232, § 1.

124 Canon 2261, § 2 and § 3.

125 Rainer, *Suspension of Clerics*, p. 190.

baptism is to be conferred.[126] Hence such persons do not have the power of conferring this right to baptize upon any priest whom they ask. His right to act must arise, not merely from their request for him to do so, but from some form of residence which these people here and now have within his territory. It would be needless repetition to note that, where several national parishes exist within the confines of a territorial English-speaking parish, it is only one of these several pastors who is qualified to confer the baptism licitly.[127] Moreover, since the pastor of the place of residence has the right to baptize its inhabitants solemnly, he likewise has the power to permit another priest to perform the ceremony.

It is certain that those whom the Code designates as *vagi* do not always lead an unstable life, and that consequently the term need not necessarily be understood in a derogatory sense. But there is the possibility that some of the *vagi* who present their children for baptism may have habits which, if known, will reveal their character to be as unstable as their abodes. In such instances it is the specific duty of the minister of baptism to assure himself that the Catholic education of the offspring is properly guaranteed. For this end it seems warranted to insist upon the presence of some good Catholic friend of the family as sponsor, rather than to lay upon the housekeeper or sexton the burden of sponsoring a child whom in all probability she or he will not see again. There are those, however, who would not go to such lengths, and who content themselves with the thought that

126 Canon 94, § 2. Proprius vagi parochus vel Ordinarius est parochus vel Ordinarius loci in quo vagus actu commoratur.

§ 3. Illorum quoque qui non habent nisi dioecesanum domicilium vel quasi-domicilium parochus proprius est parochus loci in quo actu commorantur.

127 Bouuaert-Simenon, *Manuale Juris Canonici,* II, n. 19; Vermeersch-Creusen, *Epitome,* II, n. 22.

baptism is justifiable if these Catholic parents want it, or even do not object to it, since in such instances there is a probability that the child will be made conscious at some time or other of its Catholic baptism and attendant obligations. This, they believe, under God's mercy offers a thousand chances for the Catholic life of the child, independently of the active faith of the parents or sponsors.[128]

II. *Peregrini*

So zealously does the Code guard the proper pastor's right solemnly to baptize those over whom he is given competence in this matter that only reluctantly does it free a travelling person from the obligation of seeking solemn baptism at the hands of his own proper pastor. A *peregrinus* must return to his own parish for the licit reception of solemn baptism if such a journey can be undertaken conveniently and without delay (*facile et sine mora*).[129] Hence, unless the person is excused in view of the circumstances of inconvenience and delay, his own proper pastor retains the right solemnly to baptize him regardless of his nearness to or distance from his proper parish church.

That a person be obliged to return to his own parish, however, both of the conditions mentioned by the legislator must be present simultaneously. If either one of them is lacking, e. g., if one could go back conveniently but only after an undue delay, or if one could return immediately but only with unavoidable inconvenience, then the person may receive solemn baptism from the local pastor, inasmuch as the approach to the proper pastor no longer remains a matter of duty.[130] It seems that the judgment concerning the

128 "Baptism of vagrant children"—*AER*, L (1914), 344-345.

129 Canon 738, § 2. Etiam peregrinus a parocho proprio in sua paroecia sollemniter baptizetur, si id facile et sine mora fieri potest; secus peregrinum quilibet parochus in suo territorio potest sollemniter baptizare.

130 Blat, *Commentarium,* Lib. III, pars I, n. 21.

existence of these circumstances rests solely with the subject for baptism or with his parents or guardian.

Regarding the two excusing factors indicated by the Code there exists much latitude of interpretation precisely because it remains a difficult task sharply to determine when a journey back to one's parish church may or must be considered a matter of inconvenience. In the case of an infant the delicate condition of its health is a factor that should never be overlooked. There are also to be considered, for adults as well as for infants, such factors as the element of distance, the condition of the roads, the availability of transportation, the kind of weather, the consumption of time, the amount of expense, the selection of approved sponsors, the probable emergence of ill will, the sacrifice of appreciable material gain, etc. In the case of an adult the distance from his home parish must ordinarily be greater and the exposure of his health must of course be more definite than in the case of an infant before any acceptable excuse is had for the reception of solemn baptism from the local pastor.[131]

With respect to the avoidance of delay authors are in agreement that the phrase *sine mora* should be interpreted as identical in meaning with the word *quamprimum* of canon 770.[132] The common opinion regards the administration of baptism as taking place *sine mora* or *quamprimum* as long as it is conferred within three to eight days.[133] Woywod, however, maintains that common sense

[131] Augustine, *Commentary,* IV, 39; Ayrinhac, *Legislation on the Sacraments,* p. 18; Bouuaert-Simenon, *Manuale Juris Canonici,* II, n. 19, sub. II.

[132] "Infantes quamprimum baptizentur; ..."

[133] S. C. de Prop. Fide, litt. (ad Vic. Coreae), 11 sept. 1841—*Coll.,* n. 939 and *Fontes,* n. 4795; Cappello, *De Sacramentis,* I, n. 149; Augustine, *Commentary,* IV, 86; Merkelbach, *Summa Theologiae Moralis,* III, n. 148; Aertnys-Damen, *Theologia Moralis,* II, n. 55; *et alii.* Sabetti-Barrett (*Compendium Theologiae Moralis,* n. 662, quaes. 7) set a maximum period of three weeks.

forbids an interpretation which limits the extension of time to a period of but three days. He holds that, unless the diocesan statutes rule otherwise, the second Sunday after birth still falls within the indicated time for the conferring of baptism *quamprimum.* He concedes that even this extended period may at times prove too much of a limitation inasfar as it involves any exposure of the child to uncontrollable risks, for all related eventualities must be duly weighed and every pertinent circumstance must be judiciously considered. No law, so he asserts, can absolutely set one or two weeks from the day of birth as the maximum limit within which baptism must in every case be conferred.[134]

When it is determined that one's own pastor cannot be reached conveniently and without delay, then any local pastor whatsoever may within his parish solemnly baptize the *peregrinus.* Thus, through the presence of the excusing factors, pastors who previously had no competence for the lawful administration of solemn baptism in respect to the *peregrinus* now have equal rights, so that the conferring of the baptism is recognized as being governed by the principle "*Locus regit actum.*"

Unless the circumstances of inconvenience and delay are present, however, any pastor who, apart from a canonically authorized permission,[135] confers solemn baptism upon a *peregrinus* acts unlawfully. The Second Plenary Council of Baltimore (1866) condemned as a very serious abuse the practice of priests who accepted for baptism children belonging to another parish to which they could easily be brought without delay.[136]

[134] Woywod, "How soon must newly born infants be taken to church for baptism?"—*Homiletic and Pastoral Review,* XXV (1925), 652.

[135] Canons 738, § 1, and 744 point to this possible alternative.

[136] *Acta et Decreta,* n. 227.

Moreover, since the Code is so strict in requiring that a *peregrinus* return to his own parish when this is possible for him, it may here be noted that *a fortiori* it would frown upon any practice whereby a child which is born in its own parish would be transported without cause or necessity to another parish to be later baptized there on the score that it would be difficult to return the child to its proper parish.[137]

Frequently the pastor will discover that *peregrini* who fall within his potential competence for baptism are children who are born in hospitals or maternity houses located within the limits of his parochial territory. It is frequently asked who has the right to baptize such children? Certainly the children's own pastor cannot come into an outside parish and baptize them lawfully unless he has received permission from the local pastor or Ordinary.[138] True it is that the pastor of the children's domicile or quasi-domicile retains his right over these *peregrini,* but it is a right which cannot be exercised immediately and which will vanish through an undue delay of their baptism. In those instances wherein the mother and child are to be in the hospital for several weeks, or even over ten days, and the child cannot be taken to his proper pastor, then the pastor in whose territory the institution is situated has the right lawfully to administer solemn baptism. In fact, if he possesses this right and if the child, because of distance or other reasons, cannot be brought to his parochial church without grave inconvenience or danger, the local pastor may baptize the child in any other church or public oratory within the confines of his parish, even though such church or public oratory does not possess a baptismal font.[139] Indeed, the Ordinary can per-

[137] De baptismo in paroecia aliena"—*Ius Pontificium,* I-II (1921-1922), 109.

[138] Canon 739.

[139] Canon 775.

mit him to baptize the child solemnly in the hospital chapel or in some other fitting place, in an extraordinary case when there is a just and reasonable cause for so acting.[140]

If the child were baptized privately in the hospital because it appeared to be in danger of death, it appears that the pastor of the territory in which the hospital is situated does not in view of this fact acquire the right to supply the ceremonies. But if such a child recuperated enough to be brought to the parish church of the territory in which the hospital lies, though not to its own proper church, and if there is still danger that it may die before it can be brought to its own pastor, or if it will have to remain in the hospital a long time, then the pastor of the hospital could supply the ceremonies. Though these ceremonies are certainly not necessary for salvation, and hence can be delayed much longer than baptism itself, yet the Church does desire that they be supplied after private baptism. When the necessity of a very long delay or the danger of death is present, the rights of the proper pastor should yield in this matter also to the good of the child to be derived from the ceremonies.[141]

In hospitals and maternity homes which have their own permanent chaplain, the question will arise as to what right he has to baptize the inmates, all of whom are *peregrini*, and whether this right can be exercised independently of the pastor of the parish in whose territory the institution is located. It must be borne in mind that before either the chaplain or the local pastor can habitually baptize in the chapel of such a place, that chapel must be known to possess the status of a church [142] or a public oratory.[143]

140 Canon 776, § 1, 2° and § 2.

141 *AER*, LXXXVII (1932), 306-307.

142 Canon 1161.

143 Canon 1188, § 2, 1°.

Such a status is necessary in case the chaplain baptizes there, since only a church or public oratory may possess a baptismal font.[144] On the other hand, if the local pastor chooses to baptize there because the parish church is too far distant, such a privilege is his only in regard to churches or public oratories within the limits of his parish.[145] Any permission the Ordinary may grant him to baptize solemnly in places other than these can be given only in extraordinary circumstances and in individual cases.[146]

Mothon [147] thinks that when the Code speaks of public oratories in reference to the right to have a baptismal font it is using the term in a general way in contradistinction to private oratories, and consequently he maintains that a semi-public oratory can likewise possess a baptismal font. In this opinion he appears to be alone among the authors, and certainly the language of the Code gives no warrant for such a deduction.[148]

Ordinarily the chaplain of an institution is not a pastor. However, if one of the exempt religious orders should establish a hospital, this would be exempt from the local parish priest.[149] Even then the Ordinary could put some restric-

144 Canon 773. Proprius baptismi sollemnis administrandi locus est baptisterium in ecclesia vel oratorio publico.

145 Canon 775.

146 Canon 776, § 1, 2°; S. C. de Sacr., "De facultate baptismi domi conferendi extra mortis periculum," 22 iul. 1925—*AAS*, XVII (1925), 452.

147 *Institutions canoniques* (3 vols., Paris: Desclée, de Brouwer & Cie, 1922-1924), II, art. 1696 and 1698.

148 Blat, *Commentarium*, Lib. III, pars I, n. 65; Feldhaus, *Oratories*, The Catholic University of America Canon Law Studies, n. 42 (Washington, D. C.: The Catholic University of America, 1927), p. 116; Koudelka, *Pastors, Their Rights and Duties*, p. 76; Augustine, *Commentary*, IV, 88; Merkelbach, *Summa Theologiae Moralis*, III, n. 170; Aertnys-Damen, *Theologia Moralis*, II, n. 78; Ayrinhac, *Legislation on the Sacraments*, p. 58.

149 Canon 497, § 2 and § 3.

tive conditions upon the religious, as to the sacred ministry, when granting permission for the establishment. In those cases wherein the institution is not entrusted to religious, and it possesses a church or public oratory, the chaplain is to be compared to the rectors of churches.[150]

But since the Code does not clearly define the rights and duties of chaplains attached to churches or public oratories of non-exempt institutions the extent of their authority must be determined from the diocesan statutes or the letter of appointment sent them by the bishop. In the following three cases of possible modes of appointment it will be shown how the chaplain can be permitted to baptize solemnly in the institution without infringing upon the rights of the local pastor.

First, the chaplain could be appointed "*simpliciter*", i. e., without the specification of any particular powers to be enjoyed by virtue of being chaplain, but with the determination at the same time that he is constituted as a *vicarius cooperator ad hoc* of the pastor of the parish in which the hospital is located. In this instance he does not trespass upon the pastor's right to baptize also, but he merely acquires a right for himself. Under such circumstances he could baptize exclusively in the chapel of the institution, and it would not be necessary for the infants to be taken to the local parish church.[151]

Secondly, it is possible for the Ordinary, for a just and grave cause, to withdraw these charitable institutions from the jurisdiction of the local pastor.[152] Then he can constitute them parishes in themselves and appoint the chaplain

[150] Canons 479-486.

[151] Canon 775.

[152] Canon 464, § 2. Potest Episcopus iusta et gravi de causa religiosas familias et pias domos, quae in paroeciae territorio sint et a iure non exemptae, a parochi cura subducere.

to them as a pastor *pleno iure.* The chaplain in this case has parochial jurisdiction over all those who reside in the institution. His right as to the patients who are only temporarily there should be defined by diocesan regulations. Even if this is not done by statute, he would still have the right to baptize them as *peregrini,* when they could not return to their own pastor conveniently and without delay.[153] At any rate no other priest could solemnly baptize within such an institution without the chaplain's permission.

Thirdly, the Ordinary can simply appoint the chaplain with full pastoral power. This is not as satisfactory an arrangement as the preceding method, for the chaplain would not be a pastor, exercising the pastoral functions in his own name, but a delegate of the Ordinary with full pastoral powers. Since the ordinary appointment as chaplain does not of itself carry with it full pastoral power, this type of chaplain must possess definite proof of such a grant of jurisdiction in his document of appointment.[154] For though his pastoral jurisdiction would be attached to his office as chaplain, yet it would be delegated and not ordinary jurisdiction. Ordinary jurisdiction is attached to an office *ipso iure,*[155] while the jurisdiction which would be attached in this instance would not be *a iure* but *ab homine.* Such a chaplain, therefore, acts as a delegate of the Ordinary; he may be removed at will; his rights may be curtailed or withdrawn by a simple revocation.

As a closing remark, in reference to the chaplain's authority, it may be observed that even if he has no parochial jurisdiction whatsoever, and hence no right to administer baptism solemnly within the institution, yet if solemn bap-

[153] Canon 738, § 2.

[154] Canon 200, § 2. Ei, qui delegatum se asserit, incumbit onus probandae delegationis.

[155] Canon 197, § 1.

tism is conferred in that chapel by or with the permission of the pastor in whose territory the institution is located, the priest performing the ceremony should feel bound by courtesy not to act without first speaking to the chaplain, if possible. This is only right, since by his very position he has been made responsible for the religious rites and ceremonies performed within the hospital.[156]

III. Orientals

In the usual order of events the pastor of a Latin church has no right to baptize indiscriminately Orientals living within the confines of his parish, since the Code explicitly states that such are to be baptzed in their own proper rite.[157] At the same time the Code realizes that there are three possible contingencies under which the baptism of a child of parents of an Oriental rite can be factually undertaken by a pastor of the Latin rite. It may be that he baptizes such a child (a) as the result of his deceitful representations; (b) by reason of necessity; (c) in view of an Apostolic dispensation.[158]

[156] Woywod, "Baptism in Catholic hospital"—*Homiletic and Pastoral Review,* XXIX (1929), 535; C. Augustine, O.S.B., "Hospitals—Their Chaplains, Confessors, Pastors,"—*AER*, LXVI (1922), 185-192; "Jurisdiction in charity institutions"—*AER*, LXXVI (1927), 94-95; "Baptism in a hospital"—LXII (1920), 74-75 and 315-318. The question of a chaplain's rights has been discussed frequently in Catholic periodicals, but very few worthwhile solutions have been advanced.

[157] Canon 756, § 1. Proles ritu parentum baptizari debet.

Canon 756, § 2. Si alter parentum pertineat ad ritum latinum, alter ad orientalem, proles ritu patris baptizetur, nisi aliud iure speciali cautum sit.

Canon 756, § 3. Si unus tantum sit catholicus, proles huius ritu baptizanda est.

[158] Canon 98, § 1. Inter varios catholicos ritus ad illum quis pertinet, cuius caeremoniis baptizatus fuit, nisi forte baptismus a ritus alieni ministro vel fraude collatus fuit, vel ob gravem necessitatem, cum sacerdos proprii ritus praesto esse non potuit, vel ex dispensatione apostolica, cum facultas data fuit ut quis certo quodem ritu baptizaretur, quin tamen eidem adscriptus maneret.

(a) When baptism is conferred by a Latin pastor upon an Oriental by fraudulently convincing the person that he is the proper minister of the sacrament, such a baptism is conferred illicitly.[159] Moreover, this baptism in no way changes the rite or status of the victim of the deception.[160]

(b) The Code recognizes that the spiritual welfare of the Orientals will oftentimes demand the ministrations of a Latin priest, when one of the Oriental discipline is not available. Imminent danger of death, an unreasonable delay of baptism, a long journey or grave impending difficulties in reaching a church or in procuring the proper priest may all be cited as cases of necessity which make it legitimate for a Latin priest to confer solemn baptism.[161] Such cases occur so frequently in the United States and Canada that the Holy See has seen fit to instruct the Greek Ruthenians of these countries that under such conditions they are obliged to have the sacrament administered by a priest of another rite.[162] Thus, when the Latin pastor baptizes Oriental *peregrini* and *vagi*, it is not in virtue of the general power which he receives over such from the Code, but rather because by necessity these Orientals, no matter what their canonical status may be, must approach him for the administration of the sacraments.

(c) The third contingency under which a pastor may solemnly baptize an Oriental is had in view of an Apostolic

159 Duskie, *The Canonical Status of the Orientals in the United States*, The Catholic University of America Canon Law Studies, n. 48 (Washington, D. C.: The Catholic University of America, 1928), p. 74.

160 Canon 98, § 1; Code Commission, 16 oct. 1919, ad 11 — *AAS*, XI (1919), 478.

161 Duskie, *op. cit.*, p. 75; Alexius Petrani, *De Relatione Iuridica Inter Diversos Ritus in Ecclesia Catholica* (Romae: Marietti, 1930), p. 61.

162 S. C. pro Eccl. Orient., decr., 1 mart. 1929—*AAS*, XXI (1929), 157. Found in Bouscaren's *Canon Law Digest*, I, 13; S. C. pro Eccl. Orient., decr., 24 maii. 1930—*AAS*, XXII (1930), 348. Found in Bouscaren's *Canon Law Digest*, I, 36.

dispensation. The lawful administration of such a solemn baptism in the absence of necessity presupposes a dispensation from the Holy See for every individual case, for the Code does not provide for any exceptions.

Certainly the children are to be baptized in the rite of the parents, if both are and remain Orientals. But what is to be done in case the parents change their rite? The Code makes no provision for such an unusual case, though it could be interpreted as desiring that the children be baptized in the rite which the parents are following at the time the baptism is to be administered. In view of the decree of Pope Benedict XIV which provided that, if both parents changed their rite, only the children who had not yet attained the use of reason were to follow the rite of the parents, perhaps the same regulation may be used as a solution for similar cases occurring after the promulgation of the Code.[163]

In regard to the offspring of marriages of mixed rite the Code lays down the general principle that the children follow the rite of the father. As a general principle this causes no difficulty in interpretation. But a question may be raised concerning such a child whose father has died before its birth but whose mother belongs to the Latin rite. Does such a child in the given supposition follow the rite of its mother in baptism? Duskie and Petrani think that an affirmative answer to this question does not furnish the correct solution for the case.[164] They hold that the mother is

[163] Benedictus XIV, const. "*Praeclaris*", 18 mart. 1746: "...Sua Santità ...concede a tutti la medesima licenza di seguitare il rito latino quando lo vogliono, oppure di ritornare al rito greco: colla condizione però che quelli tra *latinizzati* i quali non sono ancora giunti all' uso della ragione, seguano il rito de' loro genitori, se questi avranno scelto un medesimo rito, altrimenti abbraccino il rito del padre."—*Fontes,* n. 366; ep. encycl. "*Demandatum*", 24 dec. 1743, § 17: "Filii vero, qui huiusmodi Parentibus post emissam ab illis praedictam declarationem nascentur, necnon ii, qui iam nati sunt, sed nondum ad usum rationis pervenerunt, sequantur conditionem Parentum, si coniuges unum eumdemque Ritum elegerint; sin minus, Patris Ritum sequantur."—*Fontes,* n. 338.

[164] Duskie, *op. cit.,* p. 87; Petrani, *op. cit.,* p. 62.

obliged to educate the child according to the rite of its father, though the latter has died and though the mother has always followed the Latin rite, or at least has returned to it upon the death of the child's father.

In canon 756, §2, the Code points to the general norm that a child is to receive baptism in the rite of its father when one of the parents is an Oriental Catholic and the other a Latin Catholic. But the Code leaves intact whatever specific provision is made to the contrary by particular law. Such a law exists and therefore is still applicable in the case of the Italo-Greeks. If the husband is an Italo-Greek and the wife a Latin, the children are indeed normally to be baptized in the rite of the father, although by particular law, when the father consents in favor of his Latin wife, the child may be baptized in the Latin rite.[165] When the child is baptized in the Latin rite it remains subject to the jurisdiction of the Latin pastor.

At one time Greek Ruthenians in the United States were governed by the same law as that which was enacted for the Italo-Greeks.[166] Subsequent legislation changed this special permission, so that now they are governed by the same rule as that stated in the Code.[167] If illegitimate children

[165] Benedictus XIV, const. "*Etsi Pastoralis*", 26 maii 1742, II, n. 10: "Si vero pater sit Graecus, et mater latina, liberum erit eidem Patri, ut Proles, vel ritu Graeco baptizetur, vel etiam ritu Latino, si Uxor Latina praevaluerit, idest si in gratiam Uxoris Latinae, consenserit Graecus Pater, ut latino ritu baptizetur."—*Fontes*, n. 328. The two following regulations also prove noteworthy in the same instruction. II, n. 8: "Infantes nati ex Patre, et Matre Graecis, ritu Graeco, nisi aliter Parentes, accedente Ordinarii consensus, voluerint, baptizari debent." II, n. 9: "Nati vero ex Patre Latino, et Matre Graeca, latinis sunt caeremoniis baptizandi; proles enim sequi omnino debet Patris Ritum, si sit Latinus."—*Fontes*, n. 328.

[166] Pius X, litt. apost. "*Ea Semper*", 14 iun. 1907, art. 34, 35—*ASS*, XLI (1908), 10.

[167] S. C. de Prop. Fide pro Negotiis Ritus Orientalis, 17 aug. 1914, cap. IV, art. 32: "Nati in regione Statuum Foederatorum Americae Septentrionalis ex parentibus diversi ritus, ritu patris sunt baptizandi: proles enim utriusque sexus sequi omnino debet patris ritum." Art. 33: "Baptismus in alieno

are born of a couple of mixed rite they will follow the rite of their mother,[168] unless the father publicly acknowledges his paternity and promises to educate them in the catholic religion.[169]

ART. 3. "... VEL ALII SACERDOTI DE EIUSDEM PAROCHI VEL ORDINARII LOCI LICENTIA ..."

Though it has been stated repeatedly by authors that the proper minister for baptism is he who has parochial jurisdiction over the person, the use of the term "jurisdiction" must be interpreted widely and must be in no way confused with that real jurisdiction which is so absolutely necessary in the administration of the sacrament of Penance. If the term be understood in this wide sense one can readily realize that a simple authorization by the pastor or local Ordinary for the purpose of permitting a priest to baptize one whom otherwise he has no legal right to baptize is not called delegation in the canonical sense of the term; it is rather a permission or license granted to another. However, the fact that it is not a strictly canonical delegation does not minimize its importance. It is so necessary that without it the unauthorized minister acts unlawfully.

ritu ob gravem necessitatem susceptus, cum nimirum infans morti proximus esset vel natus esset in loco in quo, tempore nativitatis, parochus proprius patris non aderat, ritus mutationem non inducit; et sacerdos, qui baptizavit, proprio parocho testimonium baptismatis remittere debet."—*AAS*, VI (1914), 463; S. C. pro Ecclesia Orientali, decr., 1 mart 1929, cap. IV, art. 41 (this is identical with art. 32 cited above)—*AAS*, XXI (1929), 159.

[168] S. C. pro Ecclesia Orientali, decr., 1 mart. 1929, cap. IV, art. 43: "Infantes ad eius parochi iurisdictionem pertinent, cuius ritus est eorum pater, exceptis natis ex illegitimo thoro, qui sequuntur ritum matris."—*AAS*, XXI (1929), 159; cf. also: Paul J. Sandalgi, "Oriental and Latin Sacramental Rites"—*AER*, LXI (1919), 225-238; [?], "Marriage ceremony for Catholics of mixed rite and the baptism of their children"—*AER*, LXXIII (1925), 313.

[169] Petrani, *De Relatione Iuridica Inter Diversos Ritus in Ecclesia Catholica*, p. 63.

It must be remembered that only he who has the actual right to minister in the place where the baptism is going to occur can grant this permission. So a pastor whose subject is in an institution in another section of town cannot grant another priest permission to go to that institution to baptize. True it is that the domiciliary pastor has a right to baptize so long as it is evident that the person can conveniently and without delay be brought to him, but he possesses a right which cannot be exercised outside his territory. He could, on the other hand, waive his rights in such a case in favor of the pastor of the parish in which the institution is situated. Hence, if any other priest desired to baptize that person lawfully two permissions would be necessary—the permission of the domiciliary pastor in order that he might act licitly in regard to the subject, and the permission of the pastor in whose territory the institution is located in order that he might act licitly in regard to the place.

No priest, no matter how much right he had to baptize the person, could, apart from a case of necessity, give permission to a priest who pertains to a rite different from that of the parents.

For the granting of this permission or delegation the law does not require that it be committed to writing or that it be even verbal. Such permission can be given tacitly; it is deducible from the actions or attitude of the pastor.[170] Some think that the furnishing of a written permission is the safer policy to follow in practice.[171]

It must be noted that the Code does not require that there be any reason for granting this permission to a priest, for every priest by virtue of his ordination is the proper minister of baptism, and hence any particular act of baptiz-

[170] Bouuaert-Simenon, *Manuale Juris Canonici*, II, n. 19; Blat, *Commentarium*, Lib. III, pars I, n. 21.

[171] Woywod, "Delegation for baptism"—*Homiletic and Pastoral Review*, XL (1940), 1138.

ing pertains to a pastor only insofar as he is unwilling to yield to another priest that which the Code reserves for him as his pastoral right.[172]

ART. 4. ". . . QUAE IN CASU NECESSITATIS LEGITIME PRAESUMITUR."

With such solicitude does the Church seek the baptism of children of Catholic parents and desire that it be fruitful in its reception, that she permits any priest to baptize solemnly even without the permission of the proper pastor or the local Ordinary, so long as a case of necessity exists wherein he can lawfully presume that such permission would be given him under the circumstances.

The necessity in question in canon 738, § 1, of the Code is clearly not that of the extreme kind which arises in view of danger of death. It is rather to be understood as a *necessitas communis,* and examples of it as suggested by authors are: if it is feared that baptism will be neglected unless it is administered at once; [173] if the people came a great distance and found only a visiting priest in the rectory and not the pastor; if the child were ill and the pastor was not at hand; if the parish priest visited this mission only at long intervals. But mere convenience, or also the considerations of friendship or relationship, would not of themselves constitute the necessity here contemplated in the Code.[174] Some authors think that a priest could baptize if the pastor would not be present for at least three days.[175] This could be supported in a general way to some degree by a strict interpretation of the term *quamprimum* in canon 770, but would scarcely seem to constitute a plausible necessity according to the customs of this country.

[172] Fanfani, *De Iure Parochorum,* n. 233, sub B.

[173] Vermeersch-Creusen, *Epitome,* II, n. 22.

[174] Augustine, *Commentary,* IV, 38.

[175] Bouuaert-Simenon, *Manuale Juris Canonici,* II, n. 19; Blat, *Commentarium,* Lib. III, pars I, n. 21.

In those cases, which frequently happen in urban parishes, wherein people present their children for baptism at a parish to which they mistakenly think they belong, the priest would generally be justified in conferring baptism. Otherwise the people would be placed at a great inconvenience in transporting the child to the other parish, and there is also a great probability that the cermony might have to be deferred at least another week, and so the parents as well as the child and the sponsors would suffer.

ART. 5. THE MINISTER OF SOLEMN BAPTISM IN PLACES WITHOUT PARISHES OR QUASI-PARISHES

In canons 738 and 739 the legislator has determined with accuracy the proper minister of solemn baptism in parishes. Equal with the pastor in this regard is the priest who is in charge of a quasi-parish, for the quasi-parish is a territorial division of a prefecture or vicariate apostolic, similar in all possible respects to the parish as a territorial division of a diocese.[176] These, then, the parish and the quasi-parish, are both governed by the same law.

In canon 740 the Code has reference chiefly to missionary districts where the establishment of the Church is still in the process of formation, so that even quasi-parishes have not yet been established. In such cases one must take into account the specific local statutes and received or approved customs in determining who besides the Ordinary enjoys the right to baptize throughout the territory or in any given section of it.[177]

In this regard no reference can be found of any such legislation having been formulated for early America by the Baltimore Councils or any other American council or synod.[178]

[176] Canon 216, § 1 and § 3.

[177] Canon 740. Ubi paroeciae aut quasi-paroeciae nondum sunt constitutae, statutorum peculiarium et receptarum consuetudinum ratio habenda est, ut constet cuinam sacerdoti, praeter Ordinarium, in universo territorio vel in eius parte ius insit baptizandi.

[178] Augustine, *Commentary*, IV, 40.

CHAPTER VI

The Extraordinary Minister of Solemn Baptism

Canon 741. **Extraordinarius baptismi sollemnis minister est diaconus; qui tamen sua potestate ne utatur sine loci Ordinarii vel parochi licentia, iusta de causa concedenda, quae, ubi necessitas urgeat, legitime praesumitur.**

Art. 1. "Extraordinarius baptismi sollemnis minister est diaconus . . ."

By virtue of his sacred ordination the deacon possesses the power to administer solemn baptism.[1] But the law restricts him so rigorously in the use of this power that he is the extraordinary rather than the ordinary minister. In this connection Saint Thomas thought that this legal restriction was justified because the administration of the sacrament of baptism does not pertain to the deacon as a principal function flowing from his very office, but only insofar as he ministers to the bishops and priests, and so he is only a subsidiary or extraordinary minister of the sacrament.[2]

At any rate, when the deacon is permitted to administer solemn baptism, he can and must confer it with all the ceremonies prescribed in the Roman Ritual. The only restriction upon his power in this regard is that he cannot bless

[1] *Pontificale Romanum, De ordinatione diaconi*, has the following words which the bishop addresses to the candidate: "Cogitate magnopere ad quantum gradum Ecclesiae ascenditis: diaconum enim oportet ministrare ad Altare, baptizare et praedicare." This allocution also bears a reference to Acts, VIII: 12, according to which text Philip the deacon baptized and preached.

[2] *Summa Theologica*, Pars III, q. LXVII, art. 1: "Et sic ad diaconum non pertinet, quasi ex proprio officio, tradere sacramentum baptismi, sed in collatione huius sacramenti et aliorum assistere, et ministrare maioribus."

the salt and the water which are used. These must have been blessed previously by a priest or by the local Ordinary.[3] There are authors, however, who maintain that deacons can validly bless these two things if there are no priests present to do so.[4] Yet it is difficult to see how such an opinion can be substantiated.

Deacons can validly and licitly bless only those things which the law expressly permits them to bless.[5] Hence it would have to be shown that the faculty to bless salt and water, even when priests are not present, was directly conceded to deacons. It does not suffice to argue that the liturgical books do not declare such benedictions invalid, since by the force of canon 1147 the deacons lack every power of benediction which they cannot directly prove to possess by express grant of the law. As a matter of fact, the contrary can be proved from the response of the Sacred Congregation of Rites,[6] and from the fact that, inasmuch as liturgical law insists that the salt and the water be blessed by the priest,[7] the Code does not choose to make any exception and to grant the faculty to deacons under any circumstances whatsoever.[8]

[3] S. R. C., *Mariannen.*, 10 febr. 1888—*Fontes*, n. 6185; *Rituale Romanum*, Tit. II, c. 2, *ordo baptismi parvulorum*, n. 27; c. 4, *ordo baptismi adultorum*, n. 51.

[4] Stephanus Sipos, *Enchiridion Iuris Canonici* (3rd ed., Pécs: ex Typographia " Haladás R. T.", 1936), p. 440; Grosam, " Feierliche Taufspendung durch einen Diakon " — *LQS*, LXXVI (1923), 105-109; Grosam, " Der Diakon im neuen Römischen Rituale "—*LQS*, LXXIX (1926), 374-377.

[5] Canon 1147, § 4. Diaconi et lectores illas tantum valide et licite benedictiones dare possunt, quae ipsis expresse a iure permittuntur. *Rituale Romanum*, Tit. VIII, c. 1, *de benedictionibus regulae generales*, n. 1.

[6] *Mariannen.*, 10 febr. 1888—*Fontes*, n. 6185.

[7] *Rituale Romanum*, Tit. II, c. 2, *ordo baptismi parvulorum*, n. 27; c. 4, *ordo baptismi adultorum*, n. 51.

[8] Canon 2. ...Quare omnes liturgicae leges vim suam retinent, nisi earum aliqua in Codice expresse corrigatur.

Nor can these authors argue that the deacon possesses this power in virtue of canon 1153.[9] All the major commentators maintain that this canon simply states that anyone who has power to baptize or to consecrate and bless can also perform the exorcisms that accompany such rites. It presupposes that one has the power to bless, and then admits that such a one can perform the exorcisms. But in no way can it be interpreted as conferring a faculty to bless and consecrate, and anyone who would so construe its meaning would offer an erroneous interpretation.[10]

The authors do not consider what a deacon should do in the event that he has sufficient cause to baptize solemnly, but either blessed salt or blessed water is lacking and there is no priest present to bless the missing element. It would seem that if it were only the blessed salt that was lacking, the deacon could baptize solemnly and simply omit placing the salt upon the tongue of the person, since in necessity the Roman Ritual permits the omission of those prescribed rites which do not pertain to the essence of baptism.[11] The ministering of blessed salt certainly does not pertain to the essence of the sacrament and hence it is usually omitted in the Greek rite.

If it is baptismal water that is needed, it would seem that the solemn baptism must needs be deferred, if the condition of the person to be baptized permits such a delay. For the Code demands that water blessed especially for this purpose be used at solemn baptism.[12] If the person is in danger of death, then the baptism should be conferred privately.

[9] "Ministri exorcismorum qui occurrunt in baptismo et in consecrationibus vel benedictionibus, sunt iidem qui eorundem sacrorum rituum legitimi ministri sunt."

[10] Canon 18.

[11] *Rituale Romanum*, Tit. II, c. 4, *ordo baptismi adultorum*, n. 53.

[12] Canon 757, § 1.

ART. 2. "......QUI TAMEN SUA POTESTATE NE UTATUR SINE LOCI ORDINARII VEL PAROCHI LICENTIA, IUSTA DE CAUSA CONCEDENDA . . ."

The restriction placed upon the deacon in reference to the exercise of his power to baptize solemnly can be lifted quite simply through the permission of the local Ordinary or the parish priest. At first glance it would seem that both the deacon and the ordinary simple priest without pastoral rank were equal in this regard, since both need the permission of the Ordinary or of the pastor to baptize licitly. It may be asked why the simple priest, who needs the same permission, can be called the ordinary minister of solemn baptism, while the deacon is referred to as the extraordinary minister. The difference between the two consists primarily in this that the ordinary simple priest can be given permission to baptize solemnly even though no cause whatsoever exists for his so acting: the deacon, on the other hand, cannot be given permission to administer solemn baptism licitly unless a just cause be present.[13]

It must be noted that the legislator exacts only a just cause in order that permission may be given a deacon, and this must not be understood to mean a grave cause. As on other occasions, so here also the Code does not state precisely what constitutes such a just cause. But the authors intrepret the term as including the following: if the pastor is absent or sick, if at the time he has a large number of confessions to hear, if he is confronted with the task of conferring baptism to a large group of persons, or if he is preoccupied with other lawful pastoral functions, such as preaching or answering sick calls.[14] Some cite as a just

[13] Fanfani, *De Iure Parochorum*, n. 233.

[14] Cappello, *De Sacramentis*, I, n. 145; Ayrinhac, *Legislation on the Sacraments*, p. 19; Bouuaert-Simenon, *Manuale Juris Canonici*, II, n. 21; Vermeersch-Creusen, *Epitome*, II, n. 24; Noldin-Schmitt, *Summa Theologiae Moralis*, III, n. 64; Merkelbach, *Summa Theologiae Moralis*, III, n. 138.

cause the fact that a relationship exists between the deacon and the party to be baptized.[15] Fanfani includes also the case of an intimate bond of friendship or association.[16]

These causes are cited merely as examples of what may constitute a just cause for granting permission. Others just as forceable may arise. As long as a cause is judged just by the pastor or local Ordinary he can grant permission to the deacon. But if he is known to grant permission in the absence of any just cause, then the deacon would baptize validly but illicitly.

ART. 3. ". . . QUAE [LICENTIA], UBI NECESSITAS URGEAT, LEGITIME PRAESUMITUR."

In speaking of baptism Saint Thomas noted that this sacrament was of such great importance that in cases of necessity when no priests or bishops were at hand the Church permitted even deacons to administer it lawfully.[17] Certainly the Church has gone to great lengths to provide for the lawful administration of solemn baptism under varied circumstances.

As to precisely what sort of necessity must exist before a deacon can lawfully presume permission, authors are not definite. Surely it need not be a necessity as grave as that which is required for the lawful administration of a private baptism by one lacking deacon's orders.[18] On the other hand, the insistence of the Code on the presence of necessity for presuming permission seems to imply that more than a just cause must be present in this instance,[19] or that rela-

[15] Vermeersch-Creusen, *op. cit.*, II, n. 24; Noldin-Schmitt, *op. cit.*, III, n. 64. Fanfani, *De Iure Parochorum*, n. 233.

[16] *Loc. cit.*

[17] *Summa Theologica*, Pars III, q. LXVII, art. 1, ad 3am.

[18] Bouuaert-Simenon, *Manuale Juris Canonici*, II, n. 21.

[19] Ayrinhac, *Legislation on the Sacraments*, p. 19.

tively there must be a much graver cause than in the case wherein permission is positively granted by the pastor or the local Ordinary.[20] Some authors think that the causes which would allow a priest to presume the permission of the proper pastor to baptize solemnly would also in the absence of a priest, be sufficient for a deacon to presume permission and so to act lawfully.[21]

Were a deacon to baptize solemnly without permission, either express or presumed, or with a permission of which he knows that it is granted without a just cause, he would baptize validly but illicitly. He would not, however, incur any irregularity by so baptizing.[22] Since in virtue of his ordination he possesses the power to baptize solemnly, he does not incur the irregularity, for he is not performing an act of sacred orders of which he is incapable. If, however, he were prohibited by a canonical penalty from the exercise of those orders, then he would incur an irregularity even if he baptized in ordinary circumstances.[23]

20 Vermeersch-Creusen, *Epitome*, II, n. 24.

21 Augustine, *Commentary*, IV, 42; Bouuaert-Simenon, *Manuale Juris Canonici*, II, n. 21. The fact that the Code permits a deacon to presume permission settles a former controversy. Previously some theologians had held that the deacon could never presume permission to baptize solemnly.

22 Canon 985, 7°.

23 A complete discussion of this is contained in Chapter V, art. 2, C, above.

CHAPTER VII

The Minister of Private Baptism

Canon 742, § 1. **Baptismus non sollemnis, de quo in can. 759, § 1, potest a quovis ministrari, servata debita materia, forma et intentione; quatenus vero fieri potest, adhibeantur duo testes vel saltem unus, quibus baptismi collatio probari possit.**

Art. 1. "Baptismus non sollemnis, de quo in can. 759, § 1, potest a quovis ministrari . . ."

Baptism is called private (*baptismus non sollemnis*) when its administration consists solely in the application of the essential matter and form, without the attendant blessings and exorcisms prescribed in the Roman Ritual.[1] Though baptism of this nature may be administered validly at any time by anyone whatsoever, yet there are only two instances in which it is licit.

First, the local Ordinary can permit the administration of private baptism under ordinary circumstances only in the case of heretics who as adults are baptized conditionally.[2] The reason for the rigid restriction of private baptism is that the Church always desires solemn baptism in every possible case, lest otherwise persons be unduly deprived of the spiritual benefits which accompany the use of the additional ceremonies.[3]

[1] Canon 737, § 2. It is to be noted, however, that if a priest or deacon is the minister of this private baptism, he does supply the ceremonies which follow the actual baptism, but not those which precede it. This is in accordance with canon 759, § 1. But these additional ceremonies do not render the baptism solemn.

[2] Canon 759, § 2.

[3] S. C. de Prop. Fide, instr., 30 aug. 1775: "... ne baptizatus destituatur bonis spiritualibus ..., quae proveniunt ex caerimoniarum usu."—*Fontes*, n. 4569.

That the Ordinary grant this permission for the private baptism of adult heretics the Code does not exact the existence of any cause or reason. All that is required is that the baptism be one that calls for a conditional administration, and that the subject should be an adult heretic, i. e., one who has attained the use of reason.[4] The episcopal power is not limited in such a way that he can grant this permission solely in individual cases, and hence an Ordinary may impart this faculty habitually.[5]

Though the Code does not explicitly place this restriction, yet such a faculty should be given by the Ordinary only to priests and deacons. For the legislator implies such a restriction inasmuch as canon 742, § 1, permits anyone whatsoever (*a quovis ministrari*) to administer private baptism in danger of death,[6] but does not extend the permission to include the presently considered instance. It is because of this implied restriction that Noldin-Schmitt express the opinion that the faculty thus to baptize privately should be granted primarily to the pastor.[7] So if anyone other than the priest or deacon, to whom this permission to act was granted, were to baptize, such a private baptism, unless other extraordinary circumstances necessitating such an action intervened, would be valid but illicit. The one who administered it, however, would not incur an irregularity.[8]

The second instance in which the Code permits the administration of private baptism is had when the recipient of this sacrament is in danger of death. When such a situation arises any human being whatsoever who possesses both the sufficient use of reason for forming the necessary inten-

[4] Canons 745, § 2, 2°; 88, § 3.

[5] Augustine, *Commentary*, IV, 72.

[6] Canon 759, § 1.

[7] *Summa Theologiae Moralis*, III, n. 64, sub 3.

[8] Canon 985, 7°.

tion and the capability of applying the matter and form can administer the sacrament validly and licitly. This teaching that any person, no matter whether he be Jew, infidel, heretic or schismatic, can validly and lawfully administer private baptism under these circumstances is an article of faith,[9] and consequently binds the Oriental as well as the Latin Church.[10]

Though all admit that anyone possessing the use of reason can in theory baptize validly, yet there has long been a discussion among canonists and theologians as to what degree of physical incapacity would render a person incapable of such a sacramental action. All agree that one could in no way administer valid baptism if he were incapable of applying the matter. The same may likewise be said in regard to the form, but here there is some discussion. Generally the question is resolved in the light of the questioned capability of a deaf-mute to proffer a form sufficient for the validity of the sacrament. Many authors maintain that such a person is physically incapable of being the minister of valid baptism, even in cases of extreme necessity, in view of his inability to pronounce the form audibly. They refer to the decree of Pope Eugene IV [11] and insist upon his reference to words as constituting the form. So they believe that a mute cannot validly baptize since his absence of speech constitutes an impediment similar to the lack of any other essential element, such as natural water, for the performance of the sacramental rite.[12]

[9] Conc. Trident., sess. VII, *de baptismo*, can. 4.

[10] Canon 1.

[11] Const., "*Exultate Deo*", (in Conc. Florentin.), 22 nov. 1439, § 9: "Haec omnia sacramenta tribus perficiuntur, videlicet rebus tanquam materia, verbis tanquam forma, et persona ministri conferentis sacramentum cum intentione faciendi quod facit Ecclesia; quorum si aliquod desit, non perficitur sacramentum."—*Fontes*, n. 52.

[12] "Baptism administered by a deaf mute"—*Australasian Catholic Record*, I³ (1924), 31; "Can baptism be administered by persons deprived

Those who aver that a deaf-mute can baptize validly say that the sign language which the mute employs constitutes for him the vernacular by which he interprets definitely the meaning and purpose of the outward act designed as a means for salvation. Words are conventional signs for the expression of ideas, and the same may be said for the signs of the deaf-mute. The " word " is not necessarily the audible expression of a thought to others. True it is that most men speak by sounds, but the deaf-mute speaks by signs. Yet his speech is really composed of " words ", and words which definitely correspond to the intelligence of those around him; they imply a precise application of terms to definite objects and concepts. The fact that such words lack sound does not take away the principal element of their signification of a specified matter and of their application to distinct and well-understood uses. One can hardly object that such signs are not universally understood—no language is. However, due to the uncertainty that exists among theologians and canonists as to the validity of a baptism administered with the sign language, in practice conditional baptism later is advisable. But in those cases wherein the deaf-mute has been taught by modern methods a system of distinct articulation of words and pronounces the form for baptism in this way, there can be no serious doubt as to the validity of any baptism he confers, even though his pronunciation cannot always be understood.[13]

of the faculty of speech? "—*Homiletic and Pastoral Review*, XXIV (1924), 1064. Many other articles contain the same arguments.

[13] " Can a dumb person administer valid baptism? "—*AER*, XVI (1897), 189; " Baptism administered by a deaf mute "—*AER*, LV (1916), 194-196; " Baptism by a deaf mute " —*AER*, XCVII (1937), 594; " On baptism administered by deaf mutes " — *Homiletic and Pastoral Review*, XXV (1925), 523; Tanquerey, *Synopsis Theologiae Dogmaticae* (3 vols., Parisiis: Desclée et Socii, 1930-1934), III (23rd ed., 1934), 248: " Signum sacramentale duplici constat elemento, scilicet *rebus* et *verbis*. *Res* autem hic adhibetur *lato sensu*... Pariter nomine *verbi* intelligitur non solum verbum *ore* prolatum, sed etiam *gestus* verbo aequivalens quoad mentis manifestationem."

While it is true that in a case of necessity all have a right to administer private baptism, yet when there are several potential ministers present the Code and the Roman Ritual recognize a definite hierarchy among the available persons. So a priest is preferred to a deacon, a deacon to a subdeacon, a cleric to a layman, and a man to a woman, unless the woman knows the form better than the man, or unless some serious reason, such as decency, would demand a preference for her.[14]

There was a time when this order of precedence among Catholic ministers was considered to bind strictly under pain of mortal sin. Canonically such an opinion is of no value, but it is noteworthy that today theologians do not incline to so strict a view, unless there be question of a definite transgression of the rights of a priest. This modern opinion is quite logical, since the canon itself suggests motives for inverting the order in favor of women, and surely reasons can and do arise for changing the rest of the order.[15] Thus a lay person is preferred to any priest or deacon under censure after condemnatory or declaratory sentence has been passed,[16] and always to a heretical or schismatical priest.[17] A woman is preferred not only to a simple layman but even to a priest when decency demands such a preference.[18] She is preferred to a man, moreover, when the only man present is the father of the one to be baptized.[19]

[14] Canon 742, § 2. This canon is incorporated in the *Rituale Romanum*, Tit. II, c. 1, *de sacramento baptismi rite administrando*, n. 16.

[15] Bouuaert-Simenon, *Manuale Juris Canonici*, II, n. 23.

[16] Canon 2261; 2275, 2°; 2284.

[17] S. C. S. Off., 20 aug. 1671: "Non permittat [episcopus] schismaticis administrare sacramentum baptismatis nisi in casu necessitatis, et deficiente quacumque alia persona catholica."—*Fontes*, n. 746.

[18] Blat, *Commentarium*, Lib. III, pars I, n. 25.

[19] Canon 742, § 3. Patri aut matri suam prolem baptizare non licet, praeterquam in mortis periculo, quando alius praesto non est, qui baptizet.

The continued insistence upon the old law that the mother and father should not baptize their offspring even in a case of necessity, if there be someone else available, can no longer be satisfactorily explained in the manner in which this was done previously, namely, on the grounds that from such an action there would result a spiritual relationship which would prohibit the exercise of the marital right between the parties, for the Code has now definitely removed the impediment of spiritual relationship which formerly arose between the minister and the parents of the one who received baptism.[20] The reason for the continued prohibition would seem rather to lie in the fact that the Church is reluctant to have both the natural and spiritual parenthood coalesce in one and the same person.[21] In view of this supposed reason for the legislation the prohibition is not compellingly grave and would certainly yield if there were a probability that any other minister might baptize invalidly. For the phrase in the canon, "*quando alius praesto non est, qui baptizet*", must be understood as referring to a person who is at the same time capable of baptizing validly and willing to baptize lawfully.[22] When one likewise considers the Church's logical preference for a Catholic minister over a non-Catholic, and the possibility which is ever present that such a non-Catholic may lack the proper intention or make a mistake in uttering the form, then it seems not only probable, but even certain, that one of the parents should always be preferred to a Jew, a pagan, or a heretic.[23]

[20] Canon 768. Ex baptismo spiritualem cognationem contrahunt tantum cum baptizato baptizans et patrinus.

[21] Bouuaert-Simenon, *Manuale Juris Canonici*, II, n. 23; Vermeersch-Creusen, *Epitome*, II, n. 26.

[22] Vermeersch-Creusen, *loc. cit.*; Augustine, *Commentary*, IV, 44.

[23] Davis, *Moral Theology*, III, 47: "It is certainly preferable that a parent should baptize a child if, by allowing another to do so, the baptism were likely to be invalidly conferred."

It may be questioned, however, whether the rule which requires that preferably to any other person not of the faith a Catholic be called to baptize an infant in danger of death holds also when the intervention of surgical aid is needed for this act, in which case the non-Catholic physician or nurse will be the best judge of whether or how the baptismal water will effectually reach the child. Common sense dictates that preference must yield to the necessity of reality, and that, when the purpose and wish of the parent to have the child baptized has been explained sufficiently to the doctor or the nurse, the performance of the baptism should be left to them, provided that they know that the pouring of the water and the accompanying words are essential for the effective administration of the rite.[24]

The administration of private baptism, in order to be lawful as well as valid, must not take place except when the recipient is in danger of death. This danger of death does not have to be immediate or certain; a positive probability or a well-founded fear constitutes sufficient grounds for judging such an administration imperative.[25] Some authors[26] state that the phrase " danger of death " can be taken in a wide sense, since several decisions of the Sacred Congregation for the Propagation of the Faith approved a practice existing among missionaries of instructing their catechists or better-educated Christians to baptize newly-born children when no priest was expected or could be reached within ten days.[27]

24 "Administration of baptism *in utero* by physicians or trained nurses" —*AER*, XXVI (1902), 340.

25 S. C. S. Off., 11 ian. 1899: "Urgendum est ut Baptismus quam citius administretur: tunc vero permitti poterit ut obstetrix illum conferat, quando periculum positive timeatur ne puer dilationis tempore sit moriturus."—*Fontes*, n. 1214.

26 Augustine, *Commentary*, IV, 43; Ayrinhac, *Legislation on the Sacraments*, p. 20; Fanfani, *De Iure Parochorum*, n. 235.

27 (C. P. pro Sin.), 21 ian. 1788—*Fontes*, n. 4618; (C. P. pro Sin.), 16 ian. 1804—*Fontes*, n. 4677; litt. (ad Vic. Ap. Coreae), 11 sept. 1841—*Fontes*,

But most of the authors maintain that such a broad interpretation is lawful only for missionary regions inasmuch as these decisions were adopted in their regard, and so it is quite generally held that the phrase "danger of death" must be interpreted strictly in our well-organized districts.[28]

On the basis of these responses of the Sacred Congregation for the Propagation of the Faith Genicot-Salsmans extend the permission which the Code grants to baptize privately in danger of death to include the case wherein the mother finds it difficult to present her child at the church for baptism because of the opposition of her husband.[29] Certainly such an extension is not warranted by any phrase of the Code, since it is impossible to understand how such a situation could constitute a danger of death. In practice, moreover, it is seldom if ever necessary to resort to such extreme measures. The safer and saner solution seems to be for the mother to consult the parish priest in order that he may set an acceptable time for her to bring the child to the church secretly, or in order that he may receive permission from the local Ordinary to baptize the child at home solemnly at some opportune moment when the father is not at hand.[30] As a general rule either of these solutions in practice will answer the needs attaching to such a case, and repeated opportunities will present themselves for either action.

n. 4795. All of these decisions, however, in some part at least suppose that the life of the infant is endangered in view of the parents' custom of placing their newly-born infants in the same bed with them.

28 Vermeersch-Creusen, *Epitome*, II, n. 25; Aertnys-Damen, *Theologia Moralis*, II, n. 53; Merkelbach, *Summa Theologiae Moralis*, III, n. 139.

29 *Institutiones Theologiae Moralis*, II, n. 140.

30 Canon 776, § 1. In domibus autem privatis baptismus sollemnis administrari non debet, nisi hisce in adiunctis: 2°. Si loci Ordinarius, pro suo prudenti arbitrio et conscientia, iusta ac rationabili de causa, in casu aliquo extraordinario id concedendum censuerit.

ART. 2. ". . . SERVATA DEBITA MATERIA, FORMA ET INTENTIONE . . ."

Every sacrament essentially consists of three elements for validity: matter, form and the intention of the minister.[31] As a consequence of the necessity of each of these elements in the administration of any sacrament, the Code in permitting all to baptize privately in a case of necessity at the same time insists upon the faithful observance of the essentials.

A discussion in detail as to what constitutes the valid matter and form and right intention in the minister is more a question of Dogmatic and Moral Theology than Canon Law. But it does require some mention canonically, since it is upon an exact understanding of what constitutes these three elements that the canonist must always base his decision as to the validity of any baptism that has been conferred.

A. *Matter*

In discussing the sacraments theologians generally speak of the matter of each as being remote and proximate. The remote matter for baptism is true and natural water, and the proximate matter is the ablution made with that water.[32] Any true and natural water in a liquid state constitutes valid matter for private baptism, but for lawfulness it

[31] Eugenius IV (in Conc. Florentin.), const., "*Exultate Deo*", 22 nov. 1439, ad 9: "Haec omnia sacramenta tribus perficiuntur, videlicet rebus tanquam materia, verbis tanquam forma, et persona ministri conferentis sacramentum cum intentione faciendi quod facit Ecclesia; quorum si aliquod desit, non perficitur sacramentum."—*Fontes*, n. 52.

[32] Canon 737, § 1. Baptismus . . . valide non confertur, nisi per ablutionem aquae verae et naturalis . . . Conc. Trident., Sess. VII, *de baptismo*, c. 2: "Si quis dixerit, aquam veram et naturalem non esse de necessitate baptismi, atque ideo verba illa Domini nostri Jesu Christi: *Nisi quis renatus fuerit ex aqua et Spiritu Sancto*, ad metaphoram aliquam detorserit; anathema sit."

should be pure and without the admixture of any foreign substance. For solemn baptism the remote licit matter is water specially blessed for baptism and thus referred to as baptismal water.[33] When baptismal water is not available for solemn baptism, natural water is to be used in preference to holy water.[34] Though this baptismal water is not prescribed for the administration of private baptism, yet when it can easily be had it should be used. Failure to use it would not render the private baptism unlawful.[35]

There are many varieties of natural water, and chemistry has its own principles for determining what constitutes the element called water. But as far as the remote matter of private baptism is concerned, the common and popular acceptation of what is or is not considered water must be the guiding principle,[36] for it is in the common acceptation of the meaning of the words that Our Lord spoke. Hence according to common opinion the various liquids will be considered as either certainly valid, doubtfully valid, or certainly invalid matter for the administration of private baptism.[37] Matter that is certainly invalid may never be

[33] Canon 757, § 1. In baptismo sollemni adhibenda est aqua ad hoc benedicta. *Rituale Romanum,* Tit. II, c. 1, *de sacramento baptismi rite administrando,* n. 5.

[34] S. C. S. Off., 20 iun. 1883—*Fontes,* n. 1082.

[35] Noldin-Schmitt, *Summa Theologiae Moralis,* III, n. 59; Davis, *Moral Theology,* III, 42; *et alii.*

[36] Schmalzgrueber, *Ius Canonicum Universum,* Lib. III, tit. 42, n. 12.

[37] The following classification has been compiled from the various canonists and theologians previously cited in this work:

Certainly valid matter: all natural water from wells, springs, rivers, lakes, the sea, pools and cisterns; all rain, melted snow or ice or hail, mineral or sulphur water, dew, condensation, muddy water mixed with foreign matter (provided the water predominates), putrid water which still remains in the common estimation true water, distilled water, chemically produced water.

Doubtfully valid matter: unmelted ice and snow, liquid produced from salt, lye, soapsuds, the sap exuding from trees, water expressed and con-

employed. Doubtfully valid matter may be used in cases of extreme necessity when certainly valid matter cannot be obtained, but the baptism is then to be conferred under the condition: *Si haec materia sit valida.* Later, if the subject recovers or if certainly valid matter is obtained, the sacrament should be repeated under the condition: *Si non es baptizatus.*[38]

Worthy of particular note is the concession made by the Sacred Congregation of the Holy Office whereby it is recognized as valid and licit to use a solution of one part of corrosive sublimate (bichloride of mercury) to a thousand parts of natural water in the administration of uterine baptisms in order to ensure proper safeguard against the extant danger of possible infection.[39]

Some discussion has been raised as to whether the amniotic fluid which surrounds the foetus and which flows out in parturition can be considered valid matter for private baptism. The fluid is known to consist chemically of water and one per cent of other matters. The question has value since in difficult deliveries the attendant physician could easily baptize with this liquid when he cannot baptize at all or only with great difficulty with natural water.

It is most probable that this fluid does not constitute a valid matter, for it seems to be in a class with such human secretions as saliva and urine, which by general consensus are not considered valid matter. But it cannot definitely be stated that such a fluid is certainly invalid, for it is not

densed from flowers or plants, rose water, thin soup or broth, very limpid beer, weak coffee or tea.

Certainly invalid matter: strong coffee or tea, wine, glutinous beer, thick, soup, oil, milk, blood, saliva, tears, perspiration, urine, the juice of flowers or roots, mud, ink.

38 Cappello, *De Sacramentis,* I, n. 131; *Rituale Romanum,* Tit. II, c. 1, *de sacramento baptismi rite administrando,* n. 9.

39 21 aug. 1901—*Fontes,* n. 1256.

definite that in the common opinion of people it is considered to be not a form of water.

So in a case of necessity, when no other matter can be had, a doctor could use this fluid for conditional baptism; but he is not bound to do so. If he does use it he must take care that the fluid really flows, and hence it will be necessary for him to be sure that the infant, or at least the part of the body upon which the child is baptized, is outside the amniotic fluid.[40]

The proximate matter of baptism consists in the ablution of the subject with water.[41] This ablution can take place with its desired valid effect either by immersion, infusion or pouring, and aspersion or sprinkling.[42] Each of these modes offers a basis for valid baptism. Under restricted circumstances each of these modes may also lend itself for the lawful administration of baptism. But infusion is the method which is now generally in use.

In infusion it is essential that the water be poured in such manner that it will flow over and touch successively distinct parts of the bodily surface of the one who receives baptism. In aspersion it is requisite that the water be sprinkled in such fashion that it will make a simultaneous motile contact on distinct parts of the recipient's body. The water must actually be in contact with the skin. It is not enough that the water simply wet the hair of the subject. Baptism by infusion is to be conferred on the head of the person, for the head signalizes the principal part of the body of man. If baptism be conferred upon other parts of the body its

40 Aertnys-Damen, *Theologia Moralis,* II, n. 47.

41 Canon 737, § 1. Baptismus . . . valide non confertur nisi per ablutionem . . .

42 Canon 758. Licet baptismum conferri valide possit aut per infusionem, aut per immersionem, aut per aspersionem, primus tamen vel secundus modus, aut mixtus ex utroque, qui magis sit in usu, retineatur, secundum probatos diversarum Ecclesiarum rituales libros.

efficacy remains in doubt, even though there is a degree of probability that the baptism is valid. The infusion at baptism must be performed with a threefold separate pouring of water.[43]

The infusion must be made by the same person who pronounces the form, so that the words "I baptize thee" are actually verified. The minister of baptism must be responsible in some active way for the ablution. If one person pours the water and another pronounces the form, the baptism is invalid; but if the one who pronounces the form actively directs the water over the body of the one to be baptized by means of his hand or with an instrument, then the baptism is valid. In like manner one cannot confer baptism upon a person who is standing in the rain or under flowing water which issues from a fountain or from a waterspout, unless the one who pronounces the form at the same time holds the person to be baptized under that water, for by so holding the person the minister of the baptism becomes the direct instrumental cause in achieving the effect of ablution.[44]

B. *Form*

The form prescribed for baptism in the Latin rite runs as follows: "I baptize thee, in the name of the Father and of the Son and of the Holy Ghost." These words must be uttered in connection with the actual ablution. If they are pronounced before or after the ablution, but within an interval of time during which they can be considered as morally united with the act of ablution, the baptism is valid. The Greek form is: "The servant of Christ is baptized in the name of the Father and of the Son and of the Holy

[43] Payen, *Casus de Baptismo* (Zi-Ka-Wei, 1920), pp. 13-20.

[44] Davis, *Moral Theology*, III, 44; Genicot-Salsmans, *Institutiones Theologiae Moralis*, II, n. 125; Merkelbach, *Summa Theologiae Moralis*, III, n. 124; Cappello, *De Sacramentis*, I, nn. 136-137; Payen, *op. cit.*, pp. 23-27; S. C. de Sacr., 17 nov. 1916—*AAS*, IX (1916), 479.

Ghost." The latter form can be used validly by a minister of the Latin rite, but not licitly.[45]

The form employed in baptism must contain four distinct and essential elements if it is to render valid the sacramental act:

1. The term designating the person baptizing;
2. The term which specifies the distinct purpose of the act of pouring (or immersion in) water as a rite intended for christian baptism;
3. The term designating the person to be baptized;
4. The terms signalizing explicitly and intelligibly the unity of nature in the Trinity of Divine Persons.

Any intentional substantial change or any protracted interruption between the act of pouring the water and the pronouncement of the form will render the administration of the sacrament invalid. Though the wording of the required form is drawn up in the present tense, still its validity could not be called into question if the minister employed the past tense, either because he did not advert to the use of the wrong tense or because the particular language lends itself to the use of the past tense for signifying a present action.[46] Mere slips of the tongue or a garbling of the form through ignorance, haste or defective speech do not necessarily destroy the validity of the form.[47] Theolo-

[45] Cappello, *De Sacramentis*, I, n. 135.

[46] S. C. de Prop. Fide (C. P.), 27 mart. 1631—*Fontes*, n. 4446; S. C. S. Off., 8 sept. 1633—*Fontes*, n. 722.

[47] S. C. C., *Forosempronien.*, 24 maii 1823, declared valid a form which instead of "in the name" used "with the name."—*Fontes*, n. 3981. Again, the same Congregation (12 sept. 1801) stated that a form which omitted the "in" completely was nevertheless valid. Previously (*Ceneten.*, 12 maii 1753—*Fontes*, n. 3629) it had sanctioned a form which omitted the word "and" and had a corruption of the verb "to baptize". From these and like decisions some idea of the Church's liberality can be gathered, though it must be noted that these forms were used in Catholic regions by people who obviously had no intention of introducing heresy or error into the form.

gians admit, moreover, that words which have the same common significance as "baptize" can be used validly, since the intention of the minister determines as sacramental the act of washing which they signify.[48] Words which etymologically do not signify the act of ablution but which common use has determined to signify the sacred ablution of this sacrament are valid. Thus the Holy Office in 1894 approved the vernacular form, *Ia te krstim* for the Jugoslavs, although the word etymologically signifies the effect rather than the sacred ablution of baptism. As a consequence of this decision there is a dispute among theologians as to whether or not our English word *christen* can be used validly. Those who deny its validity do so with the argument that such a word not only fails to signify an ablution etymologically, but also in common usage falls short of denoting for a certainty the act of sacred ablution in baptism.[49]

Baptisms conferred with forms that are evidently invalid must be repeated absolutely.[50] If the form used was of doubtful validity, the baptism is to be repeated conditionally.[51]

[48] Aertnys-Damen, *Theologia Moralis,* II, n. 48: "Aeque ac verbum *baptizo* et similia quae sacrae huic ablutioni propria sunt, ad valorem sufficiunt verba communia *lavo, abluo* et synonyma, quum actionem abluendi significent quae intentione ministri ad esse sacramentale ablutionis determinatur."

[49] *The Clergy Review,* XV (1938), 544.

[50] Noldin-Schmitt, *Summa Theologiae Moralis,* III, n. 63, sub 2: "Invalidae sunt formae, in quibus aut non continetur, quae necessario exprimi debent, aut aliquid falsi vel haeretici continetur." The Holy Office (23 iun. 1840—*Fontes,* n. 881) declared invalid the form: "Ego volo tibi ministrare sacramentum baptismi peccatorum in nomine Patris et Filii et Spiritus Sancti. Amen."

[51] Noldin-Schmitt, *op. cit.,* III, n. 63, sub 3: "Dubiae sunt formae, quas certo non constat aut omnia exhibere, quae necessario exprimi debent, aut aliquid falsi vel haeretici continere." Thus the Holy Office (27 ian. 1892—*Fontes,* n. 1148) apparently agrees in a tacit way with the argument

C. *Intention*

In the twelfth century the discussion about the nature of the intention which the minister of a sacrament must possess when he administers the sacrament was rather vigorous. While some claimed that the will to perform exactly the ceremonies of the baptismal rite sufficed, others demanded, in addition, the intention of conferring the sacrament. It is the intention which determines the baptismal rite. So Peter Lombard said that two things were required in the administration of the sacrament: the performance of the baptismal rite and the intention to administer the sacrament.[52]

This solution was wise; still many objections were brought against it. If the performance of the sacramental rite when done conformably to the prescriptions of the Church does not suffice, but if it is further necessary that the minister have a mentally formulated intention to confer the sacrament, how can it be known that the interior intention exists, and that, therefore, the sacrament is truly conferred? Moreover, if such an intention is required, then an adversely disposed minister can baptize invalidly without anyone perceiving it. Since an infidel can baptize validly, is it reasonable to exact of him anything more than the integral observance of the baptismal rite? Up to the thirteenth century the theologians and canonists were divided in opinion. Saint Thomas adopted a middle course, which in the sixteenth century the Dominican Catharinus (1484-1553), and others who contented themselves with re-

of an Algerian missionary who thought that some doubt could be cast upon the validity of the form: "Ego te baptizo in nomine Patris nostri et Filii et Spiritus Sancti", because in the correct form the word *Patris* is used in reference to *Filii,* while the addition of the word *nostri* changes its sense to the generic paternity over all creation without emphasizing the special note to show the distinction of Persons in the Blessed Trinity.

[52] *Sententiarum libri quattuor* (Quaracchi edition), Lib. IV, dist. 6.

quiring a mere external intention, wrongly attempted to interpret in their own favor.[53] The intention of the minister, the Angelic Doctor said, is that of the Church for which he stands. But the intention of the Church is expressed by the sacramental words as pronounced by the minister. Hence there is no need to be worried about the mentally formulated intention of him who confers the sacrament, except in a case wherein it would be evident that the minister was acting in mockery.[54]

In the sixteenth century Luther gave a new turn to the controversy. Since, in his opinion, the sacrament is merely a rite intended to animate and inspire the faith of the subject, a mere external correct performance of the ceremony suffices; it matters not who performs it, nor whether the minister intends it or not, nor, *a fortiori,* whether he acts in mere pretense or derision. This time, however, the error of doctrine was plainly manifest. The minister could not be a mere passive instrument. Besides materially performing the sacramental rite instituted by Christ and perennially renewed by the Church, the minister must formally have

[53] Tanquerey, *Synopsis Theologiae Dogmaticae,* III, n. 417. According to Catharinus the external intention of doing what the Church does was present when the minister intended the correct administration of the sacramental rite according to the ceremonies, though inwardly he had the intention of not conferring the sacrament. In his opinion the exterior intention as it manifested itself in the observance of the baptismal rite was sufficient for the validity of the sacrament. He was opposed by those who taught that the interior intention was likewise required for validity. The opinion of Catharinus was never officially condemned, but it fell into discredit after the condemnation of the doctrine of Farvacques (1622-1689), whose opinion will be noted later.

[54] *Summa Theologica,* III, q. LXIV, art. 8, ad 2: "Alii melius dicunt quod minister sacramenti agit in persona totius Ecclesiae, cuius est minister; in verbis autem quae profert, exprimitur intentio ecclesiae, quae sufficit ad perfectionem sacramenti, nisi contrarium exterius exprimatur ex parte ministri vel recipientis sacramentum." The same doctrine was contained in the Bull of Pope Eugene IV (in Conc. Florentin.), const., "*Exultate Deo*", 22 nov. 1439—*Fontes,* n. 52.

the intention which acknowledges his act as the performance of the rite of a sacrament, or, in other words, in accordance with the definition of the Council of Trent, he must have the intention and the will to accomplish with the act what the Church itself accomplishes thereby (*faciendi quod facit Ecclesia.*)[55]

One can will to perform *outwardly* the baptismal rite, but *inwardly,* that is, apart from all external manifestation, have the intention of acting in mockery, or also have the positive contradictory intention of not conferring the sacrament instituted by Christ. In such a case the intention of the ministering agent in no way penetrates beyond the mere external performance of his act. It does not suffice. But if in his performance of the baptismal rite he wills to execute that rite in its character as instituted by Christ, in a word, if the minister substantially employs that rite with the view and purpose which the Church itself has when employing it, then, over and above the intention which inheres in mere externals, there is present in the minister the requisite internal intention.

According to Pallavicino (1607-1667)[56] the Council of Trent considered only the external intention, and left pending the question of the interior intention. Hence, after the Council the controversy was resumed with great intensity. However, on December 7, 1690, Pope Alexander VIII (1689-1691) condemned the proposition of Francis Farvacques of the University of Louvain which reads as follows: "That baptism is valid which is conferred by a minister who observes all the exterior rite and is faithful to the form of the

[55] Sessio VII, *de sacramentis in genere,* canon 11: "Si quis dixerit, in ministris, dum sacramenta conficiunt et conferunt, non requiri intentionem saltem faciendi quod facit ecclesia: anathema sit."

[56] *Istoria del Concilio di Trento* (4 vols., Romae, 1833), Lib. IX, cap. 6, n. 2.

sacrament, but who says resolutely to himself, 'I have no intention to do what the Church does.'"[57]

Today the common opinion—the one which is and which must be followed in practice—is that the minister must join to the exterior intention an interior intention, which, if not actual, must at least be virtual. A habitual intention, which is equivalent to the absence of all actuating interior intention, and an interpretative intention do not suffice. When the lack of at least a virtual implicit intention is evident, or, *a fortiori,* when the minister decidedly intends not to confer the sacrament, the sacrament must be considered null and void. In addition to these requisites the intention must also be absolute,[58] and determined in regard to a certain person.[59]

In view of this historical discussion of the intention necessary in the minister of a sacrament, one can readily understand that the minister could validly and licitly confer baptism without believing in the efficacy of the sacrament. Furthermore, even though the minister explicitly intends not to act as the Catholic Church acts, but rather as his own church acts, thinking it to be the true Church, he has nonetheless a sufficient intention, provided that he does not rule out what is essential in the sacrament. Even a superstitious intention or purpose does not necessarily exclude the right intention.[60] Since the minis-

[57] S. C. S. Off., decr., 7 dec. 1690, n. 28—*Fontes,* n. 760. In view of the condemnation of this proposition, and of the development of the teaching of the Church since the time of Catharinus, his opinion cannot safely be held but should be considered virtually condemned. Pope Benedict XIV (*De Synodo Dioec.,* Lib. VII, cap. 4, n. 8) said that through this condemnation it had received a grievous blow.

[58] Tanquerey, *Synopsis Theologiae Dogmaticae,* III, n. 243: "Intentio est absoluta quando non suspendit effectum sacramenti. ...Iamvero intentio conditionata aequivalet absolutae, generatim saltem, quando est de praeterito vel praesenti."

[59] Payen, *Casus de Baptismo,* pp. 67-70.

[60] S. C. S. Off., 19 sept. 1671—*Coll.,* n. 201.

ter in order to possess the proper intention must act as a serious human agent, a fictitious intention or an action in jest would be insufficient, for the Church does not act in this way, nor does the minister then wish to perform a serious rite.

Naturally no hard and fast rule by which the subject can determine when the proper intention actually exists in the minister can be stated. To allay all disquietude and anxiety in this regard, however, the Church herself has enunciated the principle that the intention of the minister to act as the Church does is to be presumed in the absence of any prudent doubt to the contrary, if evidence is at hand of the proper administration of the matter and form of the sacrament.[61]

ART. 3. ". . . QUATENUS VERO FIERI POTEST, ADHIBEANTUR DUO TESTES VEL SALTEM UNUS, QUIBUS BAPTISMI COLLATIO PROBARI POSSIT."

The sole reason which the legislator advances for requiring the presence of these witnesses at the administration of private baptism is that they may furnish testimony in regard to the baptism. That is why the insistence is placed upon one or two, since such a number is required for juridic testimony.[62] The proof which they must furnish in regard

[61] S. C. de Prop. Fide, instr. (ad Vic. Ap. Siam), 23 iun. 1830: "In illa vero disquisitione facienda de validitate vel invaliditate baptismatis, antequam sub conditionata forma iteretur, debent animarum pastores inquirere praesertim super formam et materiam adhibitam in priore baptismate. Nam relate ad intentionem, quae ex superius expositis necessaria est ad valorem baptismi, *nisi prudens de ea fuerit dubitatio, praesumenda illa est,* ut recte observavit Card. Petra inquiens de baptismo haereticorum: 'Si materiam et formam adhibeant, praesumendum est habere intentionem baptizandi, alius non baptizarent: quod etiam satis est ut baptisma collatum a calvinistis sit validum, quamvis ipsi nullam efficaciam Baptismo tribuunt." —*Fontes,* n. 4748.

[62] Canon 779. Ad collatum baptismi comprobandum, si nemini fiat praeiudicium, satis est unus testis omni exceptione maior, . . . Cf. also can. 1791.

to private baptism concerns not only the fact of the administration of baptism but also whether all the elements necessary for validity were present.

Through the use of the word *testes* the Code obviously does not intend to refer to the godparents, since elsewhere the term *patrini* is always used in reference to them.[63] Certainly nothing would prevent the same person from acting simultaneously as a witness and as a sponsor. The intended distinction between the words is important, however, inasmuch as it proves that people who are not capable of acting as sponsors validly at any baptism [64] could be used at private baptism as the witnesses required by law.

The phrase *quatenus vero fieri potest* indicates that a notable inconvenience would excuse from the necessity of having such witnesses.[65]

ART. 4. A THEORETICAL DISCUSSION OF THE VALIDITY OF NON-CATHOLIC BAPTISMS

The validity of the baptisms administered by non-Catholics in the various sects depends entirely upon the intention of the minister to do what the Church does when he applies the proper matter and pronounces the valid Trinitarian form over the subject.[66] The Council of Trent in no way demanded that this intention should be expressed or determined,—all that is necessary is the general intention

[63] Canon 762, § 2. Etiam in baptismo privato patrinus, si facile haberi queat, adhibeatur; . . .

[64] Canon 765.

[65] Blat, *Commentarium*, Lib. III, pars I, n. 25.

[66] Conc. Trident., Sessio VII, *de baptismo*, c. 4: "Si quis dixerit, baptismum, qui etiam datur ab haereticis in nomine Patris, et Filii, et Spiritus Sancti, cum intentione faciendi quod facit Ecclesia, non esse verum baptismum: anathema sit." S. C. de Sacr., *Validitatis baptismatis*, 17 nov. 1916—*AAS*, VIII (1916), 478-480.

of doing what the Church does, what Christ instituted, or what Christians do.[67]

In judging the validity of baptisms conferred in the various sects one must recall that all theologians agree that a non-Catholic minister can possess the requisite intention even though he does not intend to do what the Roman Catholic Church does, but what his own Church does, the while he believes his Church to be the true one. Moreover, the non-Catholic minister can be completely ignorant of the true nature or efficacy of the sacrament of baptism and yet possess an intention sufficient for its valid administration. In fact, he can even believe and openly aver that the rite which he is about to perform has no effect whatever upon the soul, yet, as long as he applies the proper matter and form simply with the intention of doing that which other Christians do, such a personal belief will not of itself destroy the sufficiency of his intention.[68]

With these thoughts in mind in regard to the nature of the intention required in the minister, one immediately questions the status of those baptisms which are conferred in the Protestant Churches. Do the non-Catholic sects in America which retain the rite of baptism with water and employ the Trinitarian formulary regard this as a mere external ceremony of initiation independent of any connec-

[67] S. C. S. Off., instr. (ad Custodem Terrae Sanctae), 30 ian. 1883: "Ad valorem tamen sacramenti necessariam non esse eam intentionem quam vocant expressam seu determinatam, sed sufficere intentionem tantum *genericam* nimirum *faciendi quod facit Ecclesia* seu *faciendi quod Christus instituit* vel *quod christiani faciunt*, theologi passim docent... Praeterea tunc est intentio faciendi quod facit Ecclesia, quam solam requirunt Concilium Florentinum et Tridentinum."—*Fontes*, n. 871.

[68] S. C. S. Off., instr. (ad Ep. Nesquallien.), 24 ian. 1877—*Fontes*, n. 1050; instr. (ad Vic. Ap. Oceaniae Central.), 18 dec. 1872—*Fontes*, n. 1024; instr. (ad Custodem Terrae Sanctae), 30 ian. 1833—*Fontes*, n. 871; S. C. de Prop. Fide, instr. (ad Vic. Ap. Siam), 23 iun. 1830—*Fontes*, n. 4748; instr. (ad Vic. Ap. Pondicher.), 26 iul. 1845—*Fontes*, n. 4815.

tion with Christ, or does there exist among the various sects the intention of performing that which Christ instituted?

This question is not easily answered. The increasing disregard of the sacrament of baptism among the sects of the United States is patent. It is likewise commonly known that the ministers of these non-Catholic groups frequently neglect or fail to observe all the conditions required for administering valid baptism. European theologians have observed this, and some have advanced the opinion that all baptisms administered by non-Catholics in the United States are presumptively invalid.[69] If the invalid conferring of all non-Catholic baptisms, such as they claim to obtain here in America, could be established as an *actual* custom, then the past responses of the Holy See would have to be understood as invoking the general presumption of invalidity for the baptisms thus conferred, and consequently this presumption could be utilized as an equivalent for moral certainty of non-baptism as long as no positive proof to the contrary militated against that presumption.[70] But American theologians and canonists do not admit the existence of any such actual custom capable of establishing this general presumption of invalidity.[71]

[69] Lehmkuhl, *Theologia Moralis* (9th ed., 2 vols., Friburgi Brisgoviae, 1898), II, n. 19, nota 1; Vermeersch-Creusen, *Epitome*, II, n. 38; Genicot-Salsmans, *Institutiones Theologiae Moralis*, II, n. 153.

[70] S. C. de Prop. Fide, instr. (ad Vic. Ap. Siam), 23 iun. 1830—*Fontes*, n. 4748; instr. (ad Vic. Ap. Pondicher.), 26 iul. 1845: "...non est imprudens nec insuetum, propter haereticorum incertam et suspectam praxim ..."—*Fontes*, n. 4815; S. C. S. Off., 17 nov. 1830, ad 3: "...nullum baptisma ex consuetudine actuali illius sectae..."—*Fontes*, n. 869; *Bulgariae*, 5 iul. 1853, ad 3: "Si autem certe dignoscatur invalidum esse eorum baptisma ex consuetudine actuali eiusdem sectae, . . . ut infideles esse habendos." —*Fontes*, n. 925.

[71] Sabetti-Barrett (*Compendium Theologiae Moralis*, p. 583), bear out the opinion of Lehmkuhl only in regard to certain sects. A recent discussion concerning the presumed invalidity of non-Catholic baptisms in the United States was carried on between the Rev. Joseph P. Donovan, C.M., J.C.D.,

In view of this discussion there is evidently a lack of that agreement so necessary among canonists and theologians before one can with certitude postulate the existence of a definite general presumption of invalidity regarding the baptisms conferred in the sects. Yet various responses of the Sacred Congregations and the consensus of theologians and canonists in certain instances can possibly form the basis for individual presumptions in regard to some of the sects.[72] All baptisms administered by ministers of sects

and the Rev. Valentine Schaaf, O.F.M., J.C.D., in a series of articles [*AER*, LXXIV (1926), 158-180; LXXV (1926), 136-151 and 358-370; LXXVI (1927), 155-165 and 496-504; LXXXIV (1931), 124-139 and 282-285 and 371-387]. The Rev. T. L. Bouscaren, S.J., entered the controversy long enough to state that he thought that the baptisms conferred by Baptists could not be called presumptively invalid [*Gregorianum*, VIII (1927), 41-54]. The import of this discussion seems very notably to impugn the opinion of Lehmkuhl—an opinion which Cappello (*De Sacramentis*, I, n. 174: "...*nonnisi* cum debita discretione accipiendum esse arbitramur.") considered too indiscriminate for wholesale application in actual practice.

[72] It is difficult to determine the status of individual sects in regard to their baptisms. However, the sources cited seemingly give some warrant for the conclusions here drawn:

Presumably valid: Greek Schismatics and Oriental heretics [S. C. S. Off., instr. (Pro Vic. Ap. ad Gallos), 20 iun. 1866, ad 40—*Coll.*, n. 1293; 8 sept. 1633—*Coll.*, n. 520; Leroux, "Les Baptêmes d'Adultes,"—*Revue Ecclésiastique de Liege*, XVII (1925-1926), 341-352; *AER*, LXXV (1926), 358-370], the Ritualists among the Episcopalians [Th. Bouquillon, "De la Reiteration du Baptême Conféré par les Heretiques,"—*Revue des Sciences Ecclésiastiques*, XL (1879), 145-173; *AER*, LXXIV (1926), 158-180] and the Old Catholics or members of La Petite Eglise.

Presumably invalid: Quakers and Socinians [S. C. S. Off., instr. (ad Ep. Nesquallien.), 24 ian. 1877—*Fontes*, n. 1050; S. C. de Prop. Fide, instr. (ad Vic. Ap. Pondicher.), 26 iul. 1845—*Fontes*, n. 4815], Congregationalists, Unitarians and Universalists [*Revue des Sciences Ecclésiastiques*, XL (1879), 145-173].

Presumption of Doubtful Validity: Anglicans other than the Ritualists [S. C. S. Off., 20 iul. 1840—*Nouvelle Revue Théol.*, XV (1883), 401-402; *Bombay*, 21 feb. 1883—*Fontes*, n. 1078; 20 nov. 1878—*Fontes*, n. 1058; S. C. de Prop. Fide, instr. (ad Vic. Ap. Siam), 23 iun. 1830—*Fontes*, n. 4748], Calvinists, Zwinglians and Presbyterians [S. C. S. Off., instr. (ad Custodem Terrae Sanctae), 30 ian. 1833—*Fontes*, n. 871; instr. (ad Vic.

which repudiate baptism are initially to be presumed as being at most doubtfully valid. On the other hand, those sects which prescribe baptism must first be examined with regard to their ritual before any presumption can be formed. If valid matter and form are prescribed by the ritual, the initial presumption will be for the validity of the baptism conferred as a ceremony within that sect. If the ceremony prescribed in the ritual is of doubtful validity or definite invalidity, the initial presumption will likewise be for doubtful or invalid baptism.

The presumption in these instances is said to be initial inasmuch as the Church does not permit the investigation concerning the status of a previous baptism to cease with a mere presumption regarding the ministrations of a sect. The initial presumption is of use only in determining the nature and extent of the future investigation to be made. Thus a baptism which possesses the initial presumption of validity continues to be so considered until a positive reason is discovered for regarding it as doubtful or as invalid. An initial presumption of doubtful validity in regard to a sect's baptisms retains its force until positive reasons demand that this presumption yield to the judgment that validity or invalidity is certainly present. Likewise positive reasons must be adduced before a baptism under the initial pre-

Ap. Oceaniae Central.), 18 dec. 1872—*Fontes*, n. 1024; instr. (ad Ep. Nesquallien.), 24 ian. 1877—*Fontes*, n. 1050; S. C. de Prop. Fide, instr. (ad Vic. Ap. Siam), 23 ian. 1830—*Fontes*, n. 4748], Lutherans (S. C. S. Off., Bulgariae, 5 iul. 1853—*Fontes*, n. 925) and Methodists [S. C. de Prop. Fide, instr. (ad Vic. Ap. Pondicher.), 26 iul. 1845—*Fontes*, n. 4815; S. C. S. Off., instr. (ad Vic. Ap. Oceaniae Central.), 18 dec. 1872—*Fontes*, n. 1024; instr. (ad Ep. Nesquallien.), 24 ian. 1877—*Fontes*, n. 1050].

The list here cited follows in close detail that already stated in the two moral theology books which were written with reference to America (Sabetti-Barrett, *Compendium Theologiae Moralis*, p. 583; A. Konings, C.SS.R., *Theologia Moralis* [7th ed., New York, 1889], n. 1264). Of special interest also in reference to the presumption of doubtful validity for certain sects is the discussion already referred to between the Reverend Doctors Donovan and Schaaf in the *American Ecclesiastical Review.*

sumption of invalidity yields to the presumption of doubtful or certain validity. If a baptism in an individual case cannot be examined in view of an initial presumption, its validity or invalidity must be determined solely by the evidence which the individual investigation reveals. Moreover, whenever there is a definite lack of evidence to produce moral certainty regarding either the fact of the administration of baptism, or the use of a truly valid rite, such a lack of evidence entails a presumption for considering the baptism to be doubtful.

In conclusion it must be stated that the note of necessity which attaches to baptism for eternal salvation calls for a thorough investigation to establish with certitude the status of a baptism previously conferred in a sect. Certainly one cannot adopt the attitude that all non-Catholic baptisms are either invalid or doubtfully valid, so that all converts are to be baptized either absolutely or conditionally. Such an attitude would expose the sacrament not only to needless but even to gravely interdicted repetition. Nor can one lean too heavily upon the initial presumptions. The practical lesson to be derived from a study of the present condition among Protestants who profess a Christian doctrine is that a superficial assurance regarding the validity of their baptism can hardly ever be accepted. So in addition to the initial presumption with regard to their sect each individual case must be examined carefully in respect to where, when, how and by whom the baptism was conferred. Such an investigation is not merely recommended; it is solemnly insisted upon by the Roman Congregations,[73] and by the

[73] S. C. S. Off., 20 nov. 1878: "In conversione haereticorum, a quocumque loco vel a quacumque secta venerint, inquirendum est de validitate baptismi in haeresi suscepti. Instituto igitur in singulis casibus examine, si compertum fuerit, aut nullum, aut nulliter collatum fuisse, baptizandi erunt absolute. Si autem pro tempore et locorum ratione, investigatione peracta, nihil sive pro validitate, sive pro invaliditate detegatur, aut adhuc probabile dubium de baptismi validitate supersit, tum sub conditione secreto bap-

Second Plenary Council of Baltimore (1866).[74]

tizentur. Demum, si constiterit validum fuisse, recipiendi erunt tantummodo ad abiurationem et professionem fidei."—*Fontes*, n. 1058; litt. (ad Ep. Harlemen.), 6 apr. 1859—*Fontes*, n. 950; instr. (ad Ep. Nesquallien.) 24 ian. 1877—*Fontes*, n. 1050; instr. (ad. Vic. Ap. Iaponiae Merid.), 4 feb. 1891—*Fontes*, n. 1130; 2 aug. 1901—*ASS*, XXXIV (1901-1902), 640; S. C. de Prop. Fide, instr., 17 apr. 1777—*Fontes*, n. 4575; instr. (ad Vic. Ap. Mysuren.), 31 dec. 1851—*Coll.*, n. 1069.

A satisfactory investigation has likewise been ordered by the Holy See with regard to the doubtful baptisms of individual Catholics when these baptisms were conferred in extraordinary circumstances by other than the usual ministers: S. C. C., *Ripana*, 12 dec. 1733—*Fontes*, n. 3412; *Tarvisina*, 28 apr. 1736, 4 maii 1737—*Fontes*, nn. 3458, 3475; *Sutrina*, 12 iul. 1794—*Fontes*, n. 3890; *Brixien.*, 27 aug., 17 dec. 1796—*Fontes*, n. 3902; *Brixien.*, 11 feb. 1797—*Fontes*, n. 3904; 16 mart. 1897—*Fontes*, n. 4302.

[74] "Sed in singulos, qui oblati fuerint, casus, non levi quidem aut perfunctorio, sed diligenti examine, inquirendum est explorandumque, num in singulis servata fuerit debita materia ac forma. Quod postulat tum Sacramenti dignitas, tum verba ipsa legis ecclesiasticae, quae Româ paucos ante annos ad nos transmissa fuit."—*Acta et Decreta*, n. 240. Cf. also n. 241.

CHAPTER VIII

The Minister of Solemn Baptism and Incidental Questions

ART. 1. THE OBLIGATION TO INSTRUCT THE LAITY IN REGARD TO PROPER ADMINISTRATION

The historical section of this thesis furnished ample proof of the Church's desire that others besides the clergy should know how to administer baptism properly. Councils and synods throughout the centuries required the pastors to instruct and examine in this regard all those who by the nature of their work assisted at childbirth.

The Còde, following the Roman Ritual,[1] preserves this admonition in its legislation and urges pastors to see that the faithful in general, and more particularly nurses, physicians and surgeons, are rightly instructed in the duty and mode of administering baptism in cases of necessity.[2] The obligation hereby imposed upon pastors is a grave one.[3] Since the Code requires him merely to see that such instructions are given, however, he can fulfill his obligation either personally or through another.

The pastor should not content himself with offering these instructions in a general way and solely in the church, but should take care that more particular attention is given to students who are enrolled in nursing and medical schools situated within the parish boundaries. To such parishioners a thorough course should be given in regard to their duty

[1] Tit. II, c. 1, *de sacramento baptismi rite administrando*, n. 17.

[2] Canon 743. Curet parochus ut fideles, praesertim obstetrices, medici et chirurgi, rectum baptizandi modum pro casu necessitatis probe ediscant.

[3] Cf. Davis, *Moral Theology*, III, 47.

to baptize in case of necessity, with respect to the manner in which private baptism is to be performed in various circumstances, and in reference to the advisability of securing sponsors and witnesses whenever possible. Proportionate stress should be laid on the factors involved in the proper administration of baptism in uterine cases. The instruction should likewise inform these people of the opportunity they have of baptizing the children of heretics and of infidels, even without the permission of the parents, when it is prudently foreseen that such children will die immediately or before they attain the use of reason.[4]

The laity should also be told of their obligation to notify the proper pastor of the person baptized under any of these extraordinary circumstances. Such notification serves an immediate demand; it furnishes the pastor of the person a distinct aid in his task of properly recording the fact of the baptism thus received.[5] In practice, however, few will report the baptism to any priest other than the pastor of the territory within which the sacrament was conferred, and the obligation of forwarding a simple notification to the proper pastor will then rest upon him.

ART. 2. CHRISTIAN NAMES

The right to choose the baptismal name of a child belongs primarily to the parents or guardians of the subject. If these fail to provide a name, then the pastor or any minister of baptism may do so.[6] In this regard, however, the

[4] Canons 750; 751. Helpful hints for these instructions may readily be gained from the following books: A. Bonnar, *The Catholic Doctor* (2nd ed., New York: P. J. Kenedy and Sons, 1939), pp. 89-96; Leo Gregory Fink, *Graduate Nurses* (3rd ed., New York: Paulist Press, 1938), pp. 216-220, 278-280.

[5] Canon 778. Si baptismus nec a proprio parocho nec eo praesente administratus fuerit, minister de ipso collato quamprimum proprium ratione domicilii parochum baptizati certiorem reddat.

[6] Bouuaert-Simenon, *Manuale Juris Canonici*, II, n. 43, 4°.

pastor does have a primary obligation to see that a Christian name is imposed.[7] This admonition of the Code—for it is not a rigorous precept—canonizes what had been the invariable custom of the Church from the fourth century,[8] and renews the prescriptions of the Roman Ritual.[9] In the event that the pastoral admonitions prove fruitless, baptism is not to be denied merely on that score.[10] In such a case the pastor merely adds a christian name to the one chosen by the parents or guardians and inscribes both names in the baptismal register.

Some authors state that later the pastor cannot change the parish register inscriptions, even at the request of the person baptized, unless the local Ordinary grants permission.[11] O'Rourke,[12] however, explains that their statements arise from their knowledge of a condition peculiar to some European countries. In our country the condition to which they refer does not exist, and hence the pastor by virtue of his office is able to make the necessary corrections without any reference to the Ordinary.

ART. 3. THE SPONSORS

The obligation to supply a capable and suitable sponsor for the one to be baptized is primarily incumbent upon the parents or guardians in the cases wherein the subject is an

[7] Canon 761. Curent parochi ut ei qui baptizatur, christianum imponatur nomen; quod si id consequi non poterunt, nomini a parentibus imposito addant nomen alicuius Sancti et in libro baptizatorum utrumque nomen perscribant.

[8] Ayrinhac, *Legislation on the Sacraments*, pp. 43-44.

[9] Tit. II, c. 1, *de sacramento baptismi rite administrando*, n. 70.

[10] Noldin-Schmitt, *Summa Theologiae Moralis*, III, n. 81.

[11] Cappello, *De Sacramentis*, I, n. 179; Bouuaert-Simenon, *op. cit.*, II, n. 43.

[12] *Parish Registers*, The Catholic University of America Canon Law Studies, n. 88 (Washington, D. C.: The Catholic University of America, 1934), p. 10.

infant. In the case of an adult candidate for baptism, he should be told of the obligation of having a sponsor, and be directed to have some suitable person act for him in that capacity. Hence the pastor cannot change the suitable sponsors designated by the parents or guardians, nor admit others who are not designated by them. However, if those on whom this right and obligation is primarily incumbent should refuse or neglect to exercise it, then this right and duty devolves upon the pastor or the Ordinary of the candidate, or also on the minister of the sacrament. Tantamount to the failure to provide a sponsor is the obstinate insistence of the parents on the appointment of a person who cannot act validly as a sponsor. In such a case the parents are truly deficient in the use of their right and duty.[13]

In the designation of the sponsor the pastor's chief duty consists in determining whether the sponsor selected by the parents is suitable. For a more complete and certified fulfillment of this obligation the pastor should inquire who is to act as sponsor, even before the time which is appointed for the ceremony.[14] If two sponsors are appointed the pastor should insist that one be a man and the other a woman.[15] If the parents designate more than two persons as prospective sponsors, the minister can indeed permit all

[13] Kearney, *Sponsors at Baptism According to the Code of Canon Law*, The Catholic University of America Canon Law Studies, n. 30 (Washington, D. C.: The Catholic University of America Press, 1925), pp. 20, 46, 96; Aertnys-Damen, *Theologia Moralis*, II, n. 75.

[14] Conc.. Trident., Sess. XXIV, *de ref. matrim.*, c. 2: "Before the parish priest proceeds to confer baptism, he shall carefully inquire of those whom it concerns what person or persons they have chosen to act as sponsors at the font for the one to be baptized, and he shall permit him or them only to act as such,..."—H. J. Schroeder, *Canons and Decrees of the Council of Trent: Original Text with English Translation* (Saint Louis: B. Herder Book Co., 1941), pp. 185-186.

[15] Canon 764.

of these persons to be present at the baptism, but he must advise them that only two of them, a man and a woman, and these definitely determined, can be really employed as actual sponsors and will thus contract the spiritual relationship.[16] If no fit sponsor can be had, the minister should simply baptize without one.[17]

Though the Code clearly supposes that the sponsor and minister are two distinct persons, yet it would be possible for the minister to act simultaneously as the sponsor. It is true that the Sacred Congregation for the Propagation of the Faith declared that such a practice was not to be admitted in regard to the sacrament of Confirmation,[18] but later the Sacred Congregation of Rites permitted it as long as the minister used a proxy to represent him as sponsor.[19] It seems that the minister of baptism could act in the same manner.

When the minister is certain that the sponsor or sponsors presented can validly and licitly fulfill the office, he should explain for what reason sponsors are used, what their function is, what is required of them, and what is implied by the nature of the spiritual relationship which they contract.[20]

If the pastor or minister is certain of the incapacity of the presented sponsor or sponsors to act validly or licitly, he must not permit them to function. In refusing them this honor, however, he must act kindly, so that the good name and honor of the Church will not suffer unwarranted harm in view of his undue severity. Moreover, if from such a refusal grave inconvenience would arise, the minister can permit the person to be present, but he will take care not to

[16] Bouuaert-Simenon, *Manuale Juris Canonici*, II, n. 45.

[17] Canon 762, § 1. The phrase "*quatenus fieri potest*" suggests this exception.

[18] 21 sept. 1843—*Coll.*. n. 969.

[19] 14 iun. 1873—*Fontes*, n. 6059.

[20] S. C. Sacr., instr., 25 nov. 1925—*AAS*, XVIII (1926), 47.

have such a person physically to touch the child during the act of baptizing. In this way the person who is not qualified to act as a sponsor will fail to become a true sponsor.

If it is physically or morally impossible to prevent the proposed sponsor from touching the subject, the minister may permit even this if he prudently foresees that from such an action no scandal will arise. The reason for this opinion inheres in the fact that there is question purely of an ecclesiastical law, and that such laws do not always bind under a grave inconvenience.[21] If the minister finds it impossible to reject one who may validly but not licitly act as sponsor, and if such a person fulfills the required detail of the ceremony, then he contracts the spiritual relationship and becomes a true sponsor.[22]

With a care and diligence equal to that which he must employ in declining the services of persons who cannot act validly or licitly as sponsors, the minister of the baptism should exclude women who, in presenting themselves as prospective sponsors, appear indecently attired.[23] However, in the absence of any definite statement to the contrary by the Sacred Congregation of the Council, it remains indicated that the functioning of such women in the capacity of sponsors must stand recognized in the law as a valid sponsorship. Moreover, if the use of the indecent attire does not publicly reflect a life of criminal tendency or bespeak a status of factual infamy, then it appears that the minimum requirements which the law sets up for licit sponsorship are also fulfilled at least in substance. For it cannot be gathered from the Instruction of the Congregation that it was intended to add a new prohibition which along

[21] A. Meunier, "De patrinis Baptismi,"—*Revue Ecclés. de Liege*, XXV (1933-1934), 307-308; Merkelbach, *Summa Theologiae Moralis*, III, n. 171.

[22] Kearney, *Sponsors at Baptism*, p. 96.

[23] S. C. Conc., instr., 12 ian. 1930—*AAS*, XXII (1930), 26.

with the ones mentioned in canon 766 will bar a person from licitly assuming the status of a baptismal sponsor. Rather, the disciplinary ordinance implied in the Instruction simply points to a fact which, in the light of the imminent scandal it normally involves, stands as a factor concerning which the natural law itself, and apart from all positive legislation, excludes a person from entering upon so sacred a trust as that of sponsorship. The obviation of the danger of forthright scandal is a condition which, although it be not expressly stated in law, nevertheless must always be complied with if a person is *lawfully* to assume any new status with attached duties or any new function with obligatory import.

In the event that the minister of the sacrament is doubtful whether the one presented has the essential qualifications to function validly or licitly as a sponsor, recourse must be had to the Ordinary, if time permits.[24] Such a recourse must be had whether the doubt arises from an uncertain law or from an undeterminable fact.[25] The clause "*si tempus suppetat*" in canon 767 is to be understood as the time which is normally required for any ordinary means of communication. The use of the telephone and telegraph are still considered extraordinary means.[26] Hence the time required for the making of recourse is to be computed as coincident with the usual time needed for the execution of a personal journey or for the sending of a letter plus the receiving of a reply to it.

Once resort has been made to this recourse, it is the duty of the Ordinary to decide on the admissibility of the proposed sponsor. Should the Ordinary feel certain that the

[24] Canon 767. In dubio utrum quis valide vel licite admitti possit, necne, ad patrini munus, parochus, si tempus suppetat, consulat Ordinarium.

[25] Blat, *Commentarium*, Lib. III, pars I, n. 55.

[26] Pont. Commission for the Interpretation of the Code, 12 nov. 1922—*AAS,* XIV (1922), 662-663.

necessary qualifications are lacking in the person, then he must exclude him from functioning, for from the common law the Ordinary receives no special power to dispense in such a case. If the Ordinary also remains doubtful as to whether the necessary qualifications are fulfilled in the person, then the case must be decided in accordance with the provisions of canon 15.

When time does not permit recourse to the Ordinary, the pastor may likewise employ the provisions of canon 15. So if the doubt be one which arises from the uncertain meaning of the law, he can admit the person as sponsor; if the doubt arises in consequence of an undeterminable fact, he can for a just reason presume the dispensation of the Ordinary.[27]

ART. 4. SPIRITUAL RELATIONSHIP

Spiritual relationship is a supernatural bond which, by virtue of ecclesiastical law, establishes between certain persons through the medium of the reception or the administration of the sacraments of baptism and confirmation a definite link that involves specific canonical consequences. One of the chief effects of such a spiritual relationship when contracted through baptism is the actualization of a diriment impediment to marriage between the parties so related.

The historical development of the impediment of spiritual relationship can be divided into three distinct periods: a) the period preceding the Council of Trent; b) the period following the Council of Trent up to the promulgation of the present Code; and c) the period since the promulgation of the Code. Here it is sufficient to speak of the impediment solely as it affects the minister of baptism.

Before the Council of Trent the impediment of spiritual relationship was quite extensive with regard to whom it involved. The first degree of this relationship was called

[27] Blat, *loc. cit.*; Kearney, *Sponsors at Baptism*, pp. 102-103.

paternitas, and it could be direct and indirect. Direct paternity arose between the minister and the recipient. Indirect paternity arose between the minister's wife or husband and the recipient, for the spouses were considered two in one flesh. The second degree of spiritual relationship was called *compaternitas,* and could likewise be direct and indirect. Direct compaternity arose between the minister and the sponsor, and also between the minister and the parents of the recipient. Indirect compaternity arose between the parents of the recipient and the spouse of the minister. A third degree of this relationship was called *fraternitas.* It arose between the natural children of the minister on the one hand and the recipient on the other. All these relationships constituted diriment matrimonial impediments.

The Council of Trent [28] abolished spiritual fraternity, indirect paternity and indirect compaternity. Thus, immediately prior to the promulgation of the Code spiritual relationship on the part of the minister was contracted solely with the recipient, and with the parents of the recipient.[29]

The present legislation of the Code has restricted the extent of the diriment matrimonial impediment which arises from this spiritual relationship even further. Now the minister contracts this impediment solely with the recipient of the sacrament.[30] Moreover, the Pontifical Commission for the Interpretation of the Code declared that a spiritual relationship contracted according to the law existing before the day of Pentecost, 1918, and falling outside the limits now defined by the Code, from the aforesaid day of Pente-

[28] Sess. XXIV, *de ref. matrim.*, c. 2.

[29] Kearney, *Sponsors at Baptism,* pp. 106-108.

[30] Canon 1079. Ea tantum spiritualis cognatio matrimonium irritat, de qua in can. 768. Canon 768. Ex baptismo spiritualem cognationem contrahunt tantum cum baptizato baptizans et patrinus.

cost ceased to be an impediment to marriage, although it did not cease in regard to all its other effects.[31]

It is important to note at this point that authors commonly state that this spiritual relationship does not exist when the minister is unbaptized, for such a relationship presupposes the fact of baptism in the minister as a *conditio sine qua non.*[32] The spiritual bond consists essentially in a mutual relationship, and so it can exist only when both parties are subject to the same laws of the Church.[33]

At first glance there seem to be several reasons why this relationship should exist even in an infidel minister. The first and foremost reason to be urged in this regard is that canon 768 states simply that the one baptizing contracts the spiritual bond, and hence does not exclude ministers who have themselves not been baptized. Serious as this objection may seem at first, it loses strength upon consideration of the fact that the spiritual relationship referred to in the canon is the result of a purely ecclesiastical law and hence there is no need for the canon to make any distinctions since the Code has already stated that such laws bind only baptized persons.[34]

Again it may be alleged that when baptism is conferred an act of spiritual regeneration takes place, and as a spiritual son is begotten, no matter who the minister may be, so it is logical to seek one in whom the requisite spiritual paternity exists, and who else can this be but the

[31] 3 iun. 1918, n. 8—*AAS*, X (1918), 346.

[32] Petrovits, *The New Church Law on Matrimony,* The Catholic University of America Canon Law Studies, n. 6 (Washington, D. C.: The Catholic University of America, 1919), n. 386.

[33] Ayrinhac-Lydon, *Marriage Legislation* (New York: Benziger Bros., 1936), p. 185; Bouuaert-Simenon, *Manuale Juris Canonici,* II, n. 283; Cappello, *De Sacramentis,* III, n. 558; Vermeersch-Creusen, *Epitome,* II, n. 364; De Smet, *De Sponsalibus et Matrimonio* (4th ed., Brugis: Car. Beyaert, 1927), p. 558, n. 642.

[34] Canon 12.

unbaptized minister. But such an objection arises from an erroneous interpretation of the act of spiritual regeneration. It is the sacrament, independently of the merits or status of the minister, which accomplishes the regeneration. The spiritual sonship effected by this act is primarily a filial relation towards God in Whom the spiritual paternity really exists. Baptism of itself always produces both the spiritual sonship in the subject and the primary spiritual paternity. The paternity which is attributed to the minister is secondary and so called only by analogy. Hence, if this secondary paternity is not effected in the minister, it does not destroy the existence of the spiritual sonship in its primary relation. Blat thinks that it is absurd to speak of a spiritual paternity in one who is not yet born of the Spirit.[35]

It may likewise be urged that the spiritual relationship can be communicated to the unbaptized minister through the one who is baptized. However, there can be no such thing as a communication of relationship in this sense. Relationship of itself implies something that exists mutually and cannot be conceived unless as existing on the part of both simultaneously and unless both related elements exist in the same order of being. If the relationship were communicated by the subject of baptism to the minister, there would be a time when it could be said that the subject of baptism possessed it and the unbaptized minister did not. A relationship cannot exist even for a moment solely on the part of one person only. Moreover, such a communication would seek to establish a mutual bond between two distinct orders of being—a relationship between the subject who by baptism has been placed in the spiritual order and the unbaptized minister who by his very lack of baptism exists totally outside this order. Hence it must be asserted that this relationship established by ecclesiastical law can obtain

[35] *Commentarium*, Lib. III, pars I, n. 56.

only between those persons who through baptism are subject to the same ecclesiastical law.

Neither can the subsequent conversion of the unbaptized minister in any way affect his status in this regard. The spiritual relationship cannot revive because it never existed.[36] Any assertion to the contrary would lack a solidly probable basis, in view of the general principle: "Non firmatur tractu temporis quod de iure ab initio non subsistit." [37]

Since the Code explicitly extends exemption from spiritual relationship to the sponsor in a conditionally repeated baptism when the same person has not acted as sponsor in each of the two dubious baptisms,[38] the question arises: What is to be said of the minister in the same case? Does the impediment of spiritual relationship arise between the minister of a repeated conditional baptism and the recipient of the sacrament?

Some advance the opinion that since there is only explicit mention of the sponsor in the canon, the exemption from the impediment cannot safely be extended to the minister of the sacrament, and hence the minister and the recipient in this case would be bound by a spiritual relationship doubtful in fact—not a *dubium iuris*—and if these two wish to contract marriage as long as the doubt remains unsolved, they must seek a dispensation from the impediment of spiritual relationship before contracting marriage. If the doubt arises after the marriage is contracted, the validity of the marriage is to be presumed until the contrary is proved.[39] This seems the logical solution.[40]

36 Kearney, *Sponsors at Baptism*, p. 113.

37 Reg. 18, R. J., in VI°.

38 Canon 763, § 2.

39 Canon 1014.

40 De Smet, *De Sponsalibus et Matrimonio* (2 vols., Bussum in Hollandia, 1923), I, n. 176.

Others aver that the Code seeks to restrict the impediment of spiritual relationship, and on the basis of this apparently less stringent discipline they assert that the question of the spiritual relationship between the minister and the recipient in a repeated conditional baptism would eventuate in a *dubium iuris*, according to which by the provisions of canon 15 the canonical consequences flowing from the spiritual relationship may rightfully be considered as inapplicable. In short, this opinion extends to the minister of a repeated conditional baptism the same exemption from spiritual relationship which the Code explicitly grants the sponsor.[41]

When the minister also acts as sponsor through a proxy the spiritual relationship is multiplied as an impediment to marriage.[42]

ART. 5. THE OBLIGATION TO FAST IN THE ADMINISTRATION OF BAPTISM TO ADULTS

The Code suggests that the priest who administers and the adult who receives baptism, if the latter be in sufficient health, should both be observing a natural fast, such as is done before the reception of Holy Communion.[43] This prescription is the same as that contained in the Roman Ritual.[44]

In the early days of the Church a general law required fasting both from the minister of baptism and also from the subject who received baptism. This practice was introduced no doubt with the custom of administering baptism on the vigils of Easter and Pentecost. A Council held in Mainz in 1549 still insisted that priests show proper respect

41 Cappello, *De Sacramentis*, III, n. 558; Ayrinhac, *Marriage Legislation*, p. 185; Bouuaert-Simenon, *Manuale Juris Canonici*, II, n. 48.

42 Bouuaert-Simenon, *op. cit.*, II, n. 283.

43 Canon 753, § 1. Tam sacerdotem qui adultos baptizaturus est, quam ipsos adultos qui sani sint, decet esse ieiunos.

44 Tit. II, c. 3, *de baptismo adultorum*, nn. 7 et 8.

for the sacrament of baptism by administering it in the morning, and not in the afternoon after eating and drinking.[45]

Since canon 753, § 1, states merely that it is becoming to observe such a fast, no strict obligation is thereby expressed. In canon 753, § 2, however, there is a strict obligation imposed upon the subject of baptism to receive Holy Communion as soon as possible after the reception of baptism. Hence, whenever possible the subject of baptism should be fasting when baptized in order that he may receive Holy Communion immediately thereafter.

Today, however, because of varied conditions it is frequently difficult for people to be baptized and to receive Holy Communion on the same day. So quite often adults are baptized in the evening and then receive Holy Communion the following morning. Canonists sanction this practice on the score that even though canon 753, § 2, uses the word "*statim*" in relation to the time in which the obligation to receive Holy Communion is to be fulfilled, yet all it intends to imply is that the reception must take place as soon as possible. For if the legislator intended to demand that the reception of Holy Communion follow immediately upon the administration of baptism, then canon 753, § 1, would necessarily have to demand and not merely to recommend that the subject be fasting. Hence in those cases wherein the subject finds it difficult to be baptized and receive Holy Communion on the same day canonists permit him to be baptized in the evening, since the obligation to be fasting for the reception of baptism is not a strict one, and since reception at this time assures an early fulfillment of the strict obligation to receive Holy Communion as soon as possible after the reception of baptism.[46]

[45] Canon 16—Mansi, XXXII, 1408.

[46] E. Leroux, "Les Baptêmes d'Adultes,"—*Revue Ecclésiastique de Liege*, XVII (1925-1926), 341-352; Davis, *Moral Theology*, III, 55-56.

ART. 6. REGISTRATION OF THE BAPTISM

Since the Code has made it obligatory upon pastors to maintain a baptismal register,[47] there logically follows an obligation to register therein the baptisms performed in the parish.[48] The importance of this registration cannot be overemphasized.[49]

Throughout the Code reference is constantly made solely to the pastor as the one who is obliged personally and *sub gravi* to maintain the parochial records. In consequence the authors assert that he alone should attend to the inscriptions which are to be made in the record of baptism.[50] They base his responsibility upon the fact that this obligation has been placed upon him in view of his established capacity to act as a duly qualified and competent witness in the Church. The only admitted exceptions to the personal fulfillment of this obligation are physical and mental inability or absence from home. In such cases the duty devolves on the priest in charge of the parish, or, if no particular priest had been placed in charge, on the one who solemnly administered the sacrament.[51]

[47] Canon 470, § 1. Habeat parochus libros paroeciales, idest librum baptizatorum, . . .

[48] Canon 777, § 1. Parochi debent nomina baptizatorum, mentione facta de ministro, parentibus ac patrinis, de loco ac die collati baptismi, in baptismali libro sedulo et sine ulla mora referre. Cf. *Rituale Romanum*, Tit. II, c. 2, *ordo baptismi parvulorum*, n. 34.

[49] It is unnecessary to discuss in detail how the entries should be made, for a special thesis has been written which treats of such matter. Cf. O'Rourke, *Parish Registers*. Therein are contained instructions on how to register the names of illegitimates as well as the names of children who are born of a *matrimonium conscientiae*. With reference to the questions that attend the registration of the names of illegitimate children one may also consult: McDevitt, *Legitimacy and Legitimation*, The Catholic University of America Canon Law Studies, n. 138 (Washington, D. C.: The Catholic University of America Press, 1941).

[50] Cappello, *De Sacramentis*, I, n. 188; Bouuaert-Simenon, *Manuale Juris Canonici*, II, n. 54; Vermeersch-Creusen, *Epitome*, II, n. 55.

[51] Murphy, "Parish Records"—*AER*, LXV (1921), 1-12.

The question immediately arises as to what part the parish assistant or vicar cooperator has in these affairs. Certainly from common law he has no right or duty in this regard.[52] Such a lack of juridical capacity arises as a natural consequence from the denial that a parish assistant holds an ecclesiastical office. This denial is made by the authors on the score that such an assistant enjoys only delegated powers, and that delegated powers cannot form the jurisdictional content which is associated with and inherent in an office that contains jurisdictional powers.[53] De Meester,[54] while explicitly declaring that this duty belongs to the pastor, adds that the care of such details is usually entrusted to the curate. Such a practice cannot be condemned juridically, since the determination of the assistant's rights and duties is left in the hands of the diocesan statutes, the letters of appointment from the Ordinary and the pastor's commission. Hence any difficulties from a practical standpoint may easily be removed through these agencies. Finally, De Meester [55] avers that these acts belong to the secondary class of parochial functions, and he allows the curate to presume the pastor's permission when the provisions of canon 476, § 6, have not been sufficiently utilized to care for a given situation.

When a pastor deputes another priest to baptize within his church, the pastor himself should make the entry in the register and note the fact of deputation. If the deputed minister should make the inscription, then the pastor should at least sign the register.[56]

[52] Augustine, *Commentary*, VII, 257; Chelodi, *Ius de Personis*, n. 231.

[53] Cf. Bastnagel, *The Appointment of Parochial Adjutants and Assistants*, The Catholic University of America Canon Law Studies, n. 58 (Washington, D. C.: The Catholic University of America, 1930), p. 144.

[54] *Juris Canonici et Juris Canonico-Civilis Compendium*, II, n. 887.

[55] *Op. cit.*, II, n. 892.

[56] Vermeersch-Creusen, *Epitome*, II, n. 55.

If the proper pastor does not confer the sacrament or is not present at the administration, and if the baptism is conferred in another parish church, it is the duty of the minister to bring full knowledge of his administration to the proper pastor as soon as possible, either personally or by mail.[57] Moreover, from a private response of the Sacred Congregation of the Council it is evident that the actual registration should take place in the parish where the sacrament was administered, and that a simple notification should be sent to the pastor of the territory where the recipient has his domicile.[58] Though in view of this response the domiciliary pastor would not be bound to enter such baptisms in his own register, still it would be proper for him to preserve at least some official register for the names of parishioners who were baptized elsewhere, since such a record may later eliminate worry as to whether or not a person was baptized.[59]

If a lay person performs private baptism he is bound by canon 778 to notify the proper domiciliary pastor. The canon makes no mention of the sending of a report to the pastor of the place in which the sacrament was administered. However, in view of the private response referred to above, the opinion of Fanfani,[60] namely, that it is sufficient for the lay person to inform the local pastor, so that he in turn can send a simple notification of the ceremony to the proper pastor of the subject, gains added weight.

A separate book, if necessary, should be kept for the registration of the baptisms of persons who belong to another

[57] Canon 778. Si baptismus nec a proprio parocho nec eo praesente administratus fuerit, minister de ipso collato quamprimum proprium ratione domicilii parochum baptizati certiorem reddat.

[58] S. C. Conc., 31 ian. 1927—quoted in Bouscaren, *Canon Law Digest*, II (2nd printing, 1938), 74. This response is not contained in the *AAS*.

[59] *Irish Ecclesiastical Record*, XXXV (1930), 417.

[60] *De Iure Parochorum*, n. 244, D.

rite,[61] and the proper pastor of such persons should be informed.[62] But scarcely ever will the number of such cases in the ordinary parish demand a separate register, and so the usual book may be used with a notation made therein concerning the fact of the different rite of the recipient.

Canon 777, § 1, mentions that the entry should be made "*sedulo et sine ulla mora.*" This is to say that in manner the entry should be made to include all the canonically prescribed information, set forth clearly and legibly.[63] The time within which the entry is to be made in the register is not determined in a mathematically precise manner, for various circumstances which attend the conferring of the baptism may call for some extension of the time within which the required entry is to be made. In the ordinary case, however, the recording of the fact that the baptism was conferred should follow forthwith upon the administration of the sacrament.[64] The Roman Ritual directs that the names of the one baptized and of the sponsors, along with the other items relating to the conferred baptism, be accurately entered in the baptismal register according to the duly prescribed form, even before the sponsors have left the church.[65] When delay is necessary Augustine does not permit more than a day to intervene.[66] O'Rourke contends that such an opinion is too stringent.[67] He advocates a wider interpretation in view of the fact that the law simply intends to prevent such undue delay as would result in the

61 Augustine, *Commentary*, IV, 95.

62 S. C. de Prop. Fide, decr., 6 oct. 1863, sub C, a—*Fontes*, n. 4859.

63 Augustine, *Commentary*, IV, 95; Blat, *Commentarium*, Lib. III, pars I, n. 68.

64 Blat, *loc cit.*

65 Tit. II, c. 2, *ordo baptismi parvulorum*, n. 34.

66 *Loc. cit.*

67 *Parish Registers*, p. 47.

neglect of the entry, or in the loss of the requisite information, with possible prejudicial consequences for the one baptized.

With regard to the time within which a transmission of the notification of the baptism is to be made to the proper pastor, O'Rourke [68] believes that three or four days is the widest extension of time that can be granted. Others are content with excluding voluntary and unnecessary procrastination.[69] Blat, though he stresses the gravity of the obligation, is nevertheless of the opinion that a few days' delay ordinarily constitutes a violation which does not amount to more than a venially sinful matter. He adds, however, that at times such a delay may easily become the occasion of a gravely sinful matter, particularly if the withholding of knowledge concerning the administered baptism, or also if the lack of its certification, invites imminent danger or likely harm for the parties in whose interest and for whose benefit the records must be completely entered and kept.[70] The transfer of such a notification can be made directly to the proper pastor, or, especially when there is question of another diocese, through the curia.[71] This notification takes the form of an official document with pastoral signature and parochial seal, and should not be a merely private letter.

It seems unnecessary to mention that the very nature of the parish registers requires that the persons who handle them should be in some official capacity. The Code itself cautions pastors to be careful lest the records fall into the hands of extraneous persons.[72] The necessary precautions

[68] *Op. cit.*, p. 49.

[69] Augustine, *Commentary*, V, 312; Blat, *Commentarium*, Lib. III, pars I, n. 506.

[70] *Op. cit.*, Lib. III, pars I, n. 69.

[71] Augustine, *Commentary*, V, 313.

[72] Canon 470, § 1.

for the safe-keeping of these records obviously forbid that the care of them be entrusted to sacristans, housekeepers, Sisters, etc. Furthermore, the practice of allowing them to lie about the rectory or elsewhere, perhaps even in open view, where domestics and others may have access to them and may at their desire inspect them, must be regarded as equally disallowed.[73]

If the pastor does not attend to the making of the proper entries in, or to the securing of the requisite custody of, the baptismal registers, the Ordinary has full power to determine the extent of the penalty to be imposed, but in this determination of an appropriate penalty he will, of course, be guided by a prudent judgment regarding the gravity of the fault.[74] In the event that the pastor or anyone who legitimately has the custody of the records commits acts which prevent the registers from giving clear and accurate testimony, the Ordinary is empowered to deprive such persons of their office or to inflict other grave penalties according to the gravity of the offense.[75] A refusal to draw up a baptismal record, to transmit it, or to exhibit the register to one who rightfully asks to inspect it, is punishable by privation of office or suspension from the same, together with a pecuniary fine proportionate to the offense.[76]

ART. 7. STOLE FEES

A complete discussion of the theory of stole fees with reference to the reason for their existence, the obligation of offering them, the laudable customs which determine them, and the safeguards to be invoked for the sake of keeping them free from any simoniacal aspect is out of place here.

[73] Augustine, *Commentary*, II, 555.

[74] Canon 2383.

[75] Canon 2406, § 1.

[76] Canon 2406, § 2.

Unnecessary also is a treatise on the historical development and evolution of baptismal offerings in particular. Work in detail on these matters has already been ably furnished.[77]

Of interest in this thesis is the fact that offerings are made on the occasion of baptism, and hence it remains to determine the rights which the individual ministers have with regard to such offerings.

The administration of solemn baptism is a parochial function,[78] but nowhere does the Code state that parochial functions must have a stole fee attached to them. Hence the silence of the legislator in regard to such offerings for baptism is clearly an indication that, if they are to exist legitimately, then they must be determined by other means.

In the United States the enactments of the Baltimore Councils are of particular interest, though for the greater part they were but generalizations. The VI Provincial Council (1846) [79] strictly forbade pastors to baptize the members of another parish or diocese whenever it was convenient for such people to receive the sacrament from their own pastor. The II Plenary Council (1866) [80] prohibited the demanding of money for the administration of the sacraments, but permitted the acceptance of voluntary offerings at the time of baptism. It likewise directed bishops, with the advice of their priests, to establish in their next synod, or any similarly serviceable occasion, a just method for the distribution of the revenue accruing from the administration of baptism and matrimony among the clergy residing in the same rectory, due consideration, of course, being given for

[77] Ferry, *Stole Fees*, The Catholic University of America Canon Law Studies, n. 59 (Washington, D. C.: The Catholic University of America Press, 1930), pp. 10-30.

[78] Canon 462, 1°.

[79] Decr. IV—Mansi, XLIII, 7.

[80] *Acta et Decreta*, n. 221.

the greater right and graver duties of the pastor.[81] For some reason or other this suggestion was disregarded in many dioceses. In the III Plenary Council (1884) [82] the impossibility and inexpediency of having a uniform law on stole fees was recognized and asserted. Each bishop was admonished to decide this matter for his own territory, either in diocesan synod, or otherwise, with the counsel of his diocesan consultors. Whatever schedule of fees they devised was to be submitted to the Holy See for approval.

Today stole fees can be determined by the provincial council. Pastors have no authority to depart from these norms, and should they exact more than custom or statute decrees they are bound to restitution.[83] This obligation binds in justice. However, it is not the whole offering that is to be returned, but only that part of it which is in excess of the authorized claim. Though the delinquent priest in such a case does not incur the penalties imposed by canon 2371, yet he does render himself liable for the penalties of canon 2408.[84] Voluntary offerings in excess of the customary fee may be accepted. They must result from the generosity of the faithful; the minister is not permitted either directly or indirectly to ask for more than the customary fee.[85] Moreover, though a priest has a right to the stole fees as determined by the Provincial Council, yet he should not refuse the administration of the sacraments to those who are unable [86] or unwilling to pay.

Primarily stole fees belong to the pastor. The assistant's right to participate in stole fees depends upon custom,

[81] *Acta et Decreta*, n. 94.

[82] *Acta et Decreta*, nn. 293-294.

[83] Canons 463, § 2; 1507.

[84] Fanfani, *De Iure Parochorum*, n. 182.

[85] Canon 736.

[86] Canon 463, § 4.

diocesan statute, episcopal decree or the will of his pastor. For, while the common law assigns no share to parochial assistants,[87] yet the II Plenary Council of Baltimore (1866) recommended the custom of sharing the stole fees with the assistants. But even at this late date such a custom cannot be said to have been universally adopted in the United States.

Chaplains, whether they serve in military, naval or hospital duties, have the right to the stole fee attached to any baptism which they perform licitly in virtue of their position.[88]

In the determination of the proper recipient of the stole fee it may be stated generically that every pastor has an absolute right to the stole fee attached to any baptism which can be licitly performed solely in his parochial church. Hence, even though a pastor invade the territory of another in order to baptize one of his own subjects who could easily and without delay return to his proper parish for baptism, such an act does not deprive the pastor who so baptizes of his right to the stole fee, despite his illicit procedure in the case. Also the pastors who by virtue of a privative or cumulative legal prescription baptize persons who reside in another parish have a right to the stipend. Likewise the one who by custom or statute is entitled to baptize all the converts whom he instructs shares the full right of receiving the offering.

It is to be noted that even though a pastor grant permission for another to baptize in his parish church, such a permission does not imply the surrender of his right to the stole fee. There is question of a twofold right—the pastoral right to baptize and the pastoral right to receive the stole fee. Hence there must be special mention of the yielding

87 S. C. C., *Lucana*, 17 dec. 1904—*ASS*, XXXVII (1904-1905), 701.

88 Ferry, *Stole Fees*, p. 47.

of this latter right before the one who officiates can justify any retention of the stole fee. Indeed, even if the donor gives more than the customary fee, the excess belongs to the pastor, unless it is certain that the donor intended the surplus amount in the offering for the minister himself personally. This intention on the part of the donor is not to be credulously presumed; it must be determined either from express or other unequivocal indications.[89]

In all cases wherein the minister assists without legal right the stole fee is to be returned to the proper pastor. When a question of restitution involves a plurality of pastors, Ferry suggests that it should be returned to the proper pastors in the same fashion in which the due parochial portion of a funeral perquisite must be returned.

> If therefore the child is born in one of its proper parishes and is illicitly baptized elsewhere, it would seem that the fee should be returned to the pastor of the parish where the birth occurred. If the child is born outside its proper parishes and is illicitly baptized because the conditions of inconvenience and delay are not present, it would seem that the fees should be returned to, and divided equally among, all and only those of its proper pastors to which it could have been brought conveniently and within the proper time.[90]

A final question may be raised. It concerns the administration of baptism in a case of necessity when there is no possibility either of securing the proper pastor or of obtaining his express permission. It is naturally assumed in this case that a solemn baptism may lawfully be administered in view of the proper pastor's rightfully presumed permission. To whom does the stole fee yield: to the proper pastor, or to the ministering priest? The authorities are not in unison in their attempted solution.

[89] Canon 463, § 3.

[90] *Stole Fees*, pp. 66-67.

It is not without profit to subjoin here the following statement of Ferry:

> Theoretically, therefore, it would seem that the offering must be ceded to the proper pastor even when another acts from necessity. Practically there is no obligation to follow this. As a matter of fact, not only in cases of necessity, but in other instances wherein common law permits others to assist without securing the pastor's permission, the obligation to refund the fee cannot be urged.[91]

[91] *Op. cit.*, p. 54.

CONCLUSIONS

(1) That the administration of solemn baptism in the early Church was reserved to the bishop, because even then it was implicitly considered, as the decretalists later explicitly declared, that the minister of this sacrament had to be *de iure* and *ex efficio* competent. Only the bishops, since they alone exercised true pastoral care, possessed the latter requirement. Priests and deacons, because they needed episcopal authorization or permission before they could exercise their power of orders, were but extraordinary ministers.

(2) That the priests in time became the ordinary ministers, not because greater power was attributed to their sacerdotal orders than previously, but because by reason of the parishes entrusted to their care they had become competent *ex officio.* Hence the insistence in the late centuries upon the fact that the right to baptize is parochial, and the duty to do so pastoral.

(3) That the administration of private baptism was never restricted by the Church with regard to the minister. All that was required for lawfulness was the existence of a real necessity and the correct use of the proper matter and form. Even outside of necessity, although such a practice was necessarily condemned, anyone could administer valid baptism.

(4) That the errors regarding the validity of baptisms administered by heretics, schismatics, pagans and Jews arose both from a misunderstanding of the minister's instrumentality in the constitutive formation of a sacrament and from a failure to distinguish between valid and licit administration. Thus, when Saint Augustine had clarified

these elementary concepts of the sacramental system, there was a noticeable decline of heretical doctrine concerning the minister and a more decisive acceptance in general of the validity of such baptisms when they were properly conferred.

(5) That the erroneous statements concerning the invalidity of baptisms performed by unbaptized priests were not the result of authentic conciliar legislation, but arose spuriously from two distinct texts found separately in the Penitential of Theodore of Canterbury and in the Penitential of Egbert of York.

(6) When an adult is received into the Church by conditional baptism the absolution from censure in the external forum is unnecessary.

(7) In the reception of adult converts from heresy the necessary abjuration of heresy is to be made in the presence of the local Ordinary or his delegate and two witnesses according to the norm prescribed in canon 2314, § 2, and not merely in the presence of a priest according to the norm contained in the rescript of the Holy Office to the Bishop of Philadelphia, on July 20, 1859.

(8) Any rights which chaplains of institutions have to baptize solemnly arise from special dispositions made in this regard at the time of their appointment by the Ordinary. In such instances it is necessary that the chapel in which the baptisms are to be administered have the status of a church or a public oratory.

(9) It is most probable that the amniotic fluid does not constitute a valid matter for baptism. Since it cannot be stated definitely that such a fluid is certainly invalid, in a case of necessity, when no other matter can be had, a doctor could use this fluid for conditional baptism; but he is not bound to do so.

(10) One cannot adopt the attitude that all non-Catholic baptisms are either invalid or doubtfully valid, so that all converts are to be baptized either absolutely or conditionally. A superficial assurance regarding the validity or invalidity of their baptisms can hardly ever be accepted. Each individual case must be examined carefully in respect to where, when, how and by whom the baptism was conferred. Such an investigation is not merely recommended; it is solemnly insisted upon by the Roman Congregations.

(11) It would be possible for the same person to be the minister and the sponsor in the same baptism. However, in such a case one must use a proxy to act as sponsor during the ceremony.

(12) If an unbaptized person administers baptism, no spiritual relationship is contracted between the minister and the recipient of the sacrament.

BIBLIOGRAPHY

Sources

Acta Apostolicae Sedis, Commentarium Officiale, Romae, 1909—

Acta et Decreta Concilii Plenarii Baltimorensis Tertii A. D. MDCCCLXXXIV, Baltimorae: Typis Ioannis Murphy Sociorum, 1886.

Acta et Decreta Sacrorum Conciliorum Recentiorum, Collectio Lacensis, 7 vols., Friburgi Brisgoviae: Herder and Co., 1870-1890.

Acta Sanctae Sedis, 41 vols., Romae, 1865-1908.

Bouscaren, T. Lincoln, *Canon Law Digest,* 3 vols., Milwaukee: The Bruce Publishing Co., 1934-1941.

Codex Iuris Canonici Pii X Pontificis Maximi iussu digestus Benedicti XV auctoritate promulgatus, Romae: Typis Polyglottis Vaticanis, 1934.

Codicis Iuris Canonici Fontes cura Emi. Petri Card. Gasparri Editi, 9 vols., Romae: Typis Polyglottis Vaticanis, 1923-1939. (Vol. VII, VIII et IX ed. *cura et studie Emi. Iustiniani Card. Serédi.*)

Collectanea S. Congregationis de Propaganda Fide, Romae, 1893.

Collectanea S. Congregationis de Propaganda Fide, 2 vols., Romae: Typographia Polyglotta S. C. de Propaganda Fide, 1907.

Concilii Plenarii Baltimorensis II., in Ecclesiae Metropolitana Baltimorensi, a die VII. ad diem XXI. Octobris, A. D., MDCCCLXVI., Habiti, et a Sede Apostolica Recogniti, Acta et Decreta, editio altera, Baltimorae: Ioannes Murphy, 1894.

Corpus Iuris Canonici, ed. Lipsiensis 2., Aemilius Ludouicus Richter—Aemilius Friedberg, ed. anastatice repetita, 2 vols., Lipsiae: Tauchnitz, 1928.

Corpus Iuris Civilis, vol. I, *Institutiones*—recognovit P. Krueger; vol. II, *Codex Iustinianus*—recognovit et retractavit P. Krueger; vol. III, *Novellae Constitutiones*—R. Schoell; opus Schoelli morte interceptum absolvit G. Kroll, Berolini, 1928-1929.

Corpus Scriptorum Ecclesiasticorum Latinorum, 68 vols. incomplete, Vindobonae, 1866—

Friedberg, Aemilius, *Quinque Compilationes Antiquae,* Lipsiae, 1882.

Hardouin, Jean, *Acta Conciliorum et Epistolae Decretales ac Constitutiones Summorum Pontificum,* 12 vols., Parisiis, 1715.

Jaffé, Philippus, *Regesta Pontificum Romanorum ab condita Ecclesia ad annum post Christum natum MCXCVIII,* 2nd ed. (Kaltenbrunner, Ewald, Loewenfeld), 2 vols. in 1, Lipsiae, 1885-1888.

Krueger, P., *Codex Theodosianus,* Berolini: apud Weidmannos, 1923-1926.

Labbe-Cossart, *Sacrosancta Concilia ad regiam editionem exacta,* 15 vols. in 16, Parisiis, 1671-1674.

Mansi, J. D., *Sacrorum Conciliorum Nova et Amplissima Collectio,* 53 vols. in 59, Parisiis, 1901-1927.

Migne, J. P., *Patrologiae Cursus Completus, Series Graeca,* 161 vols., Parisiis, 1856-1866.

——, *Patrologiae Cursus Completus, Series Latina,* 221 vols., Parisiis, 1884-1864.

Monumenta Germaniae Historica, 188 vols. incomplete, Hanoverae, 1826–

Scriptores Rerum Merovingicarum, (*SSRM*), 7 vols., 1884-1920.

T. I, ed. W. Arndt et B. Krusch, 1884.

Leges, T. I, ed. G. H. Pertz, 1835; T. II², ed. G. H. Pertz, 1837.

Leges in 4°, Sectio II (*Capitularia Regum Francorum*), T. I, ed. A. Boretius, 1883; Sectio III (*Concilia*), T. I, ed. F. Maassen, 1893; T. II, ed. A. Werminghoff, 1904.

Epistolae (*Ep*), 7 vols., 1887-1928. T. I, ed. Paulus Ewald, 1887.

Pallottini, S., *Collectio omnium Conclusionum et Resolutionum Quae in causis propositis apud Sacram Congregationem Cardinalium S. Concilii Tridentini interpretum Prodierunt ab eius institutione anno MCLXIV ad MDCCCLX, distinctis titulis alphabetico ordine per materias digestas,* 18 vols., Romae, 1868-1893.

Pontificale Romanum, 3 vols., Ratisbonae, 1893.

Rituale Romanum, Pauli V Pontificis Maximi iussu editum aliorumque Pontificum cura recognitum atque auctoritate SSmi. D. N. Pii Papae XI ad normam Codicis Iuris Canonici accomodatum, prima ed., Ratisbonae, 1925.

Schroeder, H. J., *Canons and Decrees of the Council of Trent: Original Text with English Translation,* St. Louis: B. Herder Book Co., 1941.

AUTHORS

Aertnys, Jos.—Damen, C. A., *Theologia Moralis,* 13th ed., 2 vols., Taurini: Marietti, 1939.

Andreae, Ioannes, *In Quinque Decretalium Libros Commentaria,* Venetiis, 1581.

Aquinas, St. Thomas, *Summa Theologica,* editio altera Romana, 6 vols., Romae, 1894.

Ayrinhac, H. A., *General Legislation in the New Code of Canon Law,* New York: Longmans, Green and Co., 1925.

——, *Legislation on the Sacraments,* New York: Longmans, Green and Co., 1928.

Ayrinhac, H. A.—Lydon, P. J., *Marriage Legislation,* revised edition, New York: Benziger Brothers, 1936.

[Bachofen], Charles Augustine, *A Commentary on the New Code of Canon Law,* 8 vols. (Vol. IV, 6th ed.), St. Louis: B. Herder Book Co., 1931.

——, *The Pastor according to the New Code of Canon Law,* 2nd ed., St. Louis: B. Herder Book Co., 1924.

Barbosa, Augustinus, *Collectanea Decretorum, tam Veterum quam Recentiorum, in Ius Pontificium Universum*, 6 vols. in 3, Lugduni, 1716.

Basso, Franciscus, *Bibliotheca Iuris Canonico-Civilis Practica*, 4 vols., Mutinae, 1757.

Bastnagel, Clement, *The Appointment of Parochial Adjutants and Assistants*, The Catholic University of America Canon Law Studies, n. 58, Washington, D. C.: The Catholic University of America, 1930.

Benedict XIV, *De Synodo Dioecesana*, 2 vols., Parmae, 1764.

Bingham, Joseph, *The Works of the Reverend Joseph Bingham*, edited by the Reverend Robert Bingham, 10 vols., Oxford: Oxford University Press, 1885. (Vol. IX, *The History of Lay Baptism.*)

Blat, Albertus, *Commentarium Textus Codicis Iuris Canonici*, 5 vols. in 6, Romae: ex Typographia Pontificia in Instituto Pii IX, 1921-1927.

Böckhn, Placidus, *Commentarius in Ius Canonicum Universum*, 5 vols. in 3, Salisburgi, 1776.

Boich, Henricus, *In Quinque Decretalium Libros Commentarius*, Venetiis, 1576.

Bonnar, A., *The Catholic Doctor*, 2nd ed., New York: P. J. Kenedy and Sons, 1939.

Bouix, Dominicus, *Tractatus de Parocho*, 3rd ed., Parisiis, 1880.

Bouuaert, F. C.—Simenon, G., *Manuale Juris Canonici*, 3rd ed., 3 vols., Gandae et Leodii: Dessain, 1930.

Caponi, Julius, *Institutiones Canonicae*, 2nd ed., 2 vols. in 1, Coloniae Allobrogum, 1734.

Cappello, F. M., *Tractatus Canonico-Moralis de Censuris*, 3rd ed., Romae: Marietti, 1933.

——, *Tractatus Canonico-Moralis de Sacramentis*, 3 vols. (Vol. I, 2nd ed.), Romae: Marietti, 1928.

Cerato, P., *Censurae Vigentes Ipso Facto a Codice Iuris Canonici Excerptae*, editio secunda recognita, Patavii, 1921.

Chardon, C., *Histoire des Sacraments*, 6 vols., Parisiis, 1745.

Chelodi, Ioannes, *Ius de Personis*, 2nd ed., Tridenti, 1927.

Connolly, Nicholas P., *The Canonical Erection of Parishes*, The Catholic University of America Canon Law Studies, n. 114, Washington, D. C.: The Catholic University of America, 1938.

Conran, Edward, *The Interdict*, The Catholic University of America Canon Law Studies, n. 56, Washington, D. C.: The Catholic University of America, 1930.

Costello, John, *Domicile and Quasi-Domicile*, The Catholic University of America Canon Law Studies, n. 60, Washington, D. C.: The Catholic University of America, 1930.

Corblet, Jules, *Histoire du Sacrament de Baptême*, 2 vols., Genève, 1881.

Davis, Henry, *Moral and Pastoral Theology*, 3rd ed., 4 vols., New York: Sheed and Ward, 1938.

De Meester, A., *Juris Canonici et Juris Canonico-Civilis Compendium*, nova edito, 3 vols. in 4, Brugis, 1921-1928.

De Smet, A., *De Sponsalibus et Matrimonio*, 4th ed., Brugis: Car. Beyaert, 1927.

Duchesne, Louis, *Histoire ancienne de l'église*, 3 vols., Paris, 1906.

Duskie, John, *The Canonical Status of the Orientals in the United States*, The Catholic University of America Canon Law Studies, n. 48, Washington, D. C.: The Catholic University of America, 1928.

Ermoni, V., *Le baptême dans l'église primitive*, Paris, 1904.

Fanfani, L., *De Iure Parochorum*, Romae: Marietti, 1924.

Feldhaus, A. H., *Oratories*, The Catholic University of America Canon Law Studies, n. 42, Washington, D. C.: The Catholic University of America, 1927.

Fermosini, N., *Opera Omnia*, ed. altera, 14 vols., Coloniae Allobrogum, 1741. (Vol. III, *De Officiis et Sacris Ecclesiae*; Vol. XI, *Criminalium*.)

Ferry, Wm., *Stole Fees*, The Catholic University of America Canon Law Studies, n. 59, Washington, D. C.: The Catholic University of America, 1930.

Fink, L. G., *Graduate Nurses*, 3rd ed., New York: Paulist Press, 1938.

Funk, F. X., *Didascalia et Constitutiones Apostolorum*, 2 vols., Paderbornae, 1905.

——, *Opera Patrum Apostolicorum*, 2 vols., Tubingae, 1887.

Genicot, E.—Salsmans, I., *Institutiones Theologiae Moralis*, 12th ed., 2 vols., Lovanii: Museum Lessianum, 1931.

Giraldi, Ubaldus, *Expositio Iuris Pontificii iuxta Recentiorem Ecclesiae Disciplinam*, nova Romana editio, 2 vols., Romae, 1830.

Grana-Nieto, Antonius, *Catena Iurium Utriusque Iurisprudentiae*, Lugduni, 1678.

Hatch, J., *The Organization of the Early Christian Church*, London: Longmans, Green and Co., 1918.

Hinschius, Paul, *Decretales Pseudo-Isidorianae et Capitula Angilrammi*, Lipsiae, 1863.

Hostiensis, Cardinalis (Henricus de Segusia), *In Quinque Libros Decretalium Commentaria*, 3 vols., Venetiis, 1581.

——, *Summa Aurea*, Venetiis, 1570.

Hyland, Francis, *Excommunication*, The Catholic University of America Canon Law Studies, n. 49, Washington, D. C.: The Catholic University of America, 1928.

Imbart de la Tour, *Les Paroisses Rurales du IVe au VIe siècle*, Paris: A. Piccard et Fils, 1900.

Jordanus, Pax, *Elucubrationes Diversae*, 3 vols., Coloniae Allobrogum et Lugduni, 1729.

Kearney, Richard, *Sponsors at Baptism according to the Code of Canon Law*, The Catholic University of America Canon Law Studies, n. 30, Washington, D. C.: The Catholic University of America, 1925.

King, James I., *The Administration of the Sacraments to Dying Non-Catholics*, The Catholic University of America Canon Law Studies, n. 23, Washington, D. C.: The Catholic University of America Press, 1924.

Konings, A., *Theologia Moralis*, 7th ed., New York, 1889.

Koudelka, Charles, *Pastors, Their Rights and Duties according to the New Code of Canon Law*, The Catholic University of America Canon Law Studies, n. 11, Washington, D. C.: The Catholic University of America, 1921.

Labauche, L., *The Three Sacraments of Initiation*, New York: Benziger and Co., 1922.

La Croix, Claudius, *Theologia Moralis*, 3 vols., Venetiis, 1761.

Lancelotti, Ioannes, *Institutiones Iuris Canonici*, Venetiis, 1704.

Lehmkuhl, A., *Theologia Moralis*, 9th ed., 2 vols., Friburgi Brisgoviae, 1898.

Lesêtre, Henri, *La Paroisse*, 3rd ed., Paris: V. Lecoffre, 1908.

Leurenius, Petrus, *Forum Ecclesiasticum*, 3 vols., Venetiis, 1729.

Mabillon, I., *Musaeum Italicum*, 2 vols., Parisiis, 1724.

MacKenzie, Eric, *The Delict of Heresy*, The Catholic University of America Canon Law Studies, n. 77, Washington, D. C.: The Catholic University of America, 1932.

Maroto, Philippus, *Institutiones Iuris Canonici ad Normam Novi Codicis*, 3rd ed., 2 vols., Romae, 1921.

Martene, Edmundus, *De Antiquis Ecclesiae Ritibus*, 4 vols., Rotomagi, 1700.

Merkelbach, B. H., *Summa Theologiae Moralis*, ed. alt., 3 vols., Parisiis: Desclée, de Brouwer et Cie, 1939.

Mothon, Jos. Pie, *Institutions canoniques*, 3 vols., Paris: Desclée, de Brouwer et Cie, 1922-1924.

McDevitt, Gilbert, *Legitimacy and Legitimation*, The Catholic University of America Canon Law Studies, n. 138, Washington, D. C.: The Catholic University of America Press, 1941.

McNeil — Gamer, *Medieval Handbook of Penance*, Records of Civilization: Sources and Studies, edited under the auspices of the Dept. of History, Columbia University, n. 29, New York: Columbia University Press, 1938.

Nicolius, Hieronymus, *Lucubrationes Utriusque Iuris*, Romae, 1662.

Noldin, H. — Schmitt, A., *Summa Theologiae Moralis*, 26th ed., 3 vols., Ratisbonae: Fridericum Pustet, 1940.

Ojetti, B., *Commentarium in Codicem Iuris Canonici*, 4 vols., Romae: Universitas Gregoriana, 1927-1931.

O'Rourke, James, *Parish Registers*, The Catholic University of America Canon Law Studies, n. 88, Washington, D. C.: The Catholic University of America, 1934.

Pallavicino, Sforza, *Istoria del Concilio di Trento*, 4 vols., Romae, 1833.

Payen, P. G., *Casus de Baptismo*, Zi-Ka-Wei, 1920.

Petrani, Alexius, *De Relatione Iuridica inter Diversos Ritus in Ecclesia Catholica*, Romae: Marietti, 1930.

Petri Lombardi Libri IV Sententiarum, studio et cura PP. Collegii S. Bonaventurae in lucem editi, Ad Claras Aquas (Quaracchi), 2nd ed., 2 vols., Ex Typographia Collegii S. Bonaventurae, 1916.

Petrovits, Joseph, *The New Church Law on Matrimony*, The Catholic University of America Canon Law Studies, n. 6, Washington, D. C.: The Catholic University of America, 1919.

Pignatelli, Jacobus, *Consultationes Canonicae*, 6 vols., Coloniae Allobrogum, 1700.

Pirhing, Ernricus, *Ius Canonicum Nova Methodo Explicatum*, 5 vols., Dilingae, 1674-1678.

Pruemmer, D. M., *Manuale Theologiae Moralis*, 2nd et 3rd ed., 3 vols., Friburgi Brisgoviae, 1923.

Rainer, Eligius G., *Suspension of Clerics*, The Catholic University of America Canon Law Studies, n. 111, Washington, D. C.: The Catholic University of America, 1937.

Realencyklopädie für Protestantische Theologie und Kirche, 24 vols., Leipzig, 1896-1913.

Sabetti, A. — Barrett, T., *Compendium Theologiae Moralis*, 27th ed., New York: Frederick Pustet Co., Inc., 1919.

Sandeus, Felinus, *In Decretalium Libros Quinque*, 3 vols., Venetiis, 1570.

Schmalzgrueber, Franciscus, *Ius Ecclesiasticum Universum*, 5 vols. in 12, Romae, 1843-1845.

Sipos, Stephanus, *Enchiridion Iuris Canonici*, 3rd ed., Pécs: ex Typographia "Haladás R. T.", 1936.

Sole, Iacobus, *De Delictis et Poenis*, Romae, 1920.

Tanquerey, A., *Synopsis Theologiae Dogmaticae*, 3 vols., Parisiis: Desclée et Socii, 1930-1934.

Thomassinus, Ludouicus, *Vetus et Nova Ecclesiae Disciplina*, 3 vols., Parisiis, 1688.

Toso, A., *Ad Codicem Juris Canonici...Commentaria Minora*, 5 vols., Romae: Marietti, 1920-1934.

Trombelli, Ioannes, *Tractatus de Sacramentis*, 5 vols., Bononiae, 1771.

Verano, Gaetano Felix, *Iuris Canonici Universi Commentarius Particularis*, 3 vols., Monachii, 1703.

Vermeersch, A. — Creusen, J., *Epitome Iuris Canonici*, 3 vols., Romae: Dessain, vol. I—1937, vol. II—1934, vol. III—1936.

——, *Theologia Moralis*, 3rd ed., 4 vols., Roma: Universitá Gregoriana, 1933.

Vlaming, Th. M., *Praelectiones Iuris Matrimonii*, 2 vols., Bussum in Hollandia, 1923.

Wernz, F. — Vidal, P., *Ius Canonicum*, 7 vols. in 8, Romae, 1923-1938.

Wex, Iacobus, *Ariadne Carolino-Canonica*, Dilingae, 1708.

Zoesius, Henricus, *Ius Canonicum Universum*, Venetiis, 1757.

Principal Articles

Achelis, "Die ältesten Quellen des Orientalischen Kirchenrechts"—Gebhardt-Harnack, *Texte und Untersuchungen zur Geschichte der altchristlichen Litteratur* (Leipzig, 1891), VI, pp. 61-62.

Augustine, "Hospitals—Their Chaplains, Confessors, Pastors"—*AER*, LXVI (1922), 185-192.

Böhm, "Taufe und Absolution von der Häresie bei Konversionen"—*LQS*, LXXXVI (1933), 787-792.

Bouquillon, "De la Reiteration du Baptême Conféré par les Heretiques"—*Revue des Sciences Ecclésiastiques*, XL (1879), 145-173.

Connell, "Priestly Ministry of the Essentials of Faith"—*AER*, LXXVI (1927), 570-579.

Grosam, "Der Diakon im neuen Römischen Rituale"—*LQS*, LXXIX (1926), 374-377.

——," Feierliche Taufspendung durch einen Diakon"—*LQS*, LXXVI (1923), 105-109.

Leroux, "Les Baptêmes d'Adultes"—*Revue Ecclésiastique de Liege*, XVII (1925-1926), 341-352.

Lydon, "The Minister of Baptism and Parental Consent"—*Homiletic and Pastoral Review*, XXV (1925), 285-292.

Meunier, "De Patrinis Baptismi"—*Revue Ecclésiastique de Liege*, XXV (1933-1934), 306-308.

Murphy, "Parish Records"—*AER*, LXV (1921), 1-12.

Sandalgi, "Oriental and Latin Sacramental Rites"—*AER*, LXI (1919), 225-238.

Seckel, Emil, "Studien zu Benedictus Levita—VII"—*Neues Archiv der Gesellschaft für ältere deutsche Geschichtskunde*, XXXIV (1908), 346-350.

——, "Studien zu Benedictus Levita—VIII"—*Neues Archiv*, etc., XLI (1917), 213.

Woywod, "The Legislation of the Code on Baptism"—*Homiletic and Pastoral Review*, XX (1920), 1037-1042.

Zorell, "Die Entwickelung des Parochialsystems bis zum Ende der Karolingerzeit"—*AKKR*, LXXXII (1902), 74-98 and 258-289.

Periodicals

Analecta Iuris Pontificii, Romae, 1852-1868; Parisiis, 1869-1891.

Archiv für katholisches Kirchenrecht, Innsbruck, 1857-1861; Mainz, 1862—

Australasian Catholic Record, The, Manly, 1923—

Clergy Review, The, London, 1931—

Ecclesiastical Review, The (originally *The American Ecclesiastical Review*), Philadelphia, 1889—

Gregorianum, Romae, 1920—

Homiletic and Pastoral Review, The, New York, 1900—

Irish Ecclesiastical Record, The, Dublin, 1864—
Ius Pontificium, Romae, 1921—
Neues Archiv der Gesellschaft für ältere deutsche Geschichtskunde, Berlin, 1876—
Nouvelle Revue Théologique, Paris, 1869—
Periodica de re canonica et morali, Brugis, 1905—; ab anno 1927: *Periodica de re canonica, morali, liturgica.*
Revue des Sciences Ecclésiastiques, Paris, 1860—
Revue Ecclésiastique de Liége, Leodii, 1908—
Theologisch-Praktische Quartalschrift, Linz, 1832—

ABBREVIATIONS

AAS—*Acta Apostolicae Sedis.*
AER—*The American Ecclesiastical Review.*
AKKR—*Archiv für katholisches Kirchenrecht.*
ASS—*Acta Sanctae Sedis.*
C.—*Codex Iustinianus.*
Coll.—*Collectanea S. C. de Propaganda Fide.*
Coll. Lac.—*Collectio Lacensis.*
C. Th.—*Codex Theodosianus.*
CV—*Corpus Scriptorum Ecclesiasticorum Latinorum.*
Fontes—*Codicis Iuris Canonici Fontes cura ... Gasparri editi.*
Hardouin—*Acta Conciliorum, etc.*
JE—Jaffé, *Regesta Pontificum Romanorum* (edited by Ewald: from 590-882).
JK—Jaffé, *op. cit.* (edited by Kaltenbrunner: from 0-590).
JL—Jaffé, *op. cit.* (edited by Loewenfeld: from 882-1198).
Labbe—Labbe-Cossart, *Sacrosancta Concilia, etc.*
LQS—*Theologisch-Praktische Quartalschrift*
Mansi—*Sacrorum Conciliorum Nova et Amplissima Collectio.*
MGH—*Monumenta Germaniae Historica.*
MPG—Migne, *Patrologia Graeca.*
MPL—Migne, *Patrologia Latina.*
SSRM—*Scriptores Rerum Merovingicarum.*

BIOGRAPHICAL NOTE

Joseph Francis Waldron was born September 6, 1914, at Philadelphia, Pennsylvania. After completing his grammar school education in Saint Veronica's School in the same city, he entered Northeast Catholic High School of Philadelphia. In 1929 he entered Saint Charles Seminary, Overbrook, Pennsylvania, where he received the degree of Bachelor of Arts in 1935. He was ordained to the Sacred Priesthood by Dennis Cardinal Dougherty at Philadelphia, Pennsylvania, June 3, 1939. In September of the same year he entered the Catholic University of America to pursue a course of studies in the School of Canon Law. In June, 1940, he received the degree of Bachelor of Canon Law, and in June, 1941, the degree of Licentiate in Canon Law.

ANALYTICAL INDEX

CANON LAW STUDIES

1. Freriks, Rev. Celestine A., C.PP.S., J.C.D., Religious Congregations in Their External Relations, 121 pp., 1916.
2. Galliher, Rev. Daniel M., O.P., J.C.D., Canonical Elections, 117 pp., 1917.
3. Borkowski, Rev. Aurelius L., O.F.M., J.C.D., De Confraternitatibus Ecclesiasticis, 136 pp., 1918.
4. Castillo, Rev. Cayo, J.C.D., Disertación Historico-Canonica sobre la Potestad del Cabildo en Sede Vacante o Impedida del Vicario Capitular, 99 pp., 1919 (1918).
5. Kubelbeck, Rev. William J., S.T.B., J.C.D., The Sacred Penitentiaria and its Relations to Faculties of Ordinaries and Priests, 129 pp., 1918.
6. Petrovits, Rev. Joseph, J.C., S.T.D., J.C.D., The New Church Law On Matrimony, X-461 pp., 1919.
7. Hickey, Rev. John J., S.T.B., J.C.D., Irregularities and Simple Impediments in the Uew Code of Canon Law, 100 pp., 1920.
8. Klekotka, Rev. Peter J., S.T.B., J.C.D., Diocesan Consultors, 179 pp., 1920.
9. Wanenmacher, Rev. Francis, J.C.D., The Evidence in Ecclesiastical Procedure Affecting the Marriage Bond, 1920 (Printed 1935).
10. Golden, Rev. Henry Francis, J.C.D., Parochial Benefices in the New Code, IV-119 pp., 1921 (Printed 1925).
11. Koudelka, Rev. Charles J., J.C.D., Pastors, Their Rights and Duties According to the New Code of Canon Law, 211 pp., 1921.
12. Melo, Rev. Antonius, O.F.M., J.C.D., De Exemptione Regularium, X-188 pp., 1921.
13. Schaaf, Rev. Valentine Theodore, O.F.M., S.T.B., J.C.D., The Cloister, X-180 pp., 1921.
14. Burke, Rev. Thomas Joseph, S.T.D., J.C.D., Competence in Ecclesiastical Tribunals, IV-117 pp., 1922.
15. Leech, Rev. George Leo, J.C.D., A Comparative Study of the Constitution, "Apostolicae Sedis" and the "Codex Juris Canonici," 179 pp., 1922.
16. Motry, Rev. Hubert Louis, S.T.D., J.C.D., Diocesan Faculties According to the Code of Canon Law, II-167 pp., 1922.
17. Murphy, Rev. George Lawrence, J.C.D., Delinquencies and Penalties in the Administration and Reception of the Sacraments, IV-121 pp., 1923.
18. O'Reilly, Rev. John Anthony, S.T.B., J.C.D., Ecclesiastical Sepulture in the New Code of Canon Law, II-129 pp., 1923.
19. Michalicka, Rev. Wenceslas Cyrill, O.S.B., J.C.D., Judicial Procedure in Dismissal of Clerical Exempt Religious, 107 pp., 1923.

20. Dargin, Rev. Edward Vincent, S.T.B., J.C.D., Reserved Cases According to the Code of Canon Law, IV-103, pp. 1924.
21. Godfrey, Rev. John A., S.T.B., J.C.D., The Right of Patronage According to the Code of Canon Law, 153 pp., 1924.
22. Hagedorn, Rev. Francis Edward, J.C.D., General Legislation on Indulgences, II-154 pp., 1924.
23. King, Rev. James Ignatius, J.C.D., The Administration of the Sacraments to Dying Non-Catholics, V-141 pp., 1924.
24. Winslow, Rev. Francis Joseph, O.F.M., J.C.D., Vicars and Prefects Apostolic, IV-149 pp., 1924.
25. Correa, Rev. Jose Servelion, S.T.L., J.C.D., La Potestad Legislativa de la Iglesia Catolica, IV-127 pp., 1925.
26. Dugan, Rev. Henry Francis, A.M., J.C.D., The Judiciary Department of the Diocesan Curia, 87 pp., 1925.
27. Keller, Rev. Charles Frederick, S.T.B., J.C.D., Mass Stipends, 167 pp., 1925.
28. Paschang, Rev. John Linus, J.C.D., The Sacramentals According to the Code of Canon Law, 129 pp., 1925.
29. Piontek, Rev. Cyrillus, O.F.M., S.T.B., J.C.D., De Indulto Exclaustrationis necnon Saecularizationis, XIII-289 pp., 1925.
30. Kearney, Rev. Richard Joseph, S.T.B., J.C.D., Sponsors at Baptism According to the Code of Canon Law, IV-127 pp., 1925.
31. Bartlett, Rev. Chester Joseph, A.M., LL.B., J.C.D., The Tenure of Parochial Property in the United States of America, V-108 pp., 1926.
32. Kilker, Rev. Adrian Jerome, J.C.D., Extreme Unction, V-425 pp., 1926.
33. McCormick, Rev. Robert Emmett, J.C.D., Confessors of Religious, VIII-266 pp., 1926.
34. Miller, Rev. Newton Thomas, J.C.D., Founded Masses According to the Code of Canon Law, VII-93 pp., 1926.
35. Roelker, Rev. Edward G., S.T.D., J.C.D., Principles of Privilege According to the Code of Canon Law, XI-166 pp., 1926.
36. Bakalarczyk, Rev. Richardus, M.I.C., J.U.D., De Novitiatu, VIII-208 pp., 1927.
37. Pizzuti, Rev. Lawrence, O.F.M., J.U.L., De Parochis Religiosis, 1927 (Not printed).
38. Bliley, Rev. Nicholas Martin, O.S.B., J.C.D., Altars According to the Code of Canon Law, XIX-132 pp., 1927.
39. Brown, Mr. Brendan Francis, A.B., LL.M., J.U.D., The Canonical Juristic Personality with Special Reference to Its Status in the United States of America, V-212 pp., 1927.
40. Cavanaugh, Rev. William Thomas, C.P., J.U.D., The Reservation of the Blessed Sacrament, VIII-101 pp., 1927.
41. Doheny, Rev. William J., C.S.C., A.B., J.U.D., Church Property: Modes of Acquisition, X-118 pp., 1927.
42. Feldhaus, Rev. Aloysius H., C.PP.S., J.C.D., Oratories, IX-141 pp., 1927.

43. Kelly, Rev. James Patrick, A.B., J.C.D., The Jurisdiction of the Simple Confessor, X-208 pp., 1927.
44. Neuberger, Rev. Nicholas J., J.C.D., Canon 6 or the Relation of the Codex Juris Canonici to the Preceding Legislation, V-95 pp., 1927.
45. O'Keefe, Rev. Gerald Michael, J.C.D., Matrimonial Dispensations, Powers of Bishops, Priests and Confessors, VIII-232 pp., 1927.
46. Quigley, Rev. Joseph, A.B., A.M., J.C.D., Condemned Societies, 139 pp., 1927.
47. Zaplotnik, Rev. Johannes Leo, J.C.D., De Vicariis Foraneis, X-142 pp., 1927.
48. Duskie, Rev. John Aloysius, A.B., J.C.D., The Canonical Status of the Orientals in the United States, VIII, 196 pp., 1928.
49. Hyland, Rev. Francis Edward, J.C.D., Excommunication, Its Nature, Historical Development and Effects, VIII-181 pp., 1928.
50. Reinmann, Rev. Gerald Joseph, O.M.C., J.C.D., The Third Order Secular of Saint Francis, 201 pp., 1928.
51. Schenk, Rev. Francis J., J.C.D., The Matrimonial Impediments of Mixed Religion and Disparity of Cult, XVI-318 pp., 1929.
52. Coady, Rev. John Joseph, S.T.D., J.U.D., A.M., The Appointment of Pastors, VIII-150 pp., 1929.
53. Kay, Thomas Henry, J.C.D., Competence in Matrimonial Procedure, VIII-164 pp., 1929.
54. Turner, Rev. Sidney Joseph, C.P., J.U.D., The Vow of Poverty, XLIX-217 pp., 1929.
55. Kearney, Rev. Raymond A., A.B., S.T.D., J.C.D., The Principles of Delegation, VII-149 pp., 1929.
56. Conran, Rev. Edward James, A.B., J.C.D., The Interdict, V-163 pp., 1930.
57. O'Neil, Rev. William H., J.C.D., Papal Rescripts of Favor, VII-218 pp., 1930.
58. Bastnagel, Rev. Clement Vincent, J.U.D., The Appointment of Parochial Adjutants and Assistants, XV-257 pp., 1930.
59. Ferry, Rev. William A., A.B., J.C.D., Stole Fees, V-135 pp., 1930.
60. Costello, Rev. John Michael, A.B., J.C.D., Domicile and Quasi-Domicile, VII-201 pp., 1930.
61. Kremer, Rev. Michael Nicholas, A.B., S.T.B., J.C.D., Church Support in the United States, VI-1930.
62. Angulo, Rev. Luis, C.M., J.C.D., Legislación de la Iglesia sobre la intención en la aplicación de la Santa Misa, VII-104 pp., 1931.
63. Frey, Rev. Wolfgang Norbert, O.S.B., A.B., J.C.D., The Act of Religious Profession, VIII-174 pp., 1931.
64. Roberts, Rev. James Brendan, A.B., J.C.D., The Banns of Marriage, XIV-140 pp., 1931.
65. Ryder, Rev. Raymond Aloysius, A.B., J.C.D., Simony, IX-151 pp., 1931.
66. Campagna, Rev. Angelo, Ph.D., J.U.D., Il Vicario Generale del Vescovo, VII-205 pp., 1931.

67. Cox, Rev. Joseph Godfrey, A.B., J.C.D., The Administration of Seminaries, VI-124 pp., 1931.
68. Gregory, Rev. Donald J., J.U.D., The Pauline Privilege, XV-165 pp., 1931.
69. Donohue, Rev. John F., J.C.D., The Impediment of Crime, VII-110 pp., 1931.
70. Dooley, Rev. Eugene A., O.M.I., J.C.D., Church Law On Sacred Relics, IX-143 pp., 1931.
71. Orth, Rev. Raymond Clement, O.M.C., J.C.D., The Approbation of Religious Institutes, 171 pp., 1931.
72. Pernicone, Rev. Joseph M., A.B., J.C.D., The Ecclesiastical Prohibition of Books, XII-267 pp., 1932.
73. Clinton, Rev. Connell, A.B., J.C.D., The Paschal Precept, IX-108 pp., 1932.
74. Donnelly, Rev. Francis B., A.M., S.T.L., J.C.D., The Diocesan Synod, VIII-125 pp., 1932.
75 Torrente, Rev. Camilo, C.M.F., J.C.D., Las Processiones Sagradas, V-145 pp., 1932.
76. Murphy, Rev. Edwin J., C.PP.S., J.C.D., Suspension Ex Informata Conscientia, XI-122 pp., 1932.
77. Mackenzie, Rev. Eric F., A.M., S.T.L., J.C.D., The Delict of Heresy in its Commission, Penalization, Absolution, VII-124 pp., 1932.
78. Lyons, Rev. Avitus E., S.T.B., The Collegiate Tribunal of First Instance, XI-147 pp., 1932.
79. Connolly, Rev. Thomas A., J.C.D., Appeals, XI-195 pp., 1932.
80. Sangmeister, Rev. Joseph V., A.B., J.C.D., Force and Fear as Precluding Matrimonial Consent, V-211 pp., 1932.
81. Jaeger, Rev. Leo A., A.B., J.C.D., The Administration of Vacant and Quasi-Vacant Episcopal Sees in the United States, IX-229 pp., 1932.
82. Rimlinger, Rev. Herbert T., J.C.D., Error Invalidating Matrimonial Consent, VII-79 pp., 1932.
83. Barrett, Rev. John D. M., S.S., J.C.D., A Comparative Study of the Third Plenary Council of Baltimore and the Code, IX-221 pp., 1932.
84. Carberry, Rev. John J., Ph.D., S.T.D., J.C.D., The Juridical Form of Marriage, X-177 pp., 1934.
85. Dolan, Rev. John L., A.B., J.C.D., The Defensor Vinculi, XII-157 pp., 1934.
86. Hannan, Rev. Jerome D., A.M., S.T.D., LL.B., J.C.D., The Canon Law of Wills, IX-517 pp., 1934.
87. Lemieux, Rev. Delisle A., A.M., J.C.D., The Sentence in Ecclesiastical Procedure, IX-131 pp., 1934.
88. O'Rourke, Rev. James J., A.B., J.C.D., Parish Registers, VII-109 pp., 1934.
89. Timlin, Rev. Bartholomew, O.F.M., A.M., J.C.D., Conditional Matrimonial Consent, X-381 pp., 1934.

90. Wahl, Rev. Francis X., A.B., J.C.D., The Matrimonial Impediments of Consanguinity and Affinity, VI-125 pp., 1934.
91. White, Rev. Robert J., A.B., LL.B., S.T.B., J.C.D., Canonical Ante-Nuptial Promises and the Civil Law, VI-152 pp., 1934.
92. Herrera, Rev. Antonio Parra, O.C.D., J.C.D., Legislación Ecclesiástica sobre el Ayuno y la Abstinencia, XI-191 pp., 1935.
93. Kennedy, Rev. Edwin J., J.C.D., The Special Matrimonial Process in Cases of Evident Nullity, X-165 pp., 1935.
94. Manning, Rev. John J., A.B., J.C.D., Presumption of Law in Matrimonial Procedure, XI-111 pp., 1935.
95. Moeder, Rev. John M., J.C.D., The Proper Bishop for Ordination and Dimissorial Letters, VII-135 pp., 1935.
96. O'Mara, Rev. William A., A.B., J.C.D., Canonical Causes for Matrimonial Dispensations, IX-155 pp., 1935.
97. Reilly, Rev. Peter, J.C.D., Residence of Pastors, IX-81 pp., 1935.
98. Smith, Rev. Mariner T., O.P., S.T.L., J.C.D., The Penal Law for Religious, VII-169 pp., 1935.
99. Whalen, Rev. Donald W., A.M., J.C.D., The Value of Testimonial Evidence in Matrimonial Procedure, XIII-297 pp., 1935.
100. Cleary, Rev. Joseph F., J.C.D., Canonical Limitations on the Alienation of Church Property, VIII-141 pp., 1936.
101. Glynn, Rev. John C., J.C.D., The Promoter of Justice, XX-337 pp., 1936.
102. Brennan, Rev. James H., S.S., A.M., S.T.B., J.C.D., The Simple Convalidation of Marriage, VI-135 pp., 1937.
103. Brunini, Rev. Joseph Bernard, J.C.D., The Clerical Obligations of Canons 139 and 142, X-121 pp., 1937.
104. Connor, Rev. Maurice, A.B., J.C.D., The Administrative Removal of Pastors, VIII-159 pp., 1937.
105. Guilfoyle, Rev. Merlin Joseph, J.C.D., Custom, XI-144 pp., 1937.
106. Hughes, Rev. James Austin, A.B., A.M., J.C.D., Witnesses in Criminal Trials of Clerics, IX-140 pp., 1937.
107. Jansen, Rev. Raymond J., A.B., S.T.L., J.C.D., Canonical Provisions for Catechetical Instruction, VII-153 pp., 1937.
108. Kealy, Rev. John James, A.B., J.C.D., The Introductory Libellus in Church Court Procedure, XI-121 pp., 1937.
109. McManus, Rev. James Edward, C.SS.R., J.C.D., The Administration of Temporal Goods in Religious Institutes, XVI-196 pp., 1937.
110. Moriarity, Rev. Eugene James, J.C.D., Oaths in Ecclesiastical Courts, X-115 pp., 1937.
111. Rainer, Rev. Eligius George, C.SS.R., J.C.D., Suspension of Clerics, XVII-249 pp., 1937.
112. Reilly, Rev. Thomas F., C.SS.R., J.C.D., Visitation of Religious, VI-195 pp., 1938.
113. Moriarty, Rev. Francis E., C.SS.R., J.C.D., The Extraordinary Absolution from Censures, XV-334 pp., 1938.

114. Connolly, Rev. Nicholas P., J.C.D., The Canonical Erection of Parishes, X-132 pp., 1938.

115. Donovan, Rev. James Joseph, J.C.D., The Pastor's Obligation in Prenuptial Investigation, XII-322 pp., 1938.

116. Harrigan, Rev. Robert J., M.A., S.T.B., J.C.D., The Radical Sanation of Invalid Marriages, VIII-208 pp., 1938.

117. Boffa, Rev. Conrad Humbert, J.C.D., Canonical Provisions for Catholic Schools, X-211 pp., 1939.

118. Parsons, Rev. Anscar John, O.F.M. Cap., J.C.D., Canonical Elections, XII-236 pp., 1939.

119. Reilly, Rev. Edward Michael, A.B., J.C.D., The General Norms of Dispensation, X-156 pp., 1939.

120. Ryan, Rev. Gerald Aloysius, A.B., J.C.D., Principles of Episcopal Jurisdiction, XII-172 pp., 1939.

121. Burton, Rev. Francis James, C.S.C., A.B., J.C.D., A Commentary on Canon 1125, X-222 pp., 1940.

122. Miaskiewicz, Rev. Francis Sigismund, J.C.D., Supplied Jurisdiction According to Canon 209, XII-340 pp., 1940.

123. Rice, Rev. Patrick William, A.B., J.C.D., Proof of Death in Prenuptial Investigation, VIII-156 pp., 1940.

124. Anglin, Rev. Thomas Francis, M.S., J.C.D., The Eucharistic Fast, VIII-183 pp., 1941.

125. Coleman, Rev. John Jerome, J.C.D., The Minister of Confirmation, VI-153 pp., 1941.

126. Downs, Rev. John Emmanuel, A.B., J.C.D., The Concept of Clerical Immunity, XI-163 pp., 1941.

127. Esswein, Rev. Anthony Albert, J.C.D., Extrajudicial Penal Powers of Ecclesiastical Superiors, X-144 pp., 1941.

128. Farrell, Rev. Benjamin Francis, M.A., S.T.L., J.C.D., The Rights and Duties of the Local Ordinary Regarding Congregations of Women Religious of Pontifical Approval, V-195 pp., 1941.

129. Feeney, Rev. Thomas John, A.B., S.T.L., J.C.D., Restitutio in Integrum, VI-169 pp., 1941.

130. Findlay, Rev. Stephen William, O.S.B., A.B., J.C.D., Canonical Norms Governing the Deposition and Degradation of Clerics, XVII-279 pp., 1941.

131. Goodwine, Rev. John, A.B., S.T.L., J.C.D., The Right of the Church to Acquire Property, VIII-119 pp., 1941.

132. Heston, Rev. Edward Louis, C.S.C., Ph.D., S.T.D., J.C.D., The Alienation of Church Property in the United States, XII-222 pp., 1941.

133. Hogan, Rev. James John, A.B., S.T.L., J.C.D., Judicial Advocates and Procurators, VIII-200 pp., 1941.

134. Kealy, Rev. Thomas M., A.B., Litt.B., J.C.D., Dowry of Women Religious, IX-152 pp., 1941.

135. Keene, Rev. Michael James, O.S.B., J.C.D., Religious Ordinaries and Canon 198.

136. Kerin, Rev. Charles A., S.S., M.A., S.T.B., J.C.D., The Privation of Christian Burial, XVI-279 pp., 1941.
137. Louis, Rev. William Francis, M.A., J.C.D., Diocesan Archives, X-101 pp., 1941.
138. McDevitt, Rev. Gilbert Joseph, A.B., J.C.D., Legitimacy and Legitimation, X-247 pp., 1941.
139. McDonough, Rev. Thomas Joseph, A.B., J.C.D., Apostolic Administrators, X-217 pp., 1941.
140. Meier, Rev. Carl Anthony, A.B., J.C.D., Penal Administrative Procedure Against Negligent Pastors, XI-240 pp., 1941.
141. Schmidt, Rev. John Rogg, A.B., J.C.D., The Principles of Authentic Interpretation in Canon 17 of the Code of Canon Law, XII-331 pp., 1941.
142. Slafkosky, Rev. Andrew Leonard, A.B., J.C.D., The Canonical Episcopal Visitation of the Diocese, X-197 pp., 1941.
143. Swoboda, Rev. Innocent Robert, O.F.M., J.C.D., Ignorance in Relation to the Imputability of Delicts, IX-271 pp., 1941.
144. Dubé, Rev. Arthur Joseph, A.B., J.C.D., The General Principles for the Reckoning of Time in Canon Law, VIII-299 pp., 1941.
145. McBride, Rev. James T., A.B., J.C.D., Incardination and Excardination of Seculars, XX-585 pp., 1941.
146. Król, Rev. John J., J.C.L., The Defendant in Contentious Trials.
147. Comyns, Rev. Joseph J., C.SS.R., J.C.L., The Papal and Episcopal Administration of Church Property.
148. Barry, Rev. Garrett Francis, O.M.I., J.C.L., Violation of the Cloister.
149. Bolduc, Rev. Gatien, C.S.V., A.B., S.T.L., J.C.L., Les études dans les religions cléricales.
150. Boyle, Rev. David John, M.A., J.C.L., The Juridic Effects of Moral Certitude on Pre-Nuptial Guarantees.
151. Canavan, Rev. Walter Joseph, M.A., Litt.D., J.C.L., The Profession of Faith.
152. Desrochers, Rev. Bruno, A.B., Ph.L., S.T.B., J.C.L., Le Premier Concile Plénier de Québec et le Code de Droit Canonique.
153. Dillon, Rev. Robert Edward, A.B., J.C.L., Common Law Marriage.
154. Dodwell, Rev. Edward John, Ph.D., S.T.B., J.C.L., The Time and Place for the Celebration of Marriage.
155. Donnellan, Rev. Thomas Andrew, A.B., J.C.L., The Obligation of the Missa pro Populo.
156. Eltz, Rev. Louis Anthony, A.B., J.C.L., Cooperators in Crimes According to Canon 2209.
157. Gass, Rev. Sylvester, Francis, M.A., J.C.L., Ecclesiastical Pensions.
158. Guiniven, Rev. John Joseph, C.SS.R., J.C.L., The Precept of Hearing Mass on Sundays and Holy Days of Obligation.
159. Gulczynski, Rev. John Theophilus, J.C.L., The Desecration and Violation of Churches.

160. Hammill, Rev. John Leo, M.A., J.C.L., The Obligations of the Traveler according to Canon 14.
161. Haydt, Rev. John Joseph, A.B., J.C.L., Reserved Benefices.
162. Huser, Rev. Roger John, O.F.M., A.B., J.C.L., The Canonical Crime of Abortion.
163. Kearney, Rev. Francis Patrick, A.B., S.T.L., J.C.L., The Principles of Canon 1127.
164. Linahen, Rev. Leo James, S.T.L., J.C.L., De Absolutione Complicis In Peccato Turpi.
165. McCloskey, Rev. Joseph Aloysius, A.B., J.C.L., The Subject of Ecclesiastical Law according to Canon 12.
166. O'Neill, Rev. Francis Joseph, C.SS.R., J.C.L., The Dismissal of Religious in Temporary Vows.
167. Prince, Rev. John Edward, A.B., S.T.B., J.C.L., The Diocesan Chancellor.
168. Riesner, Rev. Albert Joseph, C.SS.R., J.C.L., Apostates and Fugitives from Religious Institutes.
169. Stenger, Rev. Joseph Bernard, J.C.L., The Mortgaging of Church Property.
170. Waldron, Rev. Joseph Francis, A.B., J.C.L., The Minister of Baptism.
171. Willett, Rev. Robert Albert, J.C.L., The Probative Value of Documents in Ecclesiastical Trials.
172. Woeber, Rev. Edward Martin, M.A., J.C.L., The Interpellations.

www.ingramcontent.com/pod-product-compliance
Lightning Source LLC
LaVergne TN
LVHW050241080826
844660LV00012B/575
* 9 7 8 0 8 1 3 2 2 3 5 9 9 *